High-Tech Trade Wars

Pitt Latin American Series

Billie R. DeWalt, *General Editor*

G. Reid Andrews, Catherine M. Conaghan,
and Jorge I. Domínguez,
Associate Editors

High-Tech Trade Wars

U.S.–BRAZILIAN CONFLICTS
IN THE GLOBAL ECONOMY

Sara Schoonmaker

University of Pittsburgh Press

Published by the University of Pittsburgh Press, Pittsburgh, Pa., 15260

Copyright © 2002, University of Pittsburgh Press

All rights reserved

Manufactured in the United States of America

Printed on acid-free paper

10 9 8 7 6 5 4 3 2 1

Library of Congress Cataloging-in-Publication Data

Schoonmaker, Sara, 1956–

High-tech trade wars : U.S.–Brazilian conflicts in the global economy / Sara Schoonmaker.

p. cm. — (Pitt Latin American series)

Includes bibliographical references (p.   ) and index.

ISBN 0-8229-4179-1

1. Computer software industry—Brazil. 2. Computer industry—Brazil. 3. United States—Foreign economic relations—Brazil. 4. Brazil—Foreign economic relations—United States. 5. Globalization. I. Title. II. Series.

HD9696.63. B72 S36 2002

382'.45005'0981—dc21

2002000265

To Keith

Contents

Acknowledgments ix

1. Globalization, Neoliberalism, and the Brazilian Informatics Case 1
2. Information Trade Politics: From Telecommunications to Trade Policy 31
3. Who's Afraid of Brazilian Informatics? 72
4. The Double Desire: Mediation and Resistance through Software Policy 90
5. From Technological Autonomy to Neoliberalism: Constructing an Open Market 122
6. Incipient Denationalization: Brazilian Informatics in 2001 158
7. Neoliberal Globalization and Beyond: Protest, Celebration, and Alternatives to Development 171

List of Abbreviations 189
Notes 191
References 197
Index 213

Acknowledgments

WRITING THIS BOOK has been an international adventure. Doing fieldwork in Brazil was undoubtedly the most illuminating and exciting part of the project. As a new faculty member at Colgate University, I received generous support for my research through grants from the Colgate University Research Council and from a Colgate University Picker Fellowship. Peter Evans provided me with names of potential contacts in Brazil, and Beth Conklin and Howard Winant gave me advice about logistics, culture, and hand gestures. The University of Florida's Interuniversity Study Program in Brazil provided an excellent base of operations in the incredible city of Rio de Janeiro. Marcia Sá Freire was a cool Carioca Portuguese teacher and intrepid guide to Rio's night spots. Most importantly, I am indebted to the Brazilians whose gracious generosity made the fieldwork possible. Renato Archer, Fernando Calicchio, Edson Fregni, José Fernando Halfeld dos Guaranys, Josef Manasterski, Ivan da Costa Marques, Artur Pereira Nunes, Mário Dias Ripper, José Rubens Doria Porto, José Ezil Veiga da Rocha, Ricardo Saur, and Paulo Tigre provided invaluable suggestions for interview contacts as well as seasoned perspectives on the politics of informatics development. Others spent hours answering my questions about their involvement in the informatics industry, and provided access to libraries and photocopying of articles and documents. One former worker at Cobra, the state computer firm, spotted me in the library surrounded by stacks of informatics industry journals, and offered me her private collection.

Others were crucial during the writing process. Choice intellectual interventions and camaraderie came from Bob Antonio, Victoria Bernal, Cele Bucki, Jon Cruz, Avery Gordon, Padma Kaimal, Rhonda Levine, Mona Lyne, Mary Moran, Lynn Morgan, Martin Murray, Andy Rotter, Jim Salt, Paul Schervish, John Walton, Tekle Woldemikael; and from my Redlands writing group—Chuck Call, Tracy Fitzsimmons, Sharon Lang, Keith Osajima, and Pat Wasielewski. Anonymous reviewers for the University of Pittsburgh Press provided insightful feedback that allowed me to greatly improve the manuscript. Strategic emotional backing came from Chuck Barone, Chris Beach, Steve Bromer, Tad Dunlap, Marilyn Golden, Nancy Lemon, Joy Manesiotis, Ann Morrill, Milton Ospina, Lee Pelton, Pam Roby, Susie Schoonmaker, Kristen Wilson; and from my Redlands Girl Gang—Sandra Cross, Tracy Fitzsimmons, Monica Frederick, Terrell Levinson-Wickham, Erica Rosenfeld Wilson, Geri Stahly, and Lisa Usher. My parents, Ted and Hazel Schoonmaker, passed on a sense of the need to fight for social justice, and to take care of yourself in the process. My daughter, Avery, reminds me to delight in the present moment. Finally, Keith Osajima has been my partner in adventures from coast to coast, and continent to continent, for eighteen years. Thanks for helping me mix work so thoroughly with pleasure.

High-Tech Trade Wars

1
Globalization, Neoliberalism, and the Brazilian Informatics Case

IN JANUARY 2000 security forces patrolled the streets in Davos, Switzerland, to ensure that protesters would not disrupt the meeting of the elite World Economic Forum. Global economic and political leaders resolved not to allow massive protests such as those that occurred at the November 1999 meetings of the World Trade Organization (WTO) in Seattle. In Seattle activists from at least 750 organizations flooded the streets to oppose the WTO's agenda for opening markets around the world to global capital. Labor, environmental, consumer protection, and other grassroots groups forged innovative alliances. Through street theater, nonviolent resistance, and other forms of protest, they pressured trade negotiators to reconsider their views. These protesters sought to promote the interests of working people, communities, and a range of local groups that were being damaged by corporate efforts to expand into international markets (Iritani 1999).

In Davos U.S. President Bill Clinton addressed over 2,000 political leaders and business executives at the thirtieth annual World Economic Forum. He stated that his goals for the forum were to "create the conditions and provide the tools to give people on every continent the ability to solve their own problems and, in so doing, to strengthen their own lives and our global economy in the new century" (Wright 2000, A1). If those were the President's goals, then why were protesters gathered on the edge of this idyllic Alpine ski resort? Why were they breaking windows at McDonald's and throwing snowballs at police? Why would they reject an opportunity to "solve their own problems" and "strengthen their own lives," not to mention the global economy?

Answers to these questions might be found in another part of President Clinton's speech. Noting his concern for Bangladeshi textile workers and Uruguayan farmers, he argued that such disadvantaged people needed the opportunity to sell their goods on international markets. Clinton asked, "How can working conditions be improved and poverty be reduced in developing countries if they are denied these and other opportunities to grow, the things that come with participation in the world economy?" In order to assure that "the poor and those hard hit by changes are not left behind," Clinton affirmed the U.S. government's commitment to open markets and free trade. Indeed, he argued that these were the "best engine we know of to lift living standards, reduce environmental destruction and build shared prosperity" (Wright 2000, A10).

President Clinton was an exemplary proponent of free trade in the 1990s, as well as an advocate of facing the new challenges of global economic change. As the Davos experience shows, however, these positions clash with the ways that a range of grassroots groups perceive current changes in the global economy. These divergent perceptions raise questions about the nature of the globalization process and about the conflicting interests it involves. Such a profound economic transformation challenges us to question our assumptions about the nature of reality and to develop new ways of understanding the social world as it changes before our eyes. Observing the great social upheavals wrought by nineteenth-century capitalism, Marx commented, in words that are still apt, "All fixed, fast-frozen relations, with their train of ancient and venerable prejudices and opinions, are swept away, all new-formed ones become antiquated before they can ossify. All that is solid melts into air" (Tucker 1978, 476).

Marx's observations resonate with current portraits of the far-reaching effects of globalization. Globalization is commonly referred to as an inexorable force, driven by the objective logic of the market that makes government efforts to regulate economic development obsolete. International trade and investment have expanded to such an extent that national economies have been absorbed into a single worldwide economy driven by global market forces. State efforts to shape the development process are no match for the structural imperatives of the market (Hirst and Thompson 1999).

According to Hirst and Thompson (1999, xiii), globalization has become "the new grand narrative of the social sciences." While their point is well taken, Clinton's Davos speech shows that this narrative extends well beyond academe, blending with neoliberal economic policy to promote what George H. W. Bush dubbed the "new world order." Indeed, by the mid-1980s, a consensus had emerged in development policy circles that breaking down trade regulations, privatizing state companies, and other "economic liberalization" measures were the best way to promote economic development in the former Third World (Haggard and Kaufman 1992; Stallings 1992). As Gibson-Graham (1996, 120) states, globalization can be understood as "a discourse, that is, as a language of domination, a tightly scripted narrative of differential power." Theorizing globalization as a discourse can help us understand the ways in which that discourse has been forged through a process of political struggle between First and former Third World governments and multinational corporations, as well as how it has influenced the economic, political, and cultural conditions for actors to function within the global economy.

GLOBALIZATION AS DISCOURSE

Conceptualizing globalization as a discourse involves viewing it as socially constructed through a complex, volatile process of political and economic struggle. In her analysis of the globalization discourse, Gibson-Graham uses the "metaphor of a language, something that has rules of grammar but rules that can be used to say many different things" (123) to suggest alternative ways of understanding current developments in the international economy. Drawing parallels with Sharon Marcus's feminist analysis of the rape script, Gibson-Graham views globalization as a script without a fixed course or ending, one engaged in a continual process of "making and remaking ... social roles by soliciting responses and responding to cues" (124). Such an approach highlights the contradictory, complex choices that actors make as they respond to signals from each other, and the ways that those choices may eventually become part of a more familiar or standardized story. For example, multinational corporations that seek to invest in particular countries or regions may meet a variety of responses, ranging from conformity to the dictates of the World Trade Organization or the International Monetary Fund to efforts to preserve nationalist development strategies. Gibson-Graham argues that an analytical approach focused on discourse allows her to "challenge the hegemonic representation of the superior power of the [multinational corporation] by seeing how the conditions of existence of that power are constituted in language as much as in action, and even more importantly, in a complex interaction between the two" (133).

This view of power as rooted in the interaction between language and action lies at the theoretical heart of this study, which combines political economy with poststructuralism. From poststructuralism I emphasis the concept of discourse as a narrative of power and knowledge. Discourse is constituted by rules based on certain forms of knowledge. These serve to empower particular people as qualified to speak the truth in particular institutional contexts while other people and their forms of knowledge are subjugated. For Foucault (1980, 102), power is "the production of effective instruments for the formation and accumulation of knowledge—methods of observation, techniques of registration, procedures for investigation and research, apparatuses of control."

Foucault highlighted the importance of discourse in the first volume of *The History of Sexuality* (1978, 100), noting that "it is in discourse that power and knowledge are joined together." Similar to Gibson-Graham's perspective on the globalization script, Foucault argues that a variety of discursive elements may be involved in particular strategies. These discourses are not simply divided between dominant and dominated, or included and excluded; a discourse may be one of the major vehicles through which power circulates and affects people, as well as a "point of resistance and a starting point for an opposing strategy" (101). Indeed, the theorist must reconstruct the "multiplicity of discursive elements. . . . with the things said and those concealed, the enunciations required and those forbidden . . . ; with the variants and different effects—according to who is speaking, his position of power, the institutional context in which he happens to be situated" (100).

The dominant discourse of globalization is based upon four major assumptions, which assert and conceal particular things; these things contribute to its power to shape current understandings about and practices within the global economy. First, the dominant discourse of globalization is connected to the discourses of neoliberalism and neoclassical economics. These discourses share the deterministic assumption that there is an inexorable, objective economic logic that dictates the operation of the market and causes it to expand to every corner of the globe. Margaret Thatcher famously asserted that "there is no alternative" in the face of globalization and objective market laws. This deterministic logic provides the rationale for a second assumption, that neoliberalism is the most "rational" approach to economic policy. The neoliberal version of the globalization discourse recommends eliminating government policies to regulate trade and development. Such neoliberal efforts to eradicate "barriers to trade" make sense if globalization is viewed as the inevitable outcome of international market forces. Any effort to oppose it is a wrongheaded denial of the true nature of economic activity. The neoliberal globalization discourse also implies a third assumption about the nature of the state as an impediment to market operations. Block (1996) describes this "conventional wisdom" as based upon a powerful metaphor depicting the state as a vampire draining the lifeblood from the economy. Within the neoliberal globalization discourse, this "evil vampire" state stands in the way of market forces. Neoliberal economic theory thus exhorts the state to step aside and let the market lead the way to economic growth. If this advice is followed, the state loses its sovereign power to the global rule of the market.

In addition to the traits just described, the dominant globalization discourse is ahistorical. It is based upon a fourth assumption: that the expansion of international trade and production is an unprecedented, radically new development. It ignores centuries of history in the development of capitalism as a world economic system, perceiving global economic expansion as largely driven by technological change in microelectronics and telecommunications. This view fails to recognize historical developments in communications technology that have fostered the integration of world markets. Since the mid-nineteenth century, for example, world markets have been integrated through the use of underwater transoceanic cables. Modern information and communications technologies have certainly strengthened and expanded the existing infrastructure for world trade; however, the infrastructure itself is not a dramatically new development. As Hirst and Thompson (1999, 9) note, "Modern systems dramatically increase the possible volume and complexity of transactions, but we have had information media capable of sustaining a genuine international trading system for over a century.... If the theorists of globalization mean that we have an economy in which each part of the world is linked by markets sharing close to real-time information, then that began not in the 1970s but in the 1870s."

The poststructuralist perspective used in this study builds upon Escobar's (1995) work on development as a historically produced discourse constituted through relations of power and knowledge. The discourses of development and globalization share many common elements. For example, both are rooted in neoclassical economic assumptions that production, the market, labor, and development itself are quantifiable entities with a fixed material existence. Economists (as well as most sociologists and other social scientists) operate within a realist tradition, viewing their knowledge as an objective, neutral way of representing the understanding of the world they have developed through the collection and analysis of empirical data. By contrast, Escobar understands development and globalization as cultural discourses based upon values, such as rationality, that are peculiar to the modern period. They represent a complex historical process whereby individuals have come to understand production as a central part of their own activities, their relationships with others, and their larger social reality. During the eighteenth and nineteenth centuries, the institutionalization of the market system involved the creation of *homo oeconomicus,* rational economic man. As Escobar notes, "In addition to rationalizing capitalist production, ... political economy succeeded in imposing production and labor as a code of signification on social life as a whole ... modern people came to see life in general through the lens of production" (60).

Since the eighteenth century, development discourse has provided a picture of social reality as characterized by production and the market. This picture was a hallmark of modernity (Escobar 1995) and it persists today, complemented by the globalization discourse, which portrays production and trade as expanding inexorably to create a single global market. The development, globalization, and neoliberal discourses converge with a vision of the emerging prosperity to come from expanding global trade and production, as long as the state does not interfere with objective economic laws driven by the "invisible hand."

Using a poststructuralist perspective, Escobar develops an "anthropology of modernity" that views the modern Western economy as an institution consisting of systems of production, power, and signification that were central to the rise of capitalism. These systems "should be seen as cultural forms through which human beings are made into producing subjects. The economy is not only, or even principally, a material entity. It is above all a cultural production, a way of producing human subjects and social orders of a certain kind" (Escobar 1995, 59). This perspective allows us to understand what seem to be primarily economic developments, such as the rise of globalization and neoliberalism, as cultural discourses based on values such as rationality and the primacy of production. It requires us to make the familiar unfamiliar, to notice the norms and values deeply embedded in economic ideas; indeed, it requires us to notice that economics is a discourse where certain relations of power and domination are represented as normal through language, while others are subjugated by not being acknowledged. By understanding economics as culture, and as discourse, we recognize its hegemonic effect of representing a particular version of reality as normal, as truth, as science. As Escobar states, "From the classical political economists to today's neoliberals at the World Bank, economists have monopolized the power of speech. The effects of this hegemony and the damaging centrality of economics need to be exposed in novel ways" (100).

The poststructuralist perspective allows us to expose the hegemonic effects of the globalization, neoliberal, and development discourses, which share key assumptions with neoclassical economics. The poststructuralist perspective illuminates the ways in which the language we use to describe and represent the social world plays an integral part in defining social reality. The concept of discourse as a narrative of power and knowledge emphasizes that the "reality" of economic and political structures is constructed through forms of knowledge and understanding, as well as through material practices. As Escobar (1995) states, it is important to "recognize that forms of production are not independent from the representations (the 'models') of social life in which they exist." Or in other words, "forms of production and forms of representation can be distinguished only for analytical purposes" (100).

There are important analytical reasons to distinguish between forms of production and forms of representation, or discourse; and this is precisely why I have combined political economy with poststructuralism in this study. In order to theorize globalization it is useful to identify the ways that globalization is developed as a discourse. It is equally important, however, to analyze the economic changes involved with globalization and the political struggles that have shaped both the economic and discursive conditions for globalization to occur. For example, as Chapter 2 discusses, in the 1970s and 1980s First and former Third World governments and multinational corporations engaged in protracted political struggles to define the terms for telecommunications and trade policy, as well as the institutional context within which those policies would be forged. Struggles over these policy definitions were not mere semantic exercises because they affected the development of regulations governing political and economic conditions for new forms of trade in the global economy. The power to define telecommunications or trade policy was inextricably linked to economic and political power. Neoliberal definitions were designed to open markets for multinationals and increase trading opportunities for many First World governments. These conditions, however, also threatened the ability of former Third World governments to regulate economic development.

I use poststructuralism to understand the ways that the definitions of things like trade policy are part of broader political and economic struggles to establish the terms of trade and production in the global economy. The language used to define policy has implications for power relations between First and former Third World governments and multinational corporations because it implicitly defines whose interests will be served by that policy. Knowledge and power, language and action, combine to shape both our understanding of social reality and the economic and political conditions of that reality. Political economy emphasizes the economic and political dimensions of globalization while largely ignoring, or failing to theorize adequately, the discursive dimension. Combining political economy with poststructuralism is thus important in order to understand the economic, political, and discursive dimensions as equally "real," mutually constitutive parts of the globalization process.

ECONOMIC AND POLITICAL DIMENSIONS OF GLOBALIZATION

Globalization is a widely contested phenomenon. Indeed, there is great disagreement about whether contemporary changes in the international economy constitute a process of globalization. Many social and economic theorists question the concept of globalization itself. For example, world systems theorists such as Wallerstein and Arrighi emphasize the development of capitalism as an international economic system over the past 500 years. Wallerstein (1999, 21) states, "Although it is fashionable to speak of globalization today as a phenomenon that began at the earliest in the 1970s, in fact transnational commodity chains were extensive from the very beginning of the system, and global since the second half of the nineteenth century." Arrighi (1999) identifies four "systemic cycles of accumulation," developing from late-medieval Europe to the present. During each cycle, world trade and production expanded rapidly and then erupted into a crisis of overaccumulation, characterized by increased competition, financial expansion, and erosion of the organizational structures that enabled the original expansion to occur. World systems theorists thus do not view globalization as a novel condition but as part of a lengthy historical process of worldwide economic change and capitalist development.

The importance of understanding contemporary economic change from a historical perspective is supported by Hirst and Thompson (1999). They argue that the extent of the current globalization of production has been exaggerated since most firms remain tightly linked to their home bases in one of three major economic blocs: North America, Europe, and Japan. Foreign direct investment also remains highly concentrated in the First World, marginalizing the former Third World with respect to both trade and investment. The major economic blocs thus have the economic power to shape the political process whereby regulations of international trade and finance are developed.

Ahistorical, deterministic assumptions make some globalization theories highly problematic. Other theories, however, are historically grounded and complex. Indeed, they challenge neoliberal discourse by arguing that globalization is a political as well as an economic process, shaped through political struggle by actors such as the state, rather than driven by the operation of objective market laws. These more nuanced theories of globalization view the economic changes involved in a more complicated way, where the international expansion of trade and production is combined with new kinds of spatial constraints on that expansion.

In this vein, Sassen (1988, 1991) highlights the rise of specialized producer services as a new basic industry located in major core cities and supporting the centralized control and management of global production operations. These include international legal and accounting services, management consulting, and financial services. Access to such services allows firms to organize production with a large number of plants or offices in different parts of the world while monitoring those activities through a centralized managerial structure concentrated in "global cities" (Sassen 1991). The global expansion of production is thus subject to spatial constraints that shape locational decisions and lead to the concentration of producer services firms in the central business districts of major metropolitan areas. For example, producer services firms need to be located close to other firms that produce important inputs or that engage with them in joint efforts to produce some services. It is possible for an accounting firm to serve clients at a distance, but its services depend upon having access to specialists like lawyers and programmers. Many corporate transactions now require joint participation by a range of specialized firms that contribute legal, accounting, financial, public relations, management consulting, and other services (Sassen 1991).

Sassen (1988, 1991) highlights both the internationalization of production and trade occurring with the globalization process and the spatial constraints that limit corporate decisions and lead them to concentrate management and producer services activities in global cities. Equally important, Sassen emphasizes the political dimension of globalization. She questions what she calls the "zero-sum game" proposed by globalization theorists who argue that "whatever the global economy gains, the national state loses, and vice versa" (Sassen 1999, 158). She argues that states actively shape the political and economic frameworks that affect the globalization process, which creates possibilities for states to facilitate as well as to oppose that process. The state's role is particularly important because many global processes take place within national borders, and are thus subject to existing national regulations. State policy may become a battleground to establish the political and economic conditions for international trade and investment to occur. Indeed, this political dimension of globalization involves a struggle over whether states will retain control of activities within their national borders, or whether national legal regimes will be shaped to meet the interests of global capital. Sassen (1999, 159) states, "Globalization ... also has to do with the relocation of national public governance functions to transnational private arenas and with the development inside national states—through legislative acts, court rulings, executive orders—of the mechanisms necessary to accommodate the rights of global capital in what are still national territories under the exclusive control of their states."

The mechanisms Sassen refers to here largely involve the development of the discourse of globalization within national territories, through the definition and implementation of legal rulings designed to facilitate international trade and production. This discourse is also rooted in cultural values promoted by neoliberalism, such as free trade, the "objective" laws of the market, and the state as a hindrance to smooth market operations.

McMichael (2000a, 2000b) highlights this struggle between national states and global capital with his conception of globalization as a neoliberal political project, designed to eradicate state regulations on trade and to allow the "invisible hand" of the market to operate freely. Under this "globalization project," states are pressured to implement rules of global economic management by subordinating their authority to regulate trade and development policy. These rules are defined by multinational corporations and banks, multilateral financial institutions like the World Bank and the International Monetary Fund, and international bureaucratic entities like the World Trade Organization and regional free-trade agreements. The globalization project is a world order in which states implement rules of global economic management, which heightens the influence of foreign capital on local economies. Since the 1970s, it has gradually replaced the "development project" (McMichael 2000a), where economic growth was viewed primarily in national terms, to be managed by national governments and perhaps facilitated by foreign aid or loans from allies in the Cold War world. The shift from the development to the globalization project is exemplified by the World Bank's *World Development Report 1980*, which redefines "development" as participation in the world market rather than nationally managed economic growth (McMichael 2000a).

McMichael and Sassen provide the basis to conceptualize globalization as a political as well as an economic process, characterized by a struggle between states, multinational corporations and banks, multilateral financial institutions, and international bureaucratic entities. A key part of this struggle involves the extent to which states will continue to define development goals as a basis for managing their national economies, or will be pressured to implement neoliberal policies that favor global capital. This struggle thus involves the extent to which national economies, and state policies, will become denationalized in the sense of becoming oriented toward global economic activities and neoliberal (de)regulation of trade and development. Sassen (1999, 160) refers to this process as an "incipient denationalization," while McMichael (2000b, 11) views the "market as a denationalizing movement."

Krasner (1999) argues that the prospect of denationalization in the context of globalization creates new challenges to the sovereign ability of states to control activities within and across their borders. It does not, however, radically change the sovereignty of states in terms of their authority and legitimacy to govern their territories. Indeed, a particular kind of international legal sovereignty has actually been strengthened by globalization due to the increasing importance of international agreements to govern global trade, development, and political relations. Helleiner (1999) agrees, arguing that the power of states to regulate international finance has been strengthened through agreements like the Basel Accord, where G-10 central banks sought to decrease the risk of financial crisis by accepting common standards for the capital adequacy of international banks.

States may thus have the potential to strengthen their international legal sovereignty, and thus counteract tendencies toward denationalization, in the context of globalization. This potential, however, depends upon the position of states in the global economy, and on their relations with other states in the world system. Understanding the role of the state in this context involves, as Sassen (1999, 158) states, "register[ing] all the ways in which the state participates in setting up the new frameworks through which globalization is furthered." From a poststructuralist perspective, a key part of establishing these frameworks involves the development of the discourse of globalization. As Chapter 2 discusses, states were active in defining the terms for telecommunications and trade policy, which were central parts of the emerging discourses of globalization and neoliberalism.

States, however, did not just struggle to establish the terms for globalization. They also struggled to transform those terms, and to contest the dominance of global capital over their national economies. In other words, they contested the process of globalization itself. In the 1990s social movements such as the Zapatistas in Mexico formulated their political demands specifically in opposition to neoliberalism and globalization; they sought to develop alternatives to the neoliberal model of increased international trade and decreased national control over the development process (Collier and Quaratiello 1994). In the 1970s, however, former Third World governments struggled against what they viewed as a new form of information dependency. These struggles sought to counteract key aspects of what we now view as globalization: the international expansion of capital and the potential loss of control by states over their national economies; the rising importance of computer technology for trade and production; and an emerging discourse that defined the political terms for trade and production according to neoliberal cultural values of the primacy of market rule and free trade, rather than state sovereignty over national trade and development policy. These efforts to counteract information dependency were thus part of a historical process of resistance to neoliberal globalization. They helped to shape the current conditions of globalization and neoliberalism through a process of political struggle.

STRUGGLES AGAINST INFORMATION DEPENDENCY: TOWARD A NEW WORLD INFORMATION ORDER

In the 1970s, Third World demands for a new world information order were rooted in an analysis of information flows as a key facet of economic power. Information was understood in a historical context, where it was structured, used, and disseminated by multinational corporations in a global capitalist market. News, film, television, and other media purveyed commodified images of reality, imbued with the values of the former colonial powers. In addition, flows of computerized data between subsidiaries of multinational corporations allowed firms to manage production operations in distant parts of the globe from central corporate headquarters (Melody 1991; Sussman and Lent 1991; Guback 1994; Sassen 1991).

Debates over these transborder data flows were a key part of the broader struggle for a new world information order. Former Third World countries viewed the flows as part of a new form of information dependency, reinforcing the historical structure of inequality between countries in global capitalism. Information dependency arose from a lack of technologies, skills, research facilities, and industries involved with computer manufacturing and software development. As computers became an integral part of many production and distribution activities, as well as a growing economic sector in their own right, development of the resources involved with their use appeared central for global competition. Structural inequalities were emerging between countries with different levels of development of those resources (Smith 1980; Rada 1981; Murphy 1986; Piera 1986; Sauvant 1986; Wigand, Shipley, and Shipley 1984).

Beginning in the 1970s, a number of Latin American and African governments expressed concerns about the dangers of information dependency and viewed transborder data-flow policy as a way to counteract it (OECD 1979; Sauvant 1984a, 1984b; Pipe 1983, 1985; IBI 1982).[1] The Brazilian military government, however, was the only one to implement a major policy in this area. Brazilian transborder data-flow policy was part of a larger strategy to counteract information dependency by developing computer manufacturing and software industries, or "informatics" (United Nations Centre on Transnational Corporations 1983).

THE BRAZILIAN INFORMATICS STRATEGY

Initiated in the 1970s, the informatics strategy was designed to transform Brazil's position in the international division of labor by developing skills, technologies, products, and industries in informatics. This strategy built upon two earlier phases of Brazilian communications development, including the construction of a modern telecommunications system in the 1960s and the development of cultural industries in the 1970s. The formation of an informatics industry during the 1970s and 1980s thus represented a third phase in a longer process of creating communication structures in Brazil (Fadul and Straubhaar 1991). Informatics development was also facilitated by Brazil's history of scientific and technological development in nuclear and solid-state physics during the 1950s and 1960s. Although the research programs in these areas failed, they created a foundation for later success in informatics (Langer 1989).

The informatics strategy was grounded in previous efforts to use government policy as an instrument to promote industrialization. It represented a radical departure, however, from earlier import-substitution approaches. Albert Hirschman (1987) aptly characterized it as an import-preemptive strategy designed to skip the traditional import-substitution phases of importing a product, persuading foreign firms to produce it in Brazil, and then fostering the involvement of local firms. By contrast, the informatics strategy sought to promote local production from the outset, by protecting domestic firms from foreign competition (22). It was inward-oriented (Gereffi 1989), using government prohibitions on foreign investment in the mini and personal computer markets as the foundation for growth of a local industry to serve primarily the domestic market. The informatics strategy was based upon the concept of the "market reserve," which restricted foreign firms (multinationals with home bases outside Brazil) from investing in the mini and personal computer markets.

Originally established to be in effect from 1976 until 1984, the market reserve was extended for eight more years through the National Informatics Law of 1984. In addition to its focus on limiting computer production by foreign firms, the informatics law instituted controls over foreign imports and the acquisition of foreign technologies. It was designed to protect the development of a local industry until 1992 and to prepare local firms to compete in an "open" market after that time (Adler 1987, 251).

The market reserve embodied nationalist cultural values of state sovereignty over national development. It defined the Brazilian market as part of the national patrimony, a vital resource to be used to facilitate national economic growth. The market reserve, and the broader informatics strategy, formed an oppositional, nationalist development discourse where the underlying cultural values and specific policy regulations were designed to challenge efforts by global capital to control the Brazilian informatics market. The power of this discourse was highlighted in interviews with Brazilian computer executives who were deeply involved in its development and implementation. These executives noted that the mere existence of an explicitly nationalist policy seemed to irk the U.S. government and to make the Brazilian government a target for trade conflicts (Ripper 1990, interview; Fregni 1990, interview).

The Brazilian informatics strategy, and particularly the market reserve, was thus a highly controversial approach to development. It was designed to challenge structural inequalities in the global economy, in the context of technological change in computers and telecommunications that made those sectors central for global economic competition. These inequalities were reflected in the international division of labor, where high-technology development was concentrated in the First World countries. The informatics strategy sought to transform that division of labor by protecting Brazilian-owned firms from foreign competition. It contradicted the neoliberal, free-trade development approach advocated by the U.S. government. It was frequently characterized as ideological and nationalistic by its neoliberal critics, as well as by scholars like Emanuel Adler (1987, 1988) who viewed ideology as the key motivation for groups that supported the policy's development.

This controversial strategy encouraged the growth of Brazilian-owned firms in a market that had historically been dominated by a few multinational corporations, such as IBM and Burroughs. Between the mid-1970s and the mid-1980s, the informatics policy fostered the growth of a local computer industry; the local share of total computer production rose from

23 percent in 1979 to 55 percent in 1986 (Evans 1986; Inter-American Development Bank 1988).

In 1985 the momentum for informatics development was challenged. President Ronald Reagan announced an investigation of the Brazilian informatics law as potentially violating the interests of U.S. firms under Section 301 of the 1974 Trade Act. This act gave the U.S. government the authority to investigate the effects of laws in other countries that were deemed potentially damaging to the interests of U.S. firms. This was the first time a U.S. President had used his authority to initiate an investigation of such alleged violations, rather than wait to respond to complaints by U.S. firms. If the Brazilian informatics law was found to violate the interests of U.S. firms, Brazil would be subject to trade sanctions to repay the damages (Evans 1989a; U.S. House Committee on Energy and Commerce 1988). Reagan's action unleashed powerful geopolitical pressures on Brazilian state officials, who struggled to implement the informatics policy in the midst of a trade war with the United States.

The trade war over Brazilian informatics arose as the convergence of telecommunications and microelectronic technologies expanded the implications of information policy for trade and development. It was one of the battlegrounds in a global power struggle over telecommunications, information, and trade policy that I call "information trade politics." In the 1980s demands for a new world information order increasingly shifted to focus on trade and development issues, as informatics development was viewed as vital for global competition. U.S. government pressures to regulate transborder data flows as part of a broader category of trade in services, and to incorporate services trade under the neoliberal General Agreement on Tariffs and Trade (GATT), solidified this shift from telecommunications and information policy into the area of trade and development (Braman 1990; Schoonmaker 1995a).

This convergence of telecommunications, information, and trade policy was part of a political struggle over the development of the neoliberal globalization discourse. This struggle involved former Third World governments that sought to retain greater state control over trade and development policy and embraced cultural values of state sovereignty and national development as a basis for such policy. These governments clashed with many First World governments and multinational corporations, which advocated neoliberal cultural values of free trade and the objective laws of market forces as the basis for policies intended to break down national regulations on trade and open markets to multinationals. The U.S. government's investigation of Brazilian informatics, conducted under the auspices of Section 301 of the 1974 Trade Act, emerged as a bilateral dispute over whether the neoliberal or nationalist development discourse would govern global computer markets. It exemplified U.S. government opposition to efforts by former Third World countries to challenge historical patterns of power and control in global capitalism (Schoonmaker 1995b).

The trade war over Brazilian informatics provides a rich case study of the politics of globalization and neoliberalism, in the context of technological change in information technologies such as those used in computers and telecommunications systems. This book explores Brazil's controversial effort to transform the international division of labor in the information technology sector, which Evans (1995, 95) calls the "master industry of late-twentieth-century development." It examines the historical, political, and economic conditions that affected Brazilian informatics policy choices and outcomes after the initiation of the 301 case. It seeks to explain why certain policy decisions were made and why those choices had particular outcomes for development.

BRAZILIAN INFORMATICS IN GEOPOLITICAL PERSPECTIVE

This study provides a distinct perspective on the Brazilian informatics case that has not been addressed by previous works. Most importantly, this is the only study that examines Brazilian informatics development in the context of the trade war with the United States. This focus is important for two reasons.

First, the 301 investigation was part of a broader process designed to create economic, political, and discursive conditions conducive to opening world markets to global capital. This investigation, and the neoliberal globalization discourse of which it formed a part, created powerful geopolitical pressures with which Brazilian state officials had to contend as they implemented the informatics policy. In a series of works, Evans examined the evolution of U.S. policy toward Brazil during the 301 investigation (1989a), as well as the strengths and weaknesses of the Brazilian state's role in informatics development (1989b, 1992, 1995). He did not, however, analyze how U.S. actions formed part of a larger neoliberal globalization discourse, or how they influenced informatics policy development within Brazil. Since the informatics policy was dismantled between 1990 and 1992, much of the existing research has focused on policy evaluation rather than on understanding how and why the policy was implemented in particular ways (Evans, Frischtak, and Tigre 1992). None of these works highlight the influence of the neoliberal globalization discourse on the decision making of state officials or the process of policy implementation.

Second, placing the Brazilian informatics case in the context of the 301 investigation allows me to examine it as an example of the convergence of information, trade, and development policy, which was made possible by the merging of telecommunications and computer technology. I explore the implications of the Brazilian case for understanding how these technological changes shape new prospects for trade and development, as well as new arenas for political struggle. Again, this focus is different from earlier works that examined the development of the computer or communications sectors in Brazil.[2] None of these studies analyzed U.S. reactions to Brazilian informatics development, or viewed the 301 investigation as part of a broader political struggle over new prospects for trade arising from the merging of telecommunications and computer technologies.

Numerous studies have been conducted to understand why and how the Brazilian informatics policy emerged, and the subsequent process of industrial development (Tigre 1983; Benakouche 1985; Adler 1987, 1988; Evans 1986, 1995; Cline 1987; Azevedo and Zago 1989; V. Dantas 1988; M. Dantas 1989; Langer 1989). None of this research, however, has examined why and how the 1984 informatics policy was dismantled as part of Fernando Collor's sweeping plan for neoliberal economic reform after his election as Brazil's President in November 1989. Indeed, the demise of the informatics policy (two years before its originally scheduled expiration date) provides a case study of the defeat of an oppositional, nationalist approach to development in the face of neoliberal globalization.

Based upon interviews with Brazilian industrialists and state officials as this informatics policy was being dismantled between 1990 and 1992, this work highlights the complex, contradictory transition from a nationalist to a neoliberal development strategy during this period. This transition was initially viewed as a victory for foreign capital and Brazilian computer users; however, the results were not so simple. Brazilian computer firms developed new economic partnerships with foreign companies, as well as new political alliances to pressure the state to fight contraband and clarify policy changes to guide the transition period. Despite the Collor regime's commitment to the neoliberal discourse, there were pressing needs for state action to guide the transition process. These needs persisted in 2001, when the Cardoso government passed an informatics law that facilitated investment by global capital in the Brazilian market.

This research thus explores changes in Brazilian informatics policy as examples of the demise of nationalist development strategies in the context of neoliberal globalization, an approach that has not been pursued by previous studies. Evans (1995) makes a persuasive case that by the 1990s, Brazilian informatics had entered a period he calls the "new internationalization," whereby local and transnational capital form new kinds of alliances involving joint ventures, technology, and licensing agreements. Although he argues that the Brazilian state should have been encouraging capital to take on projects to deepen the process of industrial transformation during this period, he does not examine the actual process of transition from a nationalist to a neoliberal development strategy. This study fills a gap left by Evans's work, analyzing conflicts that emerged with the 1990 transition process and continued with the passage of the 2001 informatics law.

THE ARGUMENT

In recent decades, the ability to transmit computer-readable, digital signals over telecommunications links made it possible to engage in new forms of what I call "digital trade" in services and other commodities. For example, services like data processing or database access can be traded in digital form through computers over telecommunications links. In the process, communications systems serve as electromagnetic highways for what I call "digital commodities," allowing trade to occur virtually instantaneously (Schoonmaker 1993, 1994).

Chapter 2 outlines the political struggles that have arisen in response to the new possibilities for digital trade, as existing telecommunications laws took on new implications for trade and production. I trace the development of information trade politics as a global power struggle to develop a discourse governing telecommunications, information, and trade policies in the 1970s and 1980s. This struggle unfolded through three episodes of confrontation (Foucault 1978), each of which was characterized by particular policy conflicts, by struggle in national or international arenas, and by a focus on telecommunications, information, or trade policy.

In the first episode of confrontation during the 1970s, these struggles focused on national telecommunications policies that were originally designed to regulate conditions for access to the telecommunications network as well as the quality of the network. As technological change made it possible to use those networks for digital trade and communication, transnational corporations challenged the power of national governments to restrict their use of the networks to facilitate global business operations. For their part, governments in Europe and Canada, and to some extent in Latin America, clung to the telecommunications policy discourse as their only leverage over the emerging economic implications of national telecommunications systems.

Governing access to the telecommunications network, however, was not sufficient to control conditions for digital trade and communication. During the 1970s the focus of political struggles shifted from the telecommunications network itself toward transborder data flows, the digital stream of commodities and information transmitted through that network. In this second episode of confrontation over information trade politics, policy debates arose over the implications of transborder data flows for economic power and national sovereignty. They thus shifted to the arena where telecommunications policy converged with information policy. Canadian, European, Latin American, and African governments sought to counteract information dependency. In response, they were charged by the U.S. government and transnational corporations with restricting the free flow of information and free market competition. The

U.S. government eventually succeeded in defining the flows as trade in data services, in the context of broader discussions over whether to include trade in services under GATT.

This redefinition of the flows shifted conflicts over their regulation to the broader area of services trade, marking the beginning of a third episode of confrontation over information trade politics. Political struggles changed to focus on trade policy, and occurred in the international rather than the national policy-making arena. This change was part of a broader shift toward what McMichael (2000a) calls the globalization project, where states were increasingly expected to implement rules of global economic management rather than retain the authority to regulate trade and development policy. During the 1980s conflicts over information trade politics revolved around a controversial proposal by the U.S. government to incorporate services trade under GATT. This proposal was part of a U.S. government strategy to develop a neoliberal discourse to govern international trade in services, including information and other digital commodities. The Brazilian and Indian delegations led the opposition to this proposal, since they feared GATT's free-trade orientation would involve pressure to open up their services markets.

The U.S. government strategy to create a neoliberal discourse on international services trade was part of a broader effort to promote U.S. competitiveness in global telecommunications and computer markets. Bilateral trade wars over telecommunications and computers formed a key part of the third episode of confrontation over information trade politics. These global power struggles continued to focus on trade, while the terrain of policy conflict shifted from the international forum of GATT to bilateral trade negotiations. Chapter 3 examines U.S. government efforts to bolster economic competitiveness by responding to what were considered "unfair trade practices" of its major trading partners. Among the possible responses to these threats to U.S. global economic interests, retaliation against "unfair trade practices" was viewed as most effective. In the fall of 1985, President Reagan accordingly initiated investigation of four such practices under Section 301 of the 1974 Trade Act. I explore the reasons why the Brazilian informatics case was so important to the U.S. government as a battleground in the larger struggles over information trade politics.

The 301 investigation of Brazilian informatics sparked a trade war that created geopolitical pressures on the Brazilian government, which complicated its effort to implement the informatics policy. Chapter 4 examines the complex dilemmas faced by the Brazilian government as it responded to the growing foreign and domestic pressures arising from the trade conflict. I focus on what one Brazilian industrialist called the U.S. and Brazilian governments' "double desire" for Brazil to enact a software law. One of the Reagan administration's major demands was that Brazil pass a software law that included an author's copyright, to protect U.S. software firms from widespread piracy and allow them to enter the Brazilian market. For its part, the Brazilian government used software policy both to mediate the trade dispute with the U.S. government and to extend the existing informatics policy into the software sector. Extensive debates occurred over software policy in the Brazilian legislature, which eventually passed a law including an author's copyright. This was viewed as sufficient progress by the U.S. government, which suspended the threat of trade sanctions pending further discussions over the law in the Brazilian Senate.

As these discussions ensued, the Brazilian government was faced with a decision that brought conflicts with the U.S. government to a head and revealed the constraints upon the Brazilian government posed by the structure of the international software market and Brazil's history of dependence on foreign trade. Six Brazilian computer manufacturers requested to license Microsoft's MS-DOS operating system instead of using a comparable system developed by a Brazilian firm, as required under the informatics law. Brazilian government officials knew that the informatics law needed to change to keep pace with shifts in the international software market, but they did not want to penalize firms that had complied with existing law. In negotiations with the U.S. government and Microsoft, they made it clear that while the policy would eventually become more open, for now they intended to uphold the law and deny the request to license MS-DOS.

This denial sparked U.S. trade sanctions in November 1987, just as the

Brazilian Senate was reaching a compromise on the final version of the software law. The sanctions gave rise to a new set of conflicts involving Brazilian footwear, steel, and other exporters, who pressured the Brazilian government not to sacrifice their businesses for the sake of the informatics law. The licensing of MS-DOS was eventually approved in January 1988, which led to the suspension of trade sanctions the following month. This was the beginning of the end of Brazil's informatics policy, which came under increasing domestic pressure with the election of Fernando Collor as Brazil's President in November 1989.

Chapter 5 explores the last phase of the 1984 informatics policy, from Collor's election until the original date for the expiration of the market reserve in October 1992. The Collor government dismantled the 1984 informatics policy as part of a sweeping plan for neoliberal economic reform, and replaced it with the 1991 informatics law. This shift to a neoliberal development approach was initially viewed as a victory for foreign capital, which gained opportunities to operate freely in the Brazilian market; for Brazilian computer users, who enjoyed access to a broader range of products; and for Brazilian computer firms that wanted to distribute foreign products. The transition to a neoliberal development strategy, however, was fraught with conflicts and surprises. Dramatic increases in sales of famous-brand computers failed to materialize, while Brazilian computer manufacturers built on longstanding relationships with customers to tailor systems to their needs. Foreign and local firms developed new economic partnerships to complement each other's strengths and navigate the uncertainties of the changing economic environment. They also forged new political alliances to pressure the state to fight contraband, implement industrial policy in informatics, and stabilize the economy.

The Brazilian government engaged in a complex, active process of constructing an open market rather than merely disengaging itself to let market forces operate, as neoliberal economic policies dictated. It was subjected to contradictory pressures from foreign and local capital that made it difficult to act as a unified political force and led to vacillation and inconsistency. The practical need to implement a policy for the transition to an open market called for increasing state action, despite neoliberal prescriptions for minimal state intervention and free trade.

Chapter 6 explores the continuing need for state action to shape conditions for informatics development in 2000 and 2001. When the 1991 informatics law expired in October 1999, the Brazilian Congress began negotiations over a new informatics law. There was widespread agreement that the Brazilian government should pass a new law to facilitate foreign investment in the informatics sector, which was plagued by heavy dependence both upon that investment and upon imported components. President Cardoso called for Brazil to launch an ambitious program for informatics development; however, these vestiges of nationalist discourse framed a neoliberal informatics policy that clarified the terms for global capital to enter the Brazilian market.

Chapter 7 explores the possibilities for developing alternatives to neoliberal development approaches in the context of globalization. I assess these possibilities in light of the strengths and limitations of the 1984 Brazilian informatics policy, an example of an oppositional, nationalist development strategy. Escobar raises questions about whether any strategy that operates within the development discourse can fundamentally transform conditions in the former Third World. Following Foucault (1972), he characterizes such strategies as "'costly gestures' . . . ways of producing change without transforming the nature of the [development] discourse as a whole" (Escobar 1995, 216). Alternatively, Escobar proposes a process of "unmaking development" (217). This involves transforming both discursive and material practices of development: "changing the order of discourse is a political question that entails the collective practice of social actors and the restructuring of existing political economies of truth" (216). In the concluding chapter, I evaluate whether the Brazilian informatics strategy was the kind of "costly gesture" against which Escobar warns and outline lessons from the informatics case for future opportunities to challenge, and perhaps "unmake," the practices and discourses of development, neoliberalism, and globalization.

RESEARCH METHODOLOGY

This study involved a multifaceted research strategy to collect a range of data about information trade politics and struggles over the Brazilian informatics policy at the international and national levels. I gathered the primary data through thirty-one qualitative, in-depth interviews carried out during two field seasons in Brazil. I first conducted interviews in the summer of 1990, a few months after Fernando Collor began the process of dismantling the informatics policy. This was a time when business executives and government officials were reflecting about what the policy had meant for their work and for the development of Brazilian informatics. I returned in 1992, a few months before the policy's originally scheduled termination date in October of that year. I interviewed some people for a second time along with some new participants. As I discuss in Chapter 5, this was a period of great volatility, when those involved in the informatics industry were grappling with questions of how to do business during the transition to a neoliberal economic policy.

I interviewed four major categories of people during the research. In order to protect confidentiality, many participants are not identified by name in the text. Instead, I use pseudonyms or simply identify them by their positions either as entrepreneurs, representatives of industry associations or of other political groups, or as government officials holding (or having held) particular posts. I include the names of participants who gave me permission to do so.

First, I interviewed eleven industrialists in Brazilian-owned computer hardware and software firms who had participated in a range of ways in the politics of the informatics industry from the 1970s to the 1990s. My questions were designed to explore a variety of issues, including the participants' involvement in political struggles over informatics policy formation and implementation; their relationships with the government and with foreign and domestic firms; their perception of economic and political changes in the industry; and their strategies to deal with the transition from a protected to an open market. Five of the participants had been involved in developing the informatics policy during the earliest stages in the mid-1970s. They contributed a valuable historical perspective on the changes in policy and industrial development, as well as on the political tensions involved with the different stages of policy implementation. At the time of our interviews, five of the participants had official responsibilities within key organizations involved in lobbying, negotiations, and general organizing to influence informatics policy. These included the Associação

Brasileira da Indústria de Computadores e Periféricos (Brazilian Computer and Peripherals Industry Association) (ABICOMP); the Movimento Brasil Informática (Brazilian Informatics Movement) (MBI); the Associação de Empresas Brasileiras de Software e Serviços de Informática (Association of Brazilian Informatics Software and Services Firms) (ASSESPRO); and the Sociedade dos Usuários de Computadores e Equipamentos Subsidiários (Society of Computer and Subsidiary Equipment Users) (SUCESU).

Second, I conducted five interviews with business executives working for IBM and Unisys subsidiaries based in Rio and Brasília. IBM and Unisys are the two U.S. multinationals with the longest history in the Brazilian computer industry. These men were Brazilian citizens who had spent their careers working for these firms; all held managerial positions in areas such as business strategy, external relations, special projects, and external programs. These executives offered key insights into the process of developing a working relationship with the Brazilian government, in the context of implementing an industrial policy that restricted the imports and investments of U.S. firms. They also provided information about tensions within the industry during the trade conflict with the United States, and during the transition from a nationalist to a neoliberal development policy.

Third, I interviewed three Brazilian government officials who had been in charge of implementing the informatics policy during the 1985–1987 trade conflict with the United States. José Ezil Veiga da Rocha was Secretary of Informatics from 1984 to 1985, and José Rubens Doria Porto held this post from 1986 to 1988. Both men had thus been responsible for making and implementing informatics policy during the trade conflict, as well as in the periods immediately before and after that conflict. Renato Archer was the Minister of Science and Technology between 1986 and 1988. He had consulted closely with the Secretary of Informatics in the process of decision making and negotiation during the trade conflict. In addition, I explored the role of the military in informatics policy by interviewing a former military officer with a history of policy involvement in the military group on informatics. José Ezil Veiga da Rocha had also been a high-ranking military officer.

Finally, I examined domestic conflicts faced by the government during the transition from a protected to an open market. Toward this end, I interviewed a top official in the Departamento de Política de Informática e Automação (Department of Informatics and Automation Policy) (DEPIN), which was created to replace the Secretaría Especial de Informática (Special Secretariat of Informatics) (SEI) after Fernando Collor became President in 1990. He was one of the key people in charge of implementing changes in the informatics field, as the existing policy was dismantled and replaced by a neoliberal economic policy. To gain insight into the impact of the software policy discussed in Chapter 5, I interviewed DEPIN's chief of the Divisão de Programas de Computador e Serviços Técnicos (Division of Computer Programs and Technical Services).

These interviews provide rich detail about the process of policy development and implementation. The participants offer insider accounts of complex political struggles over how to respond to foreign and domestic conflicts regarding the direction of informatics policy and industrial development. Building upon the poststructuralist perspective that informs this study, I understand these interviews as providing "multiple and competing knowledge claims to 'truth' produced by groups with partial perspectives" (Collins 1990, 235). Following Collins's discussion of black feminist epistemology, I view such accounts as partial perspectives, or as situated knowledge that "exists in a situation characterized by domination" (234). Situated knowledge provides a particular perspective, rooted in the combination of experiences of oppression, as well as privilege, of specific individuals who belong to a variety of social groups. Such knowledge is not "a system of ideas divorced from political and economic reality" (236). Its claim to truth lies in its representation of a specific viewpoint, based in particular political and economic conditions. It is part of a discourse, a narrative of power and knowledge that defines particular individuals or groups as qualified to speak the "truth," thus supporting their interpretations of that "truth."

For example, government officials and business executives working for Brazilian and U.S. corporations played distinct roles in developing the informatics industry and implementing the informatics policy. They had knowledge about different parts of this process, as well as conflicting interests in situations like the trade conflict with the United States or the transition from a nationalist to a neoliberal development policy. I use the situated knowledge from each interview to interpret the complex political dynamics, the shifting interests, and conflicting partial perspectives at work in Brazilian informatics development.

I reviewed a wide range of secondary sources to complement the interview data. In Brazil I collected government documents, articles from the business press and daily newspapers, reports by the Instituto de Economia Industrial (Institute of Industrial Economy) at the Universidade Federal do Rio de Janeiro (UFRJ), and other scholarly literature from libraries at UFRJ, the Universidade Católica do Rio de Janeiro, the Biblioteca da Câmara dos Deputados (Library of the House of Deputies), and the Centro de Informática e Processamento de Dados do Senado Federal (Center of Informatics and Data Processing of the Federal Senate) in Brasília. I also consulted reports prepared by agencies like the World Bank, the International Monetary Fund, and the United Nations, particularly the UN Centre on Transnational Corporations. I conducted most of the research for Chapter 6 on the Web, where I found government documents and business press and scholarly articles on the Web pages for the Brazilian Ministério da Ciência e Tecnologia (Ministry of Science and Technology) (MCT), the Associação Brasileira da Indústria Elétrica e Eletrônica (Brazilian Association of Electrical and Electronics Industries) (ABINEE), and other organizations. I also corresponded by e-mail with policy analysts at the Ministério da Ciência e Tecnologia. Finally, I drew upon theoretical and policy analysis from a wide range of scholarly sources.

ON LANGUAGE

The transformations in the global economy over the last few decades, and the theoretical shifts that have attempted to conceptualize them, present difficult choices regarding language use for those of us who study processes of development in global capitalism. The changing organization of international economic production, shifting conditions of industrialization within particular countries, and disparate histories of integration into the global capitalist system make it difficult to find concepts that represent the complexities of these conditions. Indeed, it is hard for any set of concepts to capture broad patterns of power and oppression in relationships between countries while recognizing the great variations in historical development and contemporary processes of change.

I deal with the limitations of the available concepts in part by using the terms "First World" and "former Third World" throughout the book. I follow McMichael's (2000a, xix) reasoning for choosing the Three Worlds terminology: "Although they certainly violate a heterogeneous reality as omnibus terms, they are useful as shorthand and certainly recognizable to most people." If the tag "the former" feels a bit strange to the reader at first, I hope this unfamiliarity will remind us of the flawed nature of the language available to speak and write about these issues, and of the problems with using any "omnibus terms" to communicate the complex reality of global economic change.

All the interviews for this study were conducted in Portuguese. Throughout the text, the translations from Portuguese into English from interviews, articles, books, and other materials are my own.

2 Information Trade Politics
From Telecommunications to Trade Policy

IN THE 1970S technological change involving telecommunications and computers created new arenas for struggle over global power relations. As it became possible to link computers across the world through telecommunications networks, and to transfer data over those networks to coordinate global production activities, political struggles arose over these emerging sources of economic power. Former Third World governments feared that if they did not control their telecommunications networks and transborder data flows, they would be subjected to a new form of information dependency. Many of these governments viewed national policy regulations as their primary means to defend themselves from the dangers of information dependency. By contrast, the U.S. government and multinational corporations opposed such regulations as barriers to global economic expansion.

During the 1970s and 1980s, telecommunications, information, and trade policies became battlegrounds in a global power struggle that I call information trade politics. Building upon Foucault (1978, 102), this chapter traces the development of this struggle through three "episodes of confrontation." Each episode was characterized by particular policy conflicts, by particular terrains of struggle in national or international arenas, and by a focus on telecommunications, information, or trade policy. At stake was the power to control digital trade and communication by establishing the material and discursive conditions for access to the electromagnetic infrastructure that enabled that trade to occur. As is discussed below, the material conditions largely involved political and economic agreements forged through a process of conflict and struggle between First and former Third World governments and multinational corporations. Many of these agreements, and the struggles to achieve them, centered on the development of a discourse to govern digital trade and communication. The discursive conditions for digital trade were thus a focal point for information trade politics in the 1970s and 1980s.

Foucault's analysis of the discourse on sex in the first volume of *The History of Sexuality* provides three guidelines for this analysis. Two emerge from Foucault's (1978, 102) argument that "we must question [the discourses] on the two levels of their tactical productivity (what reciprocal effects of power and knowledge they ensure) and their strategical integration (what conjunction and what force relationship make their utilization necessary in a given episode of the various confrontations that occur)." Through the concept of strategic integration, Foucault here emphasizes the importance of understanding the "conjunctions" or "episode[s] of . . . confrontation[s]" that make certain discourses "necessary" in a particular period. Three different stages are evident in the struggle over information trade politics of the 1970s and 1980s. These stages involved periods of conflict over regulatory issues that occurred in particular institutional contexts, such as national or international policy negotiations. These stages can be conceptualized as "episodes of confrontation." Each episode involved a certain "conjunction" and set of "force relationships" that shaped the interests of First and former Third World governments and led them to advocate distinct policy positions. In other words, distinct relations of power were involved in each episode, creating conditions where the use of particular discourses became "necessary" parts of, or made a particular kind of strategic sense within, the struggle over information trade politics. This brings us to Foucault's second guideline for understanding discourses in terms of their "tactical productivity." First and former Third World governments sought to protect their economic interests largely through the process of defining telecommunications, information, or trade policy. Each policy definition had "reciprocal effects of power and knowledge" since it helped create the discursive conditions for firms and governments to engage in digital trade and communication. The power to define policy according to certain criteria of knowledge and truth was thus integrally linked to the power to engage in new forms of trade in the international economy.

Foucault (1978) provides a third guideline for understanding the development of the discourse on digital trade, as well as the power relations and institutional context that shaped struggles over information trade politics. Foucault recommends that the theorist reconstruct the "multiplicity of discursive elements . . . with the things said and those concealed, the enunciations required and those forbidden . . . ; with the variants and different effects—according to who is speaking, his position of power, the institutional context in which he happens to be situated" (100). Foucault thus emphasizes the importance of identifying the content of the discourse in terms of the elements that comprise it, as well as the relations of power between the actors involved and the institutional context within which they interact. Each episode of confrontation over information trade politics involved conflicts over how to define the content of telecommunications, information, or trade policy. Representatives of First and former Third World governments argued about which terms would be used in these definitions, all of which "said" certain things while "concealing" others. The position of power of the actors involved, and the institutional contexts in which they interacted, shaped the nature of the struggles as well as the eventual development of a discourse on digital trade.

A NEW ROLE FOR TELECOMMUNICATIONS: ELECTROMAGNETIC HIGHWAYS FOR DIGITAL TRADE AND COMMUNICATION

After 1975 striking transformations occurred in international telephone and telex systems. These were brought by technological changes involving digitalization, communication satellites, optical fibers, and the integration of telecommunications with computer technology. The ability to transmit data between computers in distant locations through telecommunications links allowed telecommunications systems to play a growing role in processes of trade and production. Transborder data flows were used by multinational corporations to coordinate business operations in different parts of the world, allowing them to reorganize and control production on a global scale. Technological innovations in microelectronics transformed the telecommunications industry, which experienced a dynamic expansion in both national and international markets. It developed into a core industry that enabled new forms of digital trade and communication to occur (United Nations Centre on Transnational Corporations 1990, 44–45).

The telecommunications infrastructure has become an electromagnetic highway facilitating the exchange of goods and services in the form of transborder data flows. Since these flows consist of computer-readable, digital signals, this involves a new form of trade that I call "digital trade." When the flows are bought and sold on the market, I refer to them as "digital commodities" (Schoonmaker 1993, 1994). For example, when users log on to services like America Online or CompuServe, they purchase a commodity that is offered in digital form, which they receive through telecommunications links to their computer systems. Financial services such as electronic cash management are also provided as digital commodities. They provide corporate treasurers with detailed information about account balances, individual transactions, and money market investments for all of a corporation's accounts scattered in countries around the world. These services give treasurers control over the transfer of funds among the firm's accounts, enabling them to invest their unused cash flow to take maximum advantage of changes in interest, inflation, and exchange rates. They are one example of a growing array of financial services that are traded in digital form and facilitate greater spreading of risk for corporate operations (Dicken 1992).

Other possibilities for digital trade arose in the banking sector as it became possible to render and transmit checks in digital form. The president of a bank-owned electronic-payment system, the National Automated Clearing House, estimates that it costs over $50 billion to print, mail, and clear the approximately 60 billion checks written in the United States every year. He notes, "Literally hundreds of tons of them are on the move every day, lugged around by truck, helicopters and planes from branches to headquarters and then to other banks over a labyrinth of routes" (Davis, Hirschl, and Stack 1997, 129). Rendering and transporting checks in digital form decreases this traffic and allows the banking sector to provide a new type of digital service to its customers.

Comparable changes emerged in other areas, reducing the need for traditional forms of transportation and creating new opportunities for digital trade. For example, the *Miami Herald* used to ship a ton of newspapers daily to a number of Latin American cities. Since 1995, however, the paper has been distributed by satellite in digital form to local printing plants, where it is printed and distributed to local markets. Similarly, Pacific Bell is testing a system to make it possible for Hollywood studios to transmit digitized movies to local theaters over high-speed phone lines. This new way of distributing new releases could reduce the distribution costs for films, costs that amount to about 25 percent of the average film budget. Instead of making hundreds, or even thousands, of prints of a film and sending them to theaters through traditional transportation means, digital trade would allow these films to be delivered more quickly and less expensively. Pacific Bell's technical manager for advanced video services describes the potential advantages of this process: "Theoretically, you could have one guy sitting in a closet anywhere in the world, programming all 25,000 theater screens in the country" (Davis, Hirschl, and Stack 1997, 129).

In a completely different economic sector, a business executive in the San Francisco Bay area established the Clos LaChance Vineyard, which he described as a "virtual winery." He states, "We buy grapes from other vineyards. We lease space at a production winery. We contract with talent for wine making and label design. We acquire materials like bottles and corks from other sources. We lease warehouse storage" (Tapscott 1996, 155). Although the wine itself is clearly not a digital commodity, the services used to market the wine are offered completely in digital form. This small vineyard has a site on the Internet that discusses the product and tells customers how to order wine electronically. The owners eventually plan to use more digital advertising, in which well-known public figures talk about how much they enjoy the wine. As one owner remarks, "We're really intrigued by the possibilities for leveling the playing field by marketing through the information infrastructure. Mondavi has a zillion dollars of advertising money and we have zero dollars. If we do a better job than Mondavi in positioning our company on the Net, we may be able to compete" (156).

Its ability to engage in digital advertising allows this small company to market its products in a completely new form, and potentially to challenge much larger competitors. Similarly, the ability to trade other digital commodities in the form of transborder data flows has made it possible for firms to enter new markets in the services field. In the 1980s there was significant growth in international trade of producer services, including financial, management, advertising, professional, and technical services. In some cases, providing these services requires no direct physical contact between buyers and sellers. Thus they represent a form of invisible international trade that allows firms to transcend all spatial and temporal barriers to their activities.

Digital trade requires telecommunications and computer systems to interconnect and provide the service of transportation in a new form. In these circumstances, telecommunications systems do much more than merely transmit information. They actually *produce* the service of transportation. Transportation and communication functions merge through the application of digital and telecommunications technologies. Information has become a commodity, and communications systems have assumed the role of the transport industry by moving commodities through space.

The connection of telecommunications and computer technologies allows the telecommunications network to play a new role as a highway for digital trade. Such trade is severely limited, however, by the practical need to meet personally with customers. Although it has become technically possible to transport them in digital form, many services cannot be offered effectively to customers without meeting them face to face. In fields like accounting and advertising, for example, personal interactions with clients are important in gaining their confidence and developing business relationships. In such cases, firms that want to expand their operations open branch offices in new locations. They use foreign investment, rather than digital trade, to develop overseas operations.

Although digital trade remains limited by the needs of businesses to serve their customers face to face, the telecommunications network still plays a vital role for all firms engaged in global business operations. These firms rely on transborder data flows for digital communication rather than trade. Digital communication facilitates corporate efforts to restructure production on a global scale, as well as to implement new forms of control over geographically dispersed activities. It makes it possible to coordinate the different phases of corporate activities located in distant corners of the world. Each step in the operation can be monitored at a distance from the actual production facilities. For example, manufacturing firms use digital communication to schedule production of product components in different parts of the world, as well as to integrate their assembly and delivery to global markets. Detailed information concerning accounts, personnel, and other fundamental business activities can be transmitted in seconds. International business operations can be conducted more efficiently when firms have almost immediate access to data about the activities of corporate branches in different parts of the world (Feketekuty 1992; Castells 1996; Tapscott 1996; United Nations Centre on Transnational Corporations 1988).

FROM TELECOMMUNICATIONS POLICY TO NETWORK ACCESS: THE FIRST EPISODE OF CONFRONTATION

The importance of telecommunications systems for these new digital forms of trade and communication has been a catalyst to transform world trade debates. These debates have shifted to emphasize the range of connections between traditional areas of telecommunications policy and new areas involving trade in services. They have also focused increasingly on the development of a discourse to govern digital trade and communication. As Robert R. Bruce, the general counsel of the Federal Communications Commission, testified before Congress in 1981, "there is also a need to cope with an emerging agenda of what might be described as information policy as opposed to telecommunications policy issues. . . . They [information policy issues] will deal primarily with the marketing of information and with the international provision of services by businesses which are highly dependent on telecommunications and computers" (U.S. House Committee on Government Operations 1981, 47–48).

What Robert R. Bruce referred to as information policy issues involves trade in services and other digital commodities, as well as digital communication. Bruce's statement exemplifies the U.S. government effort to establish a discourse for digital trade, in order to regulate new forms of trade and communication arising from the convergence of telecommunications and computer systems. Although such a framework would apply to certain uses of telecommunications equipment and services, it would need to incorporate new principles and rules to address the unique character of digital trade and communication. Its "multiplicity of discursive elements" would need to leave different "things said and ... concealed" (Foucault 1978, 100). Indeed, Bruce explicitly recommended renaming telecommunications policy, thus concealing that traditional term and replacing it with the new term "information policy." This is more than a simple semantic change since it contributes to the development of a policy discourse that extends the traditional purview of telecommunications policy to digital trade and communication.

Technological change in telecommunications and computers shaped a new social context for the development of a trade policy discourse, which was a focal point in the struggles over information trade politics. As the telecommunications system was transformed from a medium to transmit voice messages into a digital highway for international trade, national telecommunications policies took on new implications for trade and production. Traditional telecommunications policies established technical standards to operate telecommunications systems, as well as rules governing access to public and private telecommunications networks. These policies determined the quality of telecommunications systems but had no direct impact on the process of trade. But where telecommunications and computer technologies merged, existing telecommunications policies had a whole new set of implications for the process of digital trade, extending way beyond their traditional purview of basic voice transmission. By establishing the technical standards and terms for access to the telecommunications network, telecommunications policies simultaneously shaped the infrastructure for digital trade and communication.

As technological change created new possibilities for digital trade, existing telecommunications policies thus affected the conditions for that trade to occur. They effectively became trade policies, although they had not been designed as such. This changing relationship between technology, trade, and policy led to the development of information trade politics and made the development of a discourse on digital trade a central focus for political struggle. Indeed, information trade politics first emerged as a set of political struggles between national governments and multinational corporations over telecommunications policies that governed the terms for access to telecommunications networks.

The struggles focused on national telecommunications policy largely because, in most countries, telecommunications companies were either government-owned monopolies or publicly regulated. The telecommunications policy discourse took different forms in different countries; however, it was generally based upon nationalist cultural values. As Escobar (1995, 59) notes, this discourse was a "cultural production" rooted in values of national sovereignty that identified national governments as the appropriate arbiters of telecommunications policy. This discourse had a certain "tactical productivity" involving "reciprocal effects of power and knowledge" (Foucault 1978, 102) where national governments had the power to define and implement policy in the telecommunications field. Any effort to challenge this power thus involved a protracted struggle over a range of discursive elements, including policy regulations and definitions as well as the underlying cultural value of national sovereignty.

The U.S. government had economic and political reasons for engaging in such a struggle since it was concerned about the effects of telecommunications policies on multinational corporations. In the early 1980s, a number of task forces and working groups were established within the State Department and interested executive branch agencies to study issues of information and communications policy. These included the Interagency Task Force on Transborder Data Flows, chaired by the State Department's director of the Office of International Communications Policy, and the Interagency Working Group on Information and Communication, also chaired by the State Department.[1] Each of these groups focused on the activities of particular intergovernmental agencies, or were charged to prepare studies on specific issues.

In 1981 the Office of the United States Trade Representative (USTR) organized an ad hoc advisory committee to compile a report that listed barriers to transborder data flows. Working in conjunction with the Interagency Task Force on Transborder Data Flows, this committee submitted the report to the Trade Committee of the Organization for Economic Cooperation and Development. The report was entitled "International Trade

Issues in Telecommunications, Data Processing and Information Services." It outlined two major ways that telecommunications policies had raised concerns for multinational corporations (U.S. House Committee on Government Operations 1982).

The first pertained to government restrictions on private lines that firms lease from public telecommunications authorities. Some governments sought to abolish the use of private leased lines altogether; some limited their use or proposed to charge significantly more for them. Other governments considered charging for leased lines on a volume-sensitive basis rather than using a flat rate. According to the USTR report, "All of these measures could substantially increase the cost and reduce the flexibility of international telecommunications, and international trade in related services" (U.S. House Committee on Government Operations 1982, 184).

Second, the U.S. government and multinational corporations were concerned about restrictions on the type of equipment that could be connected to the public telecommunications network as well as on the procedures firms could use to link their own equipment with the public network. Such regulations limited the type, make, or design of equipment that firms were allowed to use as well as the kind of communication and data services they could provide. The USTR report warned that "governments should seriously consider entering into multilateral negotiations aimed at reaching agreement on providing open access to telecommunications equipment interconnect markets as a way of eliminating the restrictive effects of such regulations" (U.S. House Committee on Government Operations 1982, 184).

Many governments, however, did not view "open access" to their telecommunications markets as in their best interest. While existing policies had not been designed for such purposes, these governments attempted to use telecommunications policies to control the conditions for digital trade and communication. The power to control the telecommunications networks that firms were allowed to use gave national governments a foothold in these early struggles over information trade politics.

For example, German law restricted the conditions under which multinational corporations could connect their private leased lines to the German public telecommunications network. In order to connect their lines to the German network, these firms were required to use a computer that performed some data-processing activities. They were also prohibited from using the lines to transmit unprocessed data to foreign public telecommunications networks.

These policies were designed to create incentives for multinational corporations to use Germany's public telecommunications network, and thus increase earnings for the German postal, telephone, and telegraph monopoly. The trade implications of such policies were outlined in a 1981 report by an ad hoc computer group established by the U.S. Trade Representative's office. The report, entitled "Trade Barriers to Telecommunications, Data and Information Services," cited two major trade implications of government controls on telecommunications networks such as those found in Germany. First, they increased costs to users, and particularly smaller users, who had to rely on public networks and pay whatever prices were set in a particular national context. Second, in many cases, public networks did not provide the quality of service desired by multinational corporations. Requirements to use public networks thus reduced the efficiency of corporate communications while increasing their cost (U.S. House Committee on Foreign Affairs 1982, 43).

In these early struggles, governments recognized the new implications of their telecommunications policies, which led them to focus on the telecommunications discourse in their conflicts with multinational corporations and the U.S. government. They defended these policies as the only existing regulation of digital trade and communication. Such efforts conflicted with corporate attempts to gain access to the public telecommunications network, or to establish their own private networks, in order to send or receive transborder data flows. These firms challenged the cultural value of national sovereignty embedded in the telecommunications policy discourse, arguing that they should have the right to connect, or the "right to plug in," to the telecommunications networks of all the countries in which they operated.

For example, in most countries in the 1970s and 1980s, traditional telecommunications policies required governmental approval for the use of terminal equipment; this equipment had to be obtained from a government-owned telecommunications monopoly. In Japan and the European Community, governments restricted the availability of private leased telecommunications lines, in effect requiring firms to use the public telecommunications network. Such policies were designed to raise revenues for public telecommunications monopolies by generating additional business; a further objective was to support public data communications networks as well as local data processing and database service firms (U.S. House Committee on Foreign Affairs 1982, 42).

According to the USTR report, "Trade Barriers to Telecommunications, Data and Information Services," the Japanese and European policies had implications for trade similar to the German policy. Public networks often did not offer the same quality of service as the corporations' private leased lines. Being restricted to the public telecommunications network thus posed a "barrier" to the firms' operations by reducing the efficiency of their communications processes. The report also warned that "If private circuits are eliminated, advances in teleprocessing will be severely retarded and many existing teleprocessing systems will be degraded" (U.S. House Committee on Foreign Affairs 1982, 42).

National telecommunications policies thus created conflicts for multinational corporations and other large users of data communications. A number of firms objected that regulations on access to public communications networks raised costs of exporting services like data processing and database access. They argued that such increases could eventually make their current level of data communications unfeasible economically. In some cases, firms were required to establish duplicate facilities abroad in order to offer these services (United Nations Centre on Transnational Corporations 1990, 57–58; U.S. House Committee on Government Operations 1981, 108–10, 156–57; U.S. Senate Committee on Commerce, Science, and Transportation 1983, 170).

Early debates over information trade politics occurred as governments used telecommunications policy to provide some measure of regulatory control over access to the network for digital trade and communication. These efforts often posed problems for multinational corporations seeking to do business in a variety of global markets. In these cases, multinational corporations appealed to telecommunications authorities to allow the "right of non-establishment." They preferred to offer telecommunications services from abroad, in the form of cross-border trade of digital commodities, rather than establish operations in the host country.

Through such appeals, multinational corporations challenged the nationalist cultural values underlying the existing telecommunications policy discourse. These firms sought to transform this discourse by creating an alternative regulatory framework to replace national telecommunications policies, which would leave them free to engage in digital trade and communication in the ways most conducive to their global operations. Their efforts to redefine the issues at stake, as well as the nationalist cultural values that shaped them, are reflected in this statement by the Business Roundtable: "The sovereign right of nations to determine their own telecommunications policies is not the issue; rather, it is the international consequences of these national policies that may be subject to legitimate challenge by other countries whose interests are adversely affected" (Business Roundtable 1985, 6).

This statement exemplifies the initial struggles over information trade politics, which focused on who would have the power to regulate access to telecommunications networks for digital trade and communication. By redefining the telecommunications policy discourse, multinational corporations sought to wrest control over network access away from national governments. In response, governments clung to the traditional policy definitions and cultural values embedded in the telecommunications policy discourse as their only regulatory hold over this increasingly important field. Tensions over the telecommunications policy discourse were a key feature of the shift from the development to the globalization project (McMichael 2000a) discussed in Chapter 1, where states were increasingly expected to implement the rules of global economic management rather than to craft trade and development policies according to nationally defined goals. Defining the telecommunications policy discourse was vital for the establishment of economic, political, and cultural conditions for digital trade and communication.

The focus on telecommunications policy during the first episode of confrontation over information trade politics was an unintended consequence of technological change. As new telecommunications and computer technologies made it possible to merge these systems, they created new possibilities for digital trade and communication. This led the traditional telecommunications policy discourse to take on new implications for trade and production, and made it the cornerstone of the first episode of confrontation over information trade politics.

Something new was at stake in these struggles over the telecommunications policy discourse, distinguishing them from previous discussions of telecommunications regulation and marking the beginning of information trade politics. What was at stake was the power to control the conditions for digital trade and communication. And although access to the telecommunications network was necessary to exercise this power, this was merely the beginning of the struggle over digital trade. As these debates over the telecommunications policy discourse unfolded, another set of struggles emerged. They ushered in the second episode of confrontation over information trade politics in the 1970s.

In this second episode, the focus of debate shifted away from the telecommunications network itself and toward transborder data flows, the digital stream of information and commodities provided through that network. New policies were needed to regulate this electromagnetic stream used for digital trade and communication. Such policies involved much more than regulating the quality and conditions for access to the telecommunications network. Although the first episode of confrontation focused on new implications of the existing telecommunications policy discourse, the second episode focused more directly upon the emerging connections between telecommunications, information, and trade policy. These connections formed the heart of information trade politics, which shifted to focus on the development of a new discourse that would encompass telecommunications, information, and trade policy.

This change in focus from the telecommunications network to transborder data flows marked a new episode in the struggle to control the conditions for digital trade and communication. During this second episode, multinational corporations and First and former Third World governments sought to develop new policies to regulate transborder data flows, and to define the principles and norms to guide such policies. They framed the issues at stake in conflicting terms, based on distinct cultural values embedded in the struggle between the development and globalization projects. The central conflict occurred between advocates of the cultural value of national sovereignty, which corresponded to the development project's emphasis on government control over trade and development policy, and advocates of the cultural value of free market competition, which fit within the globalization project's effort to consolidate the rules of global economic management. This conflict dominated the second episode of confrontation over information trade politics, largely because transborder data flows influenced conditions for telecommunications and services development, as well as for digital trade. The flows had important economic and political implications for power relations between multinational corporations and First and former Third World countries, as well as the structure of the global economic system as a whole (Kane 1985; Feketekuty and Aronson 1984; U.S. House Committee on Government Operations 1981; U.S. House Committee on Energy and Commerce 1981; Cruise O'Brien 1983; Aronson and Cowhey 1984).

"SOVEREIGNTY DISCOURSE" ON TRANSBORDER DATA FLOWS: NATIONALIST VALUES TO RESIST INFORMATION DEPENDENCY

In the 1970s, many former Third World governments began to view transborder data flows as perpetuating a new form of economic dependency, based upon the lack of technologies, skills, scientific and research institutions, and industries involved with computer manufacturing and services. They were concerned that this "information dependency" would leave them unprepared to compete in the process of global economic restructuring and lead to dependency upon foreign data-processing capabilities. For example, foreign subsidiaries of multinational corporations located in former Third World countries often depended upon central computers at company headquarters for data processing or storage. Since these headquarters were generally located in First World countries, there was the potential for the governments of those countries to cut off the data links and disrupt the subsidiaries' operations.

Concerns about information dependency were not confined to the former Third World. Many governments raised questions about how data were stored and used by financial and insurance firms, retailers, and other employers; they wondered how data about their citizens might be used by foreign governments if they were transferred into those countries. By 1978, largely in response to these concerns, eighteen countries had either passed or were formulating laws concerning transborder data flows. In 1977 Belgium made it a criminal offense to record or transmit certain data. Spain proposed a law in 1978 that required money to be deposited in an escrow account before data files could be transmitted out of the country. And British law stipulated that the British Post Office be able to read any transmitted message; in the case of electronic data, firms were required to reveal confidential encryption methods for transborder data flows to a government agency (Eger 1978).

Canadian privacy legislation enacted in 1976 revealed concerns that transborder data flows might negatively affect national sovereignty and economic interests. The Canadian Minister for Science and Technology addressed these issues at the 1977 Conference of the International Federation of Information Processing Societies. His remarks exemplify the Canadian position at that time on the economic effects of information export: "[I]t creates the potential of growing dependence, rather than interdependence, the loss of employment opportunities, in addition to the balance of payments problems, the danger of loss of legitimate access to vital information, and the danger that industrial and social development will be largely governed by the decisions of interest groups residing in another country" (Eger 1978, 1078–79).

The risks of dependence on foreign data-processing systems were exemplified by the case of the Dresser Corporation, a major U.S. supplier of oil field and pipeline equipment and related technology. Dresser's French subsidiary conducted its engineering and design work by accessing a computer program located at corporate headquarters in the United States, using a telecommunications link. The French subsidiary had contracts with the former Soviet Union to supply equipment to construct a gas pipeline from the Urals to Western Europe. These contracts, however, violated U.S. export regulations. When the French government ordered Dresser France to fulfill the contracts, the U.S. parent firm cut the data link to corporate headquarters. Because the French subsidiary was dependent upon the data link to perform its business operations, it was unable to meet its contractual obligations with the former Soviet Union. The French government was also unable to require the firm to fulfill its contracts since it could not restore access to the necessary data-processing facilities in the United States (Sauvant 1986, 115).

The prospects for a new form of information dependency led many governments to view transborder data-flow regulations as vital to the development of a new international information order. Along with control over the media and national economic development, transborder data flows were conceived as central to national sovereignty and economic power. In 1979 the United Nations General Assembly passed a resolution supporting the new international information order, and affirming "the manifest need to change the dependent status of the developing countries in the field of information and communications" (Transnational Data Reporting Service 1980, 37).

Former Third World governments were the most vocal about the dangers of a new form of information dependency. They first articulated these concerns in 1978, when the Intergovernmental Bureau for Informatics collaborated with the United Nations Educational, Scientific and Cultural Organization (UNESCO), to sponsor the first Intergovernmental Conference on Strategies and Policies for Informatics (SPIN I), attended by delegations from seventy-eight countries. SPIN I was the first forum where former Third World countries analyzed transborder data flows as requiring international coordination and negotiation to protect national sovereignty and future prospects for economic development. They agreed on the importance of national strategies to promote informatics development. Representatives from lesser developed countries such as Bangladesh, Chad, and Niger highlighted the difficulties in implementing such strategies, although they emphasized their commitment to preparing informatics programs (Transnational Data Reporting Service 1980).

Following SPIN I, in 1979 former Third World countries participated in regional conferences on informatics in Latin America and Africa; these were sponsored by the Intergovernmental Bureau for Informatics. Conference participants passed resolutions that articulated their concerns about information dependency in more specific terms (Sauvant 1984a, 1984b; Intergovernmental Bureau for Informatics 1982).

For example, the Third Conference of Latin American Informatics Authorities passed a resolution emphasizing the links between transborder data flows and national sovereignty, as well as issues of national security and the right to privacy. This resolution conceptualized data as a "resource with real value" (United Nations Centre on Transnational Corporations 1982, 114), whose unequal global distribution perpetuated power inequalities. It warned that processing data abroad might potentially damage the interests of former Third World countries, if the data affected "national sovereignty, cultural identity and technological progress" (United Nations Centre on Transnational Corporations 1982, 115).[2] To counteract these potential problems, the resolution recommended that countries develop national data protection laws. Such laws could promote the local development of information resources, partly by limiting the extent to which data were stored and processed abroad. Regulation of data flows might also protect citizens' rights to privacy, since computer technologies made it possible to compute, store, and process unprecedented quantities of data about individuals (United Nations Centre on Transnational Corporations 1982).

The Conference on African Informatics Integration in November 1979 echoed Latin American concerns. Representatives at this conference viewed the increasing concentration of socioeconomic, geographical, scientific, and technical data in First World countries as harmful to the sovereignty of African nations. They argued that this imbalance was perpetuated by multinational corporate control over international data communication networks, which made it possible to exchange data about the economies, geography, and natural resources of African countries without their knowledge and consent. Conference participants recommended state regulations to promote the development of national data communication networks and data banks, as well as the creation of a regional body within the Organization of African Unity to support each state in creating a national informatics policy (United Nations Centre on Transnational Corporations 1982).

Former Third World governments used these regional conferences as venues to air their concerns and articulate the cultural values they viewed as most important for a transborder data-flow policy discourse. These conferences, however, did not wield any institutional power to regulate transborder data flows. Nor did most of the participating governments have the resources to develop or implement substantial policies in this area. As a result, there was a series of debates about transborder data flows but very little policy response. The policies that were enacted focused more on protecting the privacy of citizens than on resisting information dependency.

A notable exception to this lack of policy response, however, was the Brazilian military government. It formulated a policy that was designed not just to regulate transborder data flows but to promote the broader development of industries, skills, and technologies required to conduct local data-processing activities (Maciel 1981; U.S. Senate Committee on Commerce, Science, and Transportation 1983). This approach is expressed in a report on transborder data flows in Brazil prepared by the Brazilian SEI in conjunction with the United Nations Centre on Transnational Corporations. It states:

> In fact, transborder data flows are a principal vehicle through which, in the long run, the geographical distribution of information resources—and hence knowledge and intelligence—is determined. . . . such resources are key indicators of economic power and national identity. Consequently, the lack of information resources in a country can generate a serious dependence parallel to that in the area of natural resources. (United Nations Centre on Transnational Corporations 1983, 132)

The debates over transborder data flows contributed to what I call a "sovereignty discourse" on transborder data flows, which formed part of the larger call for a new international information order. This discourse was based upon the assumption that transborder data-flow policy should be rooted in the cultural values of national sovereignty and development. Governments had the right to protect their national sovereignty by regulating conditions for economic development—at least in certain sectors that were deemed most important for the economy, or where transnational corporations dominated national markets. The sovereignty discourse shared similar nationalist cultural values with the development project (McMichael 2000a) since it viewed governments as the appropriate arbiters of national trade and development policy.

Through this sovereignty discourse of the 1970s, a range of governments articulated their concerns about information dependency and posed the values they felt should inform a policy response. This discourse conflicted with what I call the "free trade" discourse on transborder data flows, which advocated the cultural values of the free flow of information and free market competition. Proponents of the free-trade discourse made a critical step that the sovereignty discourse never achieved: they gained an institutional foothold that opened up possibilities for free trade to become the guiding cultural value for an international policy on transborder data flows. They shifted the arena of struggle from discussions over values to guide transborder data-flow policy, into an international arena for making and implementing such policy. This shift was part of the rise of the globalization project (McMichael 2000a), where national trade and development policy was increasingly subjected to the rules of global economic management.

FREE-TRADE DISCOURSE ON TRANSBORDER DATA FLOWS: FROM CULTURAL VALUES TO POLICY DEVELOPMENT

The U.S. government policy discourse on international communications was rooted in the cultural value of the free flow of information throughout the postwar period. This value was first articulated in 1945 at the Inter-American Conference in Mexico City. There the U.S. government enjoined Latin American governments to incorporate the doctrine of the free flow of information and communication between nations into the final declaration of the conference (Fejes 1983).

Since then the U.S. government has consistently advocated the free flow of information as a central principle of transborder data-flow policy (Fowler 1985; Greenberg 1985; Shultz 1986; U.S. House Committee on Government Operations 1981; U.S. House Committee on Energy and Commerce 1981). In its view, the regulation of information flows threatened the ability of firms and governments to function in the world economy. U.S. government officials have argued that the free flow of information, like free trade, benefits all the parties involved (Katzenbach 1985; Coombe 1985a, 1985b; U.S. House Committee on Government Operations 1981; U.S. House Committee on Energy and Commerce 1981, 1986; U.S. House Committee on Ways and Means 1986a). Disruption of that flow was seen as potentially damaging to the economic system on a global scale (Eger 1978; U.S. House Committee on Energy and Commerce 1981).

Presentation of the free flow of information as an objective principle was a key part of the free-trade discourse on transborder flows, which had strong parallels to the discourse of neoclassical economics. Both discourses are what Escobar (1995, 59) calls "cultural forms" based upon cultural values peculiar to modernity, including the assumption that the economy is primarily a material entity governed by objective laws that dictate how markets operate. The free-trade discourse on transborder data flows drew upon these neoclassical principles, representing the free flow of information as an objective requirement of the economic system rather than as a cultural value inextricably linked to the economic interests of multinational corporations and many First World governments.

The chairman of the Senate Committee on Foreign Relations justified the U.S. government's position on the free flow of information in 1977: "One way to 'attack' a nation such as the United States which depends heavily on information and communications is to restrain the flow of information—cutting off contact between the headquarters and the overseas branches of a multinational firm; taxing telecommunications crossing borders; building information walls around a nation" (Eger 1978, 1056–57).

Multinational corporations also supported the free flow of information as the guiding principle for a transborder data-flow policy. Since the 1970s these firms have used the flows to reorganize and control global production operations. As the major users of transborder data flows, multinational corporations advocated complete freedom of movement for the flows, as well as "rights of establishment" for the communications networks to transmit them. Their main interest was in having maximum flexibility to transmit flows for whatever purposes they needed, from personnel data to new computer services like data processing or cash management (Aronson and Cowhey 1984; O'Connor 1986; O'Connor and Moser 1987).

In 1981 a Motorola executive enumerated corporate concerns about transborder data-flow regulations in congressional testimony. He argued that such regulations would require his firm to establish separate data-processing operations in different countries, in the process foregoing the benefits of a management information system that would allow the company to function competitively on a global scale. This in turn could lead to a range of problems, including dramatic increases in inventories; difficulties with information consistency; increased collection times for receivables; lower quality of customer service; extensions on monthly financial closings; impediments to the sharing of computer-aided engineering designs between the United States and Europe; and increased demands for people and computer equipment, and a possible inability to locate sufficient talented personnel to run complex computer systems in all the parts of the world where Motorola conducts its operations. Although the firm had not yet encountered any of these problems, the Motorola executive argued that the firm's ability to compete in international markets could be jeopardized if they were to occur. He summed up his concerns by saying, "the time to address the issue is now—before real problems arise. . . . Like trade in physical goods and services, 'information' . . . represents employment, economic growth, and national sovereignty and security. Consequently, any barriers to transborder data flows are limiting factors directly affecting these vital areas of our national life and interests" (U.S. House Committee on Energy and Commerce 1981, 162).

In 1983 the Senate Committee on Commerce, Science, and Transportation commissioned a report on "Long-Range Goals in International Telecommunications and Information." In this report, free competitive market enterprise was integrated with the free flow of information as a second major principle to guide U.S. telecommunications and information policy.[3] The report recommended that individual policy decisions "enhance the free (without restriction or control) flow of information across national borders" and promote international conditions where telecommunications and information facilities, services, and equipment, as well as the production and distribution of information itself, entail "maximum reliance . . . on free enterprise, open and competitive markets, and free trade and investment with minimum direct government involvement or regulation" (U.S. Senate Committee on Commerce, Science, and Transportation 1983, 12).

In this report, the U.S. government articulated its support for free trade as an underlying principle of transborder data-flow policy. During this same period, however, U.S. government officials took decisive actions that shifted struggles over information trade politics into a new arena. They changed the focus of debate away from the principles for transborder data-flow policy and in the direction of creating an international institutional framework to make and implement such policy. Furthermore, they raised the stakes in the struggle for control over digital trade and communication by seeking to institutionalize policy-making power in a way that undermined the authority of national governments to develop their own transborder data-flow policies. This emerging institutional foundation was part of the globalization project, where international bureaucratic entities like the General Agreement on Tariffs and Trade joined multinational corporations and banks, as well as multilateral financial institutions like the World Bank and the International Monetary Fund, in establishing the rules for global economic management (McMichael 2000a).

U.S. government officials began this institutionalization effort by raising the question of how to define transborder data flows. This question arose within more general discussions over whether to include services under the General Agreement on Tariffs and Trade (GATT). GATT was an international free-trade agreement based upon neoclassical economic principles. According to these principles, all trading partners were equal players in the world economy, and the free flow of goods maximized everyone's economic interests. First and former Third World countries were viewed as making rational choices on a level playing field where all trading partners should be treated alike. Many former Third World representatives to GATT deemed these assumptions to be problematic since GATT failed to recognize the disadvantages their countries faced in international trade. These representatives believed that former Third World countries should be able to protect the growth of local industries by implementing development policies, rather than be expected to open their markets to foreign capital on the same terms as their First World counterparts. As Shrirang

Shukla, India's representative to GATT, observed, "a different power spectrum" exists between participants in GATT, "and it must be recognized that simple paradigms like that of liberalization are not going to work" (Shukla 1989a, 157).

GATT's underlying assumption that free trade benefited all trading partners thus made it a controversial forum for many former Third World countries. From a poststructuralist perspective, GATT can be understood as a discourse based upon values similar to those underlying the discourses of free trade and neoclassical economics. For example, these discourses share the values of rationality and the primacy of production. The economy is viewed as an objective system where rational economic actors make choices based upon self-interest. Differences between actors rooted in the history of colonialism and unequal global power relations, such as those between First and former Third World countries, are not taken into account. Following Escobar (1995), GATT is understood here as a historically produced cultural discourse constituted through relations of power and knowledge. This discourse is rooted in particular definitions of knowledge, which view neoclassical economics as a science defining objective principles about how markets and rational economic actors operate.

Using these principles, GATT defined particular rules and decision-making procedures for actors to follow when engaged in international trade. Member governments sent ministerial delegations to represent them in rounds of negotiations to discuss which rules would be accepted to govern international trade under GATT. (Each round was named according to the country or city where it began. For example, the Uruguay Round began in 1986 in Punta del Este, Uruguay.) Ministers met every two years at a Ministerial Session of the Contracting Parties. Through this organizational structure, GATT promoted the general goal of reducing and eventually eliminating all barriers to trade (Krasner 1985; McMichael 2000a). In the context of international trade between First and former Third World countries, GATT's rules and norms for behavior have had distinct implications for relations of power among these countries.

Again, the struggle to define the discourse that would govern digital trade and communication was a vital part of establishing the economic, political, and cultural conditions for these new forms of international trade to occur. It was thus perceived as a major victory when U.S. representatives to GATT lobbied successfully to redefine transborder data flows as trade in data services. Such services include data processing, software, information storage and retrieval, and telecommunications services. In the official U.S. view, the flows represented the movement of data services in a digital stream that could be considered a form of invisible trade.

The redefinition of transborder data flows as trade in data services was a turning point in information trade politics. It was part of a larger U.S. government strategy to create an international trade agreement for services, information, and other digital commodities. This redefinition played a key part in this strategy since it enabled debates over transborder data flows to be incorporated into broader discussions over trade in services. Conflicts that had been developing over the flows then merged with those over trade in services, ushering in the third episode of confrontation over information trade politics. The links between transborder data flows and services trade were articulated in 1985 by George Shultz, then the U.S. Secretary of State: "Any government that resorts to heavy-handed measures to control, regulate or tax the flow of electronic information will find itself stifling the growth of the world economy as well as its own progress. This is one of the reasons why the United States is pressing for a new round of trade negotiations in the service fields, to break down barriers to the free flow of knowledge across borders" (*Transnational Data Report* 1985, 170).

The U.S. government's success in including transborder data flows in the broader category of services trade meant that the free-trade discourse on the flows became articulated within the institutional framework of GATT. The U.S. government was able to move debates over the flows away from a focus on principles and to claim a place on the agenda of services trade negotiations that had the potential to define internationally accepted rules. Struggles over information trade politics thus went beyond the sovereignty discourse's articulation of key concerns and underlying cultural values, shifting into the arena of GATT as the dominant cultural discourse defining the rules for international trade.

During the debates over transborder data flows, information trade politics changed focus between the articulation of policy principles and concerns and the process of policy making. Proponents of the sovereignty discourse did not develop an institutional framework where it could be put into practice on an international scale. With the definition of transborder data flows as trade in data services, however, they shifted their attention to the question of whether services should be included in GATT negotiations.

Struggles over information trade politics thus changed focus once again. Instead of featuring divergent discourses on transborder data flows, these conflicts centered on the question of services trade. The U.S. government led the effort to extend GATT's purview to services, as a way to develop a neoliberal international trade agreement for the services sector (Mahoney 1988). By contrast, GATT ministers from several former Third World countries opposed this effort. They wanted services trade to be governed by a different institutional body, so that the discourse on international services trade would be based upon the cultural values of national sovereignty and development.

VICTORY IN THE THIRD EPISODE: A NEOLIBERAL DISCOURSE ON INTERNATIONAL SERVICES TRADE

The redefinition of transborder data flows as trade in data services was part of a broader effort by the U.S. government to incorporate services under the General Agreement on Tariffs and Trade, and to establish GATT as the dominant neoliberal discourse on international services trade. U.S. government support for such an expanded definition of international trade had its roots in the Trade Act of 1974. This was the first piece of U.S. trade legislation to address the question of trade in services, by expanding the definition of international trade to include both goods and services.

After this act was passed, major multinational services firms supported the inclusion of services in GATT negotiations. These firms included American International Group (AIG) in insurance; American Express, Citibank, and Merrill Lynch in financial services; Sea-Land in shipping; and Control Data in data-processing services. Other firms in these sectors also expressed more limited interest in the prospect of GATT services talks.

The move to include services trade under GATT had important implications for relations of power and knowledge in the international economy.

It sought to shift regulatory power from the national to the international levels, from national governments to a neoliberal agreement governing international trade. GATT would thus become the dominant cultural, political, and economic discourse on international services trade, since its cultural values would shape the development of a new set of rules and procedures governing that trade. Equally important, including services trade under GATT would consolidate services trade policy within the emerging institutional framework of the globalization project (McMichael 2000a). GATT, in conjunction with multinational corporations and multilateral financial institutions like the International Monetary Fund and the World Bank, was in the process of developing global economic rules to govern the activities of national governments.

As I have discussed, Foucault (1978) provides a framework to understand the development of GATT as a neoliberal discourse on international services trade. He recommends reconstructing the various elements of the discourse, "the things said and those concealed" as well as the power relations between the actors involved and the institutional context within which they interact (1978, 100). For example, incorporating international services trade under GATT was in the interest of multinational corporations seeking to expand their global business operations. As producers of services, these firms faced a broad range of national regulatory limitations that constrained their activities in world markets. As consumers of services, they relied upon core services like telecommunications to support their international production activities. National regulations on telecommunications services potentially limited firms' access to key production inputs. In addition to these services, multinationals, IBM, and a few other manufacturing firms in high-technology sectors emphasized services as a major area for negotiation. They viewed regulations of telecommunications and other services sectors as problematic constraints upon their global market opportunities.

The U.S. government, and particularly the office of the U.S. Trade Representative, shared the corporate interest in seeing that services trade would be part of GATT negotiations. Indeed, instituting a new framework for services trade was part of their broader vision for global control over national development, which fit within the globalization project that emerged in the 1970s (McMichael 2000a). U.S. GATT delegates pressed for inclusion of services in GATT Tokyo Round when they joined those negotiations in 1975, but were urged by other ministers not to pursue the issue at that time. The Carter administration assured interested multinational firms that services would be addressed at the next GATT Round, and the Reagan administration refused to participate in the Uruguay Round unless services were placed on the agenda (Aronson and Cowhey 1984, 36–38; Feketekuty 1988, 300–310).

In November 1982, the U.S. government escalated its effort to include services in GATT. At the Ministerial Session of the Contracting Parties to GATT, the U.S. delegation proposed an initiative on services in GATT. It pressured other delegates to request that barriers to services trade be studied by GATT. The U.S. proposal was highly controversial. It sparked opposition from almost all the former Third World GATT representatives, who did not hold positions of power within the institutional context of GATT. These representatives were concerned about the expansion of foreign multinational corporations into their services markets. In an initial effort to control such expansion, these representatives argued with the definition of services trade proposed by the U.S. government and multinational corporations. In Foucault's (1978) terms, they attempted to "say things" that had been "concealed" by that definition of services trade. They fought to define services in different terms that would require services trade to be regulated within a different institutional context. They insisted that trade in services was an investment issue that could not be adequately addressed by GATT rules governing trade in goods. They also objected that including services in GATT would divert attention from needed reforms in the regime for goods trade (Jaramillo 1989; Nicolaides 1989).

As struggles over information trade politics shifted to focus on the development of a discourse for services trade, two major changes occurred. First, the debate over trade in services was completely focused on trade policy. Earlier information trade policy debates concerned how telecommunications policies affected the quality of and access to telecommunications networks, or how transborder data-flow policies affected sovereignty, information dependency, and the free flow of information. With the redefinition of transborder data flows as trade in data services, and the consideration of services trade moved onto GATT negotiating agenda, the U.S. government succeeded in shifting information trade politics debates entirely to the area of trade policy. Certain battles over the development of a discourse for services trade had thus largely been won. Defining the issue strictly in terms of trade coincided with the cultural values of the neoliberal globalization discourse. Rather than framing the issues at stake in terms of national sovereignty, power, or domination, services trade was defined in the "scientific" language of neoclassical economics that identified the "objective" laws governing its operations.

The second important change to occur was that the terrain of debate over services trade changed from the national to the international arena. Instead of national governments debating their individual telecommunications or transborder data-flow policies, or airing their concerns at international conferences with no policy-making authority, debates over services trade occurred within the institutional framework of international trade negotiations. GATT was a policy-making body with authority to develop international trade rules, not simply a forum for debate like SPIN or other informatics conferences. It was a vital part of the formation of an institutional framework for global economic management under the globalization project.

The choice of GATT as a forum for services negotiations became the new focus for conflicts over information trade politics in the early 1980s, as a range of governments resisted the rise of the globalization project and defended their rights to control trade and development policy at the national level. This choice was controversial because of GATT's historical link with the process and principles of trade liberalization, which were vital to the development of the globalization project. Since GATT was established in 1947, it defined the rules and decision-making procedures for the liberal international trade regime. Proponents of this liberal approach credit the sustained growth in the world economy since GATT's founding to the progressive liberalization of world trade under a system of transparent rules. Tendencies toward protectionism are viewed as exacerbating contemporary problems of slow growth, unemployment, and external debt in many economies. Trade-liberalization advocates see the lack of transparent rules as a key constraint on international services trade. They thus propose liberalization of services trade as a way to extend the dynamism of domestic services sectors to the international economy.

Neoliberals viewed GATT negotiations on trade in services as a key part of global economic revitalization. John Richardson, the head of the services division of the Commission of the European Communities, noted GATT's "pragmatic, unpoliticized ethos" as a key asset in this effort (Richardson 1989, 175). This assessment is consistent with neoclassical economic discourse, which presents free-trade principles as objective, scientific laws governing the functioning of all economies. In particular, the neoclassical view of the benefits of trade lent academic authority to trade-liberalization proponents and supported their policy goals and proposals. According to Richardson and his colleague, a member of the permanent delegation of the European Communities at Geneva, "unless one believes that gains come from trade and can be shared by all trading countries, one is led to a very pessimistic idea of negotiations, which is, what one country gains from trade, another country loses—in other words, the basic concept of a zero sum game. If one believes that, then one cannot expect the successful conclusion of a multilateral trade agreement" (Richardson and Scheele 1989, 151).

In fact, however, pessimism about the benefits of trade characterized the position of many former Third World GATT delegates, and formed the basis for struggles over information trade politics during this period. These delegates questioned the merits of the neoliberal trade discourse, and sought the freedom to implement strategies to control the entrance of foreign capital into their services markets. The resulting tensions belied the portrayal of free-trade principles as neutral and "unpoliticized." Rather, these principles can be understood as cultural values that support the claims to knowledge and power by multinational corporations and other proponents of the globalization project. Indeed, these principles became the focus for conflicts over the development of a discourse for international services trade, which formed part of the broader institutional framework for the globalization project. Trade talks became a terrain for political struggle, as conflicts over information trade politics focused upon the choice of GATT as an institutional forum to negotiate a framework for services trade.

Former Third World GATT delegates were concerned about the economic and political implications of such a choice for the development of their national services industries. They did not perceive GATT as a forum that would promote greater equity in the world trading system. GATT was based upon the neoclassical economic principle of promoting the efficient, free play of market forces in all economic activities. Corresponding to the tenets of the globalization project, this orientation implied limiting the role of governments in economic development, freezing perceived barriers to trade at current levels, and eventually eradicating those barriers through negotiations. Since several former Third World delegates viewed services as a sector that required government protection, they opposed the incorporation of services under the free-trade discourse of GATT. They were concerned about their comparative disadvantage in services. They feared being pressured to open their services markets, particularly in key segments like banking and insurance, as a condition for retaining their existing rights with respect to trade in goods. They thus defended the emphasis of the development project and the sovereignty discourse on the rights of national governments to formulate economic policy (Shukla 1989b).

A number of Western European governments expressed similar concerns about GATT as a forum for services trade negotiations. Their lack of competitiveness with the United States in the computer and telecommunications fields made them reluctant to join a negotiating process guided by the principle of opening markets to foreign competition. They were wary of developing a binding GATT agreement that codified current arrangements under which they were at a competitive disadvantage.

Conflicts unfolded over information trade politics as intense discussions were held between 1984 and 1986. First and former Third World delegates aired their positions about whether services negotiations should be incorporated under GATT. These conflicts reflected deeper struggles over the development and globalization projects as distinct discourses competing to guide the formation of trade and development policy, and particularly over the international agreement for services trade. Four major groups of GATT members formed around common positions concerning the inclusion of services in GATT negotiations. These groups shared similar positions of power within the institutional context of negotiations over international services trade. They struggled over whether services trade should be incorporated under GATT, largely because GATT discourse ensured different "reciprocal effects of power and knowledge" (Foucault 1978, 102) for each group. These differences in the "tactical productivity" (102) of GATT discourse for each of these groups fueled conflicts over GATT as a forum for services trade.

The first group consisted of delegations from the United States, Canada, the United Kingdom, Sweden, and Japan. This group supported the original proposal to incorporate services directly under GATT regime, at a fast pace. The strong links between the Canadian and U.S. economies fostered early Canadian support for this proposal, despite past disagreements over issues of border broadcasting, banking, and trucking. The British government was interested in open markets for its financial and insurance services industries. The Swedish government had a history of support for open markets to export both goods and services. Although Japan had not been a major services exporter, its position was changing in the areas of transportation, travel, and financial services. In 1971 the three largest banks in the world were based in the United States; by 1986, three Japanese banks held this position. The Japanese government viewed support of the U.S. services initiative as a way to gain access to foreign markets, and to respond to critics of its closed markets and trade surplus (Aronson and Cowhey 1984; Nicolaides 1989).

The second group of GATT ministers included delegates from France, West Germany, and other European countries that were more hesitant about including services in GATT. These ministers were uncertain whether a neoliberal international services trade agreement would benefit their own services markets. France had a large services trade surplus and questioned the goals and potential benefits of the U.S. proposal. The West German government was concerned about the implications of a services agreement for the Bundespost, the postal and telecommunications services monopoly that was the country's largest employer. For other European Community delegates, services were not a high priority, which made it difficult to develop a common position among the Community's twelve members. Despite these hesitations, the European Community delegation eventually supported the principle of services trade negotiations in March 1985.

A third group, comprising ten delegations from former Third World countries (the G-10), strongly opposed the U.S. position. This group was led by the Indian and Brazilian delegations, and also included ministers from Argentina, Cuba, Egypt, Nicaragua, Nigeria, Peru, Tanzania, and Yugoslavia. It continued to articulate concerns about the potential for GATT to undermine their own prospects for development and trade in the services sector. These delegates favored an international services trade agreement that would support broader state strategies to control the entrance of foreign capital into their services markets.

This group was gradually isolated, however, by the reaction of First World delegates, particularly the United States. The U.S. government used its power as a major trading partner, threatening to withdraw tariff preferences for countries that sought to exclude services from GATT talks. U.S. Trade Representative Clayton Yeutter expressed the Reagan administration position at that time: "We simply cannot afford to have a handful of countries, responsible for 5 percent of world trade, dictate the destiny of a large number of countries who deal with 95 percent of that trade" (Nicolaides 1989, 81).

Finally, a group of twenty delegates from former Third World countries (the G-20) was persuaded to discuss the terms of the U.S. proposal. The U.S. government pursued its strategy to include services negotiations in GATT by offering inducements to support its position. It expressed willingness to restructure debt arrangements for certain countries, and it lowered U.S. interest rates and the foreign exchange value of the dollar. In addition to these inducements, sanctions were threatened if countries failed to support the U.S. stance. The U.S. Trade Representative announced that the U.S. government would engage in bilateral or multilateral talks with countries favoring liberalized services trade if services were not included in GATT round. Only participating countries would share the benefits from these more limited negotiations. Such a prospect had severe economic implications for former Third World countries dependent upon foreign trade with the United States.

The combination of inducements and admonitions from the U.S. government was effective in promoting negotiations with the Group of Twenty. Ministers from Singapore, Hong Kong, the Philippines, and a number of other former Third World countries were convinced that GATT services negotiations might support their economic interests. Some key African and Latin American delegations, particularly those from Colombia and Uruguay, were persuaded to change their positions on GATT discussions. European Community ministers led a campaign to inform many African and Latin American delegations about substantial Brazilian and Indian services trade surpluses with other former Third World countries. This campaign implied that Brazilian and Indian leadership in opposing GATT services negotiations was related to their ability to earn monopolistic profits in existing protected services markets (Bhalla 1990; Marconini 1990; Aronson and Cowhey 1984; Kakabadse 1987; Nicolaides 1989).

Despite its isolation, the Group of Ten continued to implement its counter strategy by offering a compromise in 1985. The Brazilian GATT representative proposed a "dual track" whereby negotiations would occur on a "services compact" outside the purview of GATT. This approach signaled a willingness to discuss services, but not within the framework of GATT. It also revealed the importance of the choice of an institutional forum in which to discuss trade in services, an issue that became the focus for conflicts over information trade politics during this period (Braga 1990).

These conflicts reached a critical juncture in 1986, at a Special Session of the Contracting Parties in Punta del Este, Uruguay. After intense negotiations, GATT ministers eventually reached procedural and substantive compromises that were embodied in the Punta del Este Declaration of the Contracting Parties to GATT. With respect to procedural issues, the Punta del Este declaration established a "dual track" approach to services negotiations. This approach responded to the Group of Ten's resistance to including services discussions under GATT. While services negotiations would occur under the auspices and procedures of GATT, the Group of Negotiations on Services (GNS) was established as a separate subsidiary body to conduct these negotiations, through an agreement signed by the ministers as representatives of their governments rather than as official GATT contracting parties (Jaramillo 1989; Kelly et al. 1988; Shukla 1989b; Marconini 1990; Braga 1990; Nicolaides 1989; Aronson and Cowhey 1984).

The dual-track approach was a compromise position that allowed a new GATT round of negotiations to begin. It did not resolve conflicts, however, over the choice of a forum for services trade negotiations. Debates continued over the legal status of the Group of Negotiations on Services, reflecting prior differences between advocates of the free trade and sovereignty discourses. The Brazilian and Indian delegates argued that since the entities negotiating goods and services were legally separate, inclusion of services in the new round of negotiations did not imply a recognition of services as a part of GATT. From their view, the ministers' decisions in the Group of Negotiations on Services had no legal standing under the existing GATT treaty. Due to this lack of legal status, the outcome of services negotiations could not be legally binding upon GATT members. By contrast, the U.S. delegation and its supporters viewed services negotiations as a legitimate part of the broader GATT round, where the negotiating groups on goods and services operated under the same time frame and reported to an umbrella Trade Negotiations Committee (Nicolaides 1989).

As GATT negotiations proceeded during the 1980s and into the 1990s, services negotiations were given formal status and were incorporated in the final agreement. The choice of GATT as a forum for international services trade negotiations was thus a turning point in information trade politics. It was a victory for the U.S. government strategy to create a neoliberal discourse for international services trade as part of the institutional framework for the globalization project. This victory consolidated the shift from telecommunications to trade policy, and from national to international policy-making bodies as the locus of policy formation.

Once GATT was chosen as a forum for services trade negotiations, conflicts continued over the underlying cultural values that should guide the formation of the international services trade agreement. Similar to earlier conflicts, these tensions emerged between advocates of the values of development and liberalization. Former Third World delegates sought to define development as a guiding cultural value for an international services trade agreement. They succeeded to the extent that development was identified as a goal for the services talks at Punta del Este, and thus remained a key focus for debate. This achievement, however, did not diminish the support for liberalization as a principle to guide the formation of an international services agreement. Since it fostered the role of global rather than national institutions in making trade and development policy, this purportedly objective principle effectively worked to consolidate the globalization project.

After the Punta del Este meetings, the services negotiating agenda was set in January 1987. It consisted of five points, which can be understood from a poststructuralist perspective as elements of the discourse on international services trade. For example, the agenda included developing definitions of trade in services as well as concepts to guide the formulation of rules and principles of the final agreement. Such definitions, of course, say certain things and conceal others since they are based upon particular criteria of knowledge that recognize particular actors as qualified to speak the truth about the nature of social reality. These definitions are not neutral or objective; rather, they help to create a discourse of power and knowledge with disparate effects on different social groups. The services negotiating agenda included the selection of the services industries or subsectors to be covered by the multilateral framework, and it considered the existing sectoral arrangements in services, such as those established by the International Telecommunications Union, the International Civil Aviation Organization, and the United Nations Conference on Trade and Development (UNCTAD) Code of Conduct for Liner Conferences. These agenda items were vital to the development of a discourse on international services trade since they involved identifying the actors who would and would not participate in these negotiations. Equally important, these negotiating points involved decisions about which existing agreements would be honored or excluded from the emerging discourse on services trade and the extent to which they would be incorporated into a new agreement. Finally, the services negotiating agenda included discussion of measures and practices to facilitate or limit the expansion of services trade. These practices defined the rules by which the new discourse would operate, affecting the ongoing struggle over whether, or to what extent, national governments would retain the power to regulate their markets in the services field.

Differences between First and former Third World delegates on each point of GATT services agenda reflected the "reciprocal effects of power and knowledge" (Foucault 1978, 102) at stake for these delegates on each agenda item. Indeed, much of the discord involved the development and globalization projects as conflicting discourses to guide trade and development policy. As occurred in previous struggles, these conflicts focused largely on the underlying cultural values that would govern a discourse on international services trade. The value of fostering national development was consistently juxtaposed to that of promoting trade liberalization and free-market competition.

These tensions persisted throughout the meetings of the Group of Negotiations on Services. In December 1988, a Ministerial Statement on Services was negotiated in Montreal that outlined the main points that might be covered by a general services agreement. At this midterm ministerial review, former Third World delegates expressed more willingness to accept a broad framework agreement on services. They continued to insist, however, that national development goals be respected as a legitimate basis for restrictions on services trade. They reiterated the importance of considering the needs of former Third World countries within a services agreement, and rejected the expectation that they undertake reciprocal obligations with their First World trading partners (Marconini 1990; Nicolaides 1989; Cowhey and Aronson 1989). These persistent efforts by the former Third World GATT delegates produced little more than the concerns they aired about information dependency at earlier informatics conferences. Their concerns shaped debates over the services agenda but had little effect upon the content of the final agreement.

By contrast, the U.S. delegation won a strategic victory by successfully lobbying to include the concept of market access in the Montreal Ministerial Statement, a key part of the emerging discourse on international services trade. The acceptance of this concept codified a major U.S. government goal of facilitating the expansion of multinational capital into global services markets. It established that foreign firms could provide services through their "preferred mode of delivery." In other words, governments would be expected to allow firms to provide services either through trade or foreign investment, depending upon the firms' judgments about which mode of delivery would most benefit corporate operations.

Inclusion of the concept of market access sparked continued resistance to a neoliberal discourse on international services trade, and to the broader globalization project, by some former Third World delegates. They objected that market access could lead to exploitation of their economies by foreign services multinationals. In response to these concerns, three measures were included to counterbalance the potential effects of market access and retain greater government control over trade and development policy. These measures tempered the globalization project's influence in the services field by preserving some emphasis on nationally defined development goals. First, it was agreed to increase former Third World participation in world trade by promoting their service exports and access to information networks and distribution channels. Second, exceptions to market access for reasons of national security or cultural sovereignty were defined as points for future negotiations, as were safeguards against balance of payments problems. Finally, GATT delegates acknowledged the right of former Third World governments to implement new regulations that complied with their existing GATT commitments, and that addressed differences between their regulatory situations and those of their First World counterparts. Questions of investment, the movement of labor and personnel, and the transfer of technology could be regulated as part of the effort to equalize regulatory situations in different parts of the world (Marconini 1990; Nicolaides 1989; Cowhey and Aronson 1989).

Conflicts over the underlying cultural values for a discourse on international services trade were intense and protracted, due to the magnitude of the economic opportunities emerging with the expansion of services industries on a global scale. The U.S. government and its allies sought to take advantage of these opportunities by opening access for multinational capital to international services markets, through the expansion of GATT into a neoliberal international services trade agreement. This effort was part of a larger strategy to promote the globalization project and consolidate the rules of global economic management. As former Third World governments fought this effort, conflicts over information trade politics shifted from debates over transborder data flows to questions of whether GATT would be the institutional forum for services trade negotiations, and eventually to the goals and substantive agenda for services trade talks.

CONCLUSION

During the 1970s and 1980s, technological change in telecommunications and computers blurred the boundaries between what had originally constituted the separate spheres of telecommunications, information, and trade policy. These changes created conditions for a series of political struggles that I term information trade politics.

Information trade politics developed through three major episodes of confrontation. Over time, the focus of policy conflicts shifted from telecommunications to trade policy while the locus of policy debate and the power over policy formation moved from national to international institutions, as part of the broader rise of the globalization project. The role of technology in shaping policy debate and formation decreased as these stages unfolded.

In the first episode, during the 1970s, technological change played a decisive part as the merging of telecommunications and computer systems allowed telecommunications networks to play a new role in trade and production. Telecommunications systems were used to engage in digital communication as well as to trade digital commodities, creating new implications for existing telecommunications policies. These policies were originally designed to govern the conditions for access to the telecommunications network as well as its quality. The ability to use such networks for digital trade and communication meant that telecommunications policies affected the ability of corporations to take advantage of these emerging economic opportunities. Policy debates arose over the power of national governments to regulate access to and conditions of telecommunications networks. In other words, they took place on the terrain of national politics, within the framework of the development project where governments were viewed as the appropriate institutions to make trade and development policy (McMichael 2000a). Multinational corporations, however, resisted the power of individual governments and policies to establish the conditions for them to conduct their global business activities.

In the second episode of confrontation over information trade politics, the focus of struggles shifted from the telecommunications network itself to the information and commodities transported through it in the form of digital signals. Policy debates arose over the implications of these transborder data flows for economic power and national sovereignty. They thus focused on the area where the discourses on telecommunications and information policy converged. A range of governments raised concerns about the prospects of a new form of information dependency due to their lack of the technologies, industries, and communications systems required to engage in transborder data exchanges. Some passed national policies to regulate the data flows, continuing struggles over information politics on the terrain of national policy made by individual governments. Former Third World governments led the way, however, in shifting the terrain of struggle over transborder data flows to the international arena. They raised their concerns at international conferences that lacked policy-making authority but nonetheless provided a wider forum to articulate their positions.

In the third episode in the development of information trade politics, the U.S. government succeeded in redefining transborder data flows as trade in data services. This occurred in the context of negotiations over whether to include services trade within GATT negotiations. It also marked the shift of policy focus into the sphere of trade policy, as well as a change in the terrain of struggle to the international policy-making arena as part of the emergence of the globalization project (McMichael 2000a). As a discourse on international trade, GATT had institutional power to define the rules for trade. A choice of GATT as the institutional forum for services trade policy meant a shift away from the power of national governments to regulate conditions for access to their services markets. Conflicts over information trade politics during the 1980s focused on the question of whether GATT should have the power to regulate services trade. The ultimate selection of GATT signaled the formation of a neoliberal discourse on international services trade, which formed an integral part of the global economic rules guiding the globalization project. This regime challenged the regulatory power of national governments and consolidated the shift of information trade politics debates from telecommunications to trade policy.

These conflicts over information trade politics reveal key international political struggles arising with the process of technological change in microelectronics and telecommunications, and the shift from the development to the globalization projects, in the last few decades. The above analysis illuminates the effects of these technological changes on the processes of trade and production, on the content of policy debates, and on the terrains in which those debates were fought. Technological changes made it possible to engage in new forms of digital trade and allowed the telecommunications system to play a new role in transporting services and other digital commodities. They created a new context for trade and trade-policy formation, lending new implications to traditional telecommunications policies and gradually shifting the focus of policy debates from the telecommunications infrastructure to the information and commodities it was used to transport. These developments contributed to a shift in policy focus to trade in services, which became a central part of GATT Uruguay Round.

Technological changes in microelectronics and telecommunications have had significant effects both on the economic conditions for trade and production and on struggles to establish the political, cultural, and discursive terms for those processes to occur. The three episodes of confrontation over information trade politics formed the geopolitical context for further conflicts between the United States and its major trading partners. The high-tech trade war between the U.S. and Brazilian governments over Brazil's informatics policy is a prime example of a bilateral struggle over information trade politics. The Brazilian policy, based upon the cultural value of national sovereignty, conflicted with U.S. government efforts to make free trade the underlying, "objective" principle for national and international telecommunications, information, and trade policy.

3 Who's Afraid of Brazilian Informatics?

America has never been afraid to compete. When trade follows the rules, and there is equal opportunity to compete, American business is as competitive as any. This is fair trade and we will not impair it. When these conditions do not exist, it is unfair trade, and we will fight it.

THE U.S. GOVERNMENT STRATEGY to create a neoliberal international services trade regime was part of a larger effort to promote global U.S. competitiveness in the telecommunications and computer sectors. The U.S. government was concerned about falling behind in these sectors, largely due to what it called the "unfair" trade and investment policies of its major trading partners. Rather than assume that comparative advantage was a natural outcome of market forces, countries like Japan, South Korea, and Taiwan used industrial policies to promote high-technology development. They regulated trade and investment to encourage industrial development, strengthen exports, and acquire technology. In 1986 the House Committee on Energy and Commerce issued its *Report on Unfair Foreign Trade Practices,* which concluded that "unfair trade is wreaking havoc upon U.S. industries in every sector of the economy while U.S. laws, negotiated agreements, and the enforcement of those laws and agreements remain woefully inadequate to halt such practices" (U.S. House Committee on Energy and Commerce 1986, 11).[1]

This chapter examines relationships between the U.S. government and its major trading partners as a battleground in the global power struggle over information trade politics. In the 1970s and 1980s these relationships were viewed as a key reason for declining U.S. economic competitiveness. The U.S. government evaluated possible responses to "unfair trade" and deemed investigation and retaliation against such practices to be the most effective approach. This assessment set the stage for the high-tech trade war over Brazilian informatics.

"FREE" TRADE IN AN "UNFAIR" WORLD: U.S. COMPETITIVENESS UNDERMINED

According to the *Report on Unfair Foreign Trade Practices* (U.S. House Committee on Energy and Commerce, 1986), U.S. trading partners contributed to a range of U.S. economic problems by failing to pursue "free and fair trade." In countries of the former Third World, government controls over economic development fueled debt and inhibited their ability to import from the United States. Such policies contributed to drops in U.S. exports to heavily indebted countries by up to 50 percent since 1981. This congressional report recommended that these countries use market-oriented development approaches both to promote domestic economic growth and improve export opportunities for U.S. firms. It proposed opening markets to foreign investment as a way to increase competition, cut the inefficiency of protected monopolies, and generate funds to service the countries' debt burdens.

Japan and other highly industrialized countries posed different threats to U.S. economic interests. Their governments combined policies to foster industrial development with restrictions on foreign investment that prevented U.S.-based firms from entering their markets. Debates arose in government, academic, and other policy circles about the implications of these differences in economic policy. The House Energy and Commerce Committee concluded that the United States had been "victimized in the world market," and "hamstrung by a free trade ideology that ignores the realities of the world trading system" (U.S. House Committee on Energy and Commerce 1986, 3).

A U.S. Senate report titled *Long-Range Goals in International Telecommunications and Information* defended the free-trade approach as the best response to U.S. problems with its trading partners. It warned that Japan, France, West Germany, Canada, and other major trading partners were subsidizing firms to enter the U.S. telecommunications and information markets while protecting their own markets from foreign competition. The

United States was thus being doubly hurt by protectionist foreign economic policies (U.S. Senate Committee on Commerce, Science, and Transportation 1983). These concerns echoed the congressional testimony of a communications lawyer, who discussed the costs to the U.S. economy of foreign restrictions on telecommunications and information transmission. He stated, "the biggest foreign restriction is that almost every country in the world runs its telephone system as a monopoly, and it is very hard for us to enter those markets. It has been so hard that I don't think anybody has even tried to figure out the dollar volumes involved" (U.S. House Committee on Foreign Affairs 1982, 41).

As the president of AT&T International testified before Congress in 1986, this situation was largely the unintended result of a complicated series of government decisions that deregulated the U.S. telecommunications equipment market. These decisions "in essence resulted in a unilateral trade concession to foreign countries" by opening the U.S. telecommunications equipment market to foreign competition without providing similar access for U.S. firms to markets abroad (U.S. House Committee on Ways and Means 1986b, 43). The combination of deregulation in the United States, the historical nature of telecommunications as a regulated market in most other countries, and the high value of the dollar led to marked changes in the U.S. trade balance in telecommunications equipment. A $1 billion U.S. trade surplus in telecommunications equipment in 1981 became a $1.5 billion trade deficit in 1985. Imports rose from $2.1 billion to $3 billion during this period while exports rose only slightly; 60 percent of this change was due to the growth of the U.S. trade deficit with Japan in the telecommunications equipment sector.

Representative Sam Gibbons, chairman of the Subcommittee on Trade of the House Ways and Means Committee, characterized the trade situation in the aftermath of telecommunications deregulation as "dismal." Exports rose about 30 percent in five years, at about the same rate as inflation. In the same period, however, imports rose 241 percent. He expressed his surprise at the strikingly negative effects on the U.S. trade position in an area where the United States had prided itself as a world leader: "Now as I see it, we unilaterally disarmed when we deregulated AT&T. If anybody was smart enough to catch what was going to happen, they did not tell me;

and obviously I was not smart enough to tell what was going to happen" (U.S. House Committee on Ways and Means 1986b, 205).

The effects on U.S. competitiveness were particularly important because of the nature of technological change in the telecommunications field, and the position of telecommunications as a core industry that supports the growth of other industries. Many telecommunications products were at the cutting edge of technological development, and companies were required to make extensive investments in research and development in order to keep pace with shortening product life cycles. Such investments were virtually impossible to support through sales in a single national market. The rapid pace of technological change created market imperatives to globalize corporate operations. Immediate and continual access to international markets was required to recover costs and support the ongoing development of new products. And as Chapter 2 discussed, access to telecommunications infrastructures and services was vital for corporate strategies to reorganize and control production on a global scale. The state of development of the telecommunications industry had ripple effects on the competitiveness of other economic sectors.

Foreign government policies to restrict market entry in telecommunications thus impeded the ability of U.S. firms to operate in the global economy and adapt to the rapid pace of change. These policies were viewed as especially damaging after the U.S. telecommunications market opened to foreign competition. The United States represented the largest telecommunications market in the world, comprising almost half the world market in this sector, and deregulation provided an excellent opportunity for expansion by foreign firms (U.S. House Committee on Ways and Means 1986b; U.S. Senate Committee on Commerce, Science, and Transportation, 1983).

Although telecommunications deregulation undermined U.S. competitiveness with its trading partners, other factors contributed as well. The 1983 U.S. Senate report *Long-Range Goals in International Telecommunications and Information* cited a wide range of actions taken by foreign governments that challenged the U.S. economic position in the telecommunications and information sectors. As early as 1970, the Japanese government targeted the development of "knowledge-intensive industries" as part of its national economic policy. This was a prelude to a ten-year research and development program proposed in 1981 by the Japanese Ministry of International Trade and Industry (MITI), where government and industry would develop the computer and data-processing industries, which were seen as vital for long-term economic development. As will be discussed further below, the Brazilian government in the early 1970s initiated a strategy to foster the growth of telecommunications infrastructures, computer manufacturing, and services. Additional measures were taken in 1976 and 1984, with the passage of laws to promote Brazilian informatics development by restricting foreign investment in the mini and personal computer markets. In the early 1970s, Canada and several European countries passed laws to regulate transborder data flows, a move that threatened to impede the global business operations of multinational corporations. By 1979 the European Commission recommended the harmonization of standards for telecommunications and information services throughout the European Community. A European data communications network was established to provide exclusively European services for the European market (U.S. Senate Committee on Commerce, Science, and Transportation 1983).

THE EMPIRE STRIKES BACK: FIGHTING "UNFAIR" TRADE

The U.S. government responded to the challenge from its trading partners by promoting free trade as a fundamental principle for trade and development policy. The 1985 "Administration Statement on International Trade Policy" issued by the U.S. Trade Representative touted free trade as "in the best interest of the citizens of the United States and the world" (U.S. House Committee on Ways and Means 1986a, 23). It was extolled as promoting employment, growth, innovation, and increased standards of living, as well as national security. The U.S. government was credited with playing the critical role in promoting the maximum operation of market forces in the global trading system. For their part, U.S. trading partners were urged to support such a system by eradicating trade barriers, subsidies, and other unfair trading practices, and by engaging in multilateral negotiations to liberalize trade under GATT (U.S. House Committee on Ways and Means 1986a; U.S. Senate Committee on Commerce, Science, and Transportation 1983).

The U.S. government considered a variety of measures to promote free trade during the 1980s. The lack of U.S. trade restrictions made bargaining with foreign governments somewhat problematic since there were no comparable U.S. policies that could be dismantled in exchange for reductions in foreign trade barriers. This was particularly true for the deregulated U.S. telecommunications sector, although similar situations existed in the computer and electronics industries. The U.S. government followed a free-trade policy in those sectors as well, unlike the industrial targeting practices of foreign governments. The existing bargaining chips for U.S. trade negotiators were concentrated in declining industries like steel, rather than in the high-technology sectors that were viewed as more promising areas for future growth (U.S. Senate Committee on Commerce, Science, and Transportation 1983).

This lack of bargaining power provided further impetus for foreign competitors to enter the U.S. market without opening their own markets to U.S. firms. The U.S. government enjoyed little success in negotiating with foreign governments for more liberal government procurement policies and technical standards requirements, restrictions on government subsidies for research and development, or floors for export financing terms. And existing U.S. unfair-trade-practice laws provided little recourse when foreign government policies favored the development of domestic industries. Violations of these laws were generally hard to prove under existing antidumping and countervailing-duty statutes. Even if a case could be proven, prosecution took an extended period of time. Foreign trade practices might have altered market conditions to such a degree during this period that provable damages might not cover actual losses by U.S. industry. Lengthy prosecution periods and difficulty of proof were particularly problematic for high-technology industries, where the pace of technological change led to short product life cycles and imperatives to engage in ongoing research and development (U.S. Senate Committee on Commerce, Science, and Transportation 1983).

These problems in forming and enforcing trade agreements fueled support for a more aggressive U.S. government stance toward its trading partners. In the early 1980s, five major approaches were considered to address these U.S. problems with global economic competitiveness. U.S. government officials weighed the advantages of each approach as they sought to develop a strategy to promote U.S. competitiveness in the face of the "unfair" practices of its trading partners.

First, some members of Congress supported a "reciprocity" policy, and included reciprocity proposals in a range of bills. Such a policy would have made U.S. imports from a particular country contingent upon the openness of that economy to U.S. exports of the same product.[2] It was difficult to implement, however, in the context of other U.S. trade agreements. President Reagan strongly opposed this approach, which eventually led to its being discounted as a major part of U.S. trade strategy.

Second, there was general U.S. government support for GATT talks as a viable way to negotiate terms for trade in a context that reinforced the existing postwar trading system. The U.S. government advocated the framework of free-trade principles embodied in GATT as a sound basis for trade agreements. The extension of GATT to a majority of countries also appealed to negotiators interested in developing a neoliberal framework for world trade. Pursuing trade agreements within GATT, however, was a difficult way to address U.S. government complaints with individual trading partners. These negotiations were extremely lengthy. The Uruguay Round, for example, continued through most of the 1980s and into the next decade, making the talks unsuitable for crafting a timely response to U.S. economic problems with "unfair" trade. Further, some GATT ministers were reluctant to accept free-trade principles as the cornerstone of trade and development policy, particularly in new areas like services. Moreover, GATT included provisions that allowed former Third World countries to restrict imports as a means to protect infant industries, address balance of payments problems, or promote national security. The Brazilian government argued that its informatics policy was justified by those GATT provisions and thus complied with the international trade agreement. The U.S. government may have feared that GATT arbitrators would rule in Brazil's favor if the informatics case were examined under GATT's jurisdiction or that other trading partners would use similar arguments to defend their industrial policies. GATT negotiations were thus discounted as a primary vehicle to address bilateral problems between the United States and its trading partners (U.S. Senate Committee on Commerce, Science, and Transportation 1983).

Bilateral trade agreements with key foreign governments posed a third option for U.S. trade negotiators. Such agreements were viewed as particularly useful for a country like Japan, whose import barriers posed a competitive threat in key high-technology sectors. They would not, however, provide recourse when trading partners violated the agreements. The United States would remain unprotected from the dangers of "unfair" trade.

Under a fourth possible solution, "linkage" could be created between the implementation of new trade agreements in high technology industries and the relaxation of existing protective measures in declining industrial sectors. This option, however, might require U.S. trade negotiators to confront domestic political pressures. Labor, environmental, and community groups might rally to retain protections for labor-intensive industries. Trade officials would then be put in the position of defending the agreements on the grounds that they would provide greater export opportunities in expanding industries. The potential for such domestic conflicts undermined political support for this response to U.S. trade problems.

Finally, the U.S. executive branch could more actively pursue retaliatory measures against foreign trade barriers that were judged most harmful to U.S. interests. The Senate report titled *Long Range Goals in International Telecommunications and Information* recommended such an approach as potentially more effective than reciprocity legislation. This approach presented the considerable advantage of avoiding the risk of violating existing U.S. treaty obligations. It also avoided the lengthy duration and uncertain outcome of GATT talks as well as the risks of domestic opposition to the "linkage" approach. The executive branch had the discretion to select the cases and means for retaliation, adjusting its response to particular problems and political conditions involved with "unfair" foreign government policies (U.S. Senate Committee on Commerce, Science, and Transportation 1983).[3]

After weighing its options, the Reagan administration chose investigation and retaliation against "unfair" foreign trade as a central part of its strategy to open global markets and promote the competitiveness of U.S. firms. The Trade Act of 1974 established presidential authority to initiate an investigation of unfair foreign trade practices under Section 301. The Trade and Tariff Act of 1984 conferred the power to initiate an investigation to the U.S. Trade Representative. However, this authority had never been used. U.S. Presidents had always waited to respond to corporate requests to investigate potentially unfair practices. In September and October 1985, President Reagan set a precedent for U.S. trade strategy. He directed the U.S. Trade Representative to initiate investigations of Brazilian informatics, Japanese tobacco, Korean insurance, and Korean intellectual property laws as potentially unfair trade practices that harmed U.S. industry and commerce. At the same time, the President asked the Trade Representative to propose retaliatory measures unless disputes could be settled over Japanese import restrictions on leather and leather footwear, and over European Community production subsidies on canned fruit.[4] The procedures defined for a 301 investigation provided the U.S. Trade Representative one year to submit recommendations to the President about how to respond in a particular case (Evans 1989a; U.S. House Committee on Energy and Commerce 1988; U.S. House Committee on Ways and Means 1986a).

The U.S. Trade Representative and the Economic Policy Council weighed a range of factors in choosing four cases for investigation under Section 301. Criteria included the importance of a particular country as a U.S. trading partner; the amount of trade affected; the legal merits and trade principles raised by the case; U.S. competitiveness in the sector involved; and the history of negotiating efforts to settle the disputes through other means. These cases highlighted the importance of services, intellectual property, and high technology for the U.S. trade agenda (U.S. House Committee on Energy and Commerce 1988; U.S. House Committee on Ways and Means 1986a).

The Brazilian informatics case embodied a number of the concerns expressed by U.S. government officials about the threats to U.S. interests by foreign economic-development strategies. President Reagan, U.S. trade officials, and some U.S. corporations viewed Brazil's informatics policy as a major threat to U.S. interests. In announcing the initiation of the 301 case, President Reagan objected to the informatics law as "squeezing out some

American computer firms" as well as restricting U.S. exports (Riding 1986).

In explaining why the President chose to investigate Brazilian informatics, however, deputy U.S. Trade Representative Michael B. Smith presented a more complicated view of the effects of the informatics policy on U.S. firms. He testified at a congressional hearing, "We did proceed under section 301, despite—and I would underline this—despite concerns about self-initiation by some segments of the U.S. industry; notably, those with operations already established in Brazil, and therefore, most vulnerable to Brazilian countermeasures, about the likely costs and benefits of this approach" (U.S. House Committee on Energy and Commerce 1988, 3).

As this testimony indicates, a complex combination of conditions influenced the Reagan administration's decision to initiate the 301 investigation of Brazilian informatics. An equally complex set of relationships existed between U.S. computer firms and the informatics policy, which shaped their reactions to the new U.S. government strategy to investigate and retaliate against "unfair" foreign trade.

WHY BRAZILIAN INFORMATICS?

When the informatics case was first announced, it appeared to be a clear-cut trade dispute. Data on U.S. informatics trade with Brazil reveal, however, that more was at stake than opening markets for U.S. exports. Total U.S. computer-related exports to Brazil actually rose by 146 percent between 1979 and 1985; worldwide U.S. exports of computer-related products rose by 138 percent during the same period. The Brazilian informatics policy thus allowed considerable growth in U.S. exports (Evans 1989a). The Brazilian informatics case was motivated by concerns that extended well beyond the focus on exports that generally characterizes trade disputes.

These concerns were outlined by Michael B. Smith, the deputy U.S. Trade Representative, in his testimony at congressional hearings on informatics trade problems with Brazil. First, the Brazilian informatics law was viewed as unfair. As Smith explained, "We believe that, if we are to keep our market open to Brazilian labor-intensive products here in the United States, it is only reasonable that Brazil open its market to American computers software, which are symbolic of this country's comparative advantage in high-tech products and services" (U.S. House Committee on Energy and Commerce 1988, 3). This testimony equates the ability of U.S. firms to enter the Brazilian informatics market with the ability of Brazilian firms to enter the U.S. market for labor-intensive goods. It reflects the Reagan administration's effort to protect the U.S. position in the international division of labor by preserving open access to the Brazilian informatics market. This goal was diametrically opposed to the Brazilian strategy to transform its position in the division of labor by developing capacities to produce and export informatics products and services.[5]

Second, Smith voiced the Reagan administration's objections to the two principles underlying the informatics policy. The first principle was embodied in the Brazilian Law of Similars, which prohibited imports of products already manufactured within Brazil. The second principle was codified in the market reserve policy, which prohibited foreign investment in the Brazilian mini and personal computer markets. The U.S. government considered these principles problematic both in their effects on investment opportunities in Brazil and in their potential as a model for other industrializing countries. U.S. government concerns were sparked by discussions in Brazil about applying the market reserve approach to other Brazilian industries, such as pharmaceuticals, where foreign firms controlled 85 percent of the market (Vessuri 1990). A State Department official summarized these concerns in congressional testimony: "It seems that Brazil, despite its rapid growth, still sees itself as an underdeveloped country, a developing country, which needs to utilize what we call infant industry policies in order to nurture its growth. . . . We are concerned in fact that other developing countries not emulate Brazil's approach to development" (U.S. House Committee on Energy and Commerce 1988, 22–23).[6]

These objections to "infant industry" protections for Brazilian informatics echo the concerns raised in GATT debates about whether former Third World governments should be allowed to exercise greater control over domestic economic development. The infant industry model was viewed as particularly inappropriate for Brazil. The same State Department official testified that Brazil had grown to become the world's eighth-largest market economy. Brazil was a major trading country, and its policies increasingly affected the economic activities of U.S. firms. The U.S.

trade deficit with Brazil grew from $1.2 billion in 1982 to $4.5 billion in 1985. In return for this boon to Brazilian trade, the State Department official called upon Brazil to become a better market for U.S. informatics products. He criticized the Brazilian informatics policy for imposing costly limits on U.S. firms, by restricting their opportunities for sales and investment (U.S. House Committee on Energy and Commerce 1988, 1986).

Notwithstanding this testimony, export losses by U.S. firms do not provide a sufficient explanation for U.S. government opposition to the informatics policy. In fact, the Brazilian informatics policy allowed considerable growth in U.S. exports, although not as much as U.S. officials estimated was possible. According to Evans (1989a), the Brazilian informatics market tripled between 1979 and 1985. Even if U.S. exports to Brazil had also been permitted to triple during this period, they would only have been $60 million higher than their actual 1985 levels.

U.S. fears about export losses were part of a broader concern about creating favorable conditions for access to the Brazilian informatics market. The software market posed particular problems, providing a third reason for the Reagan administration to initiate the 301 investigation of Brazilian informatics. Specifically, the administration was concerned about the lack of copyright protection for computer software, which had led to piracy and a loss of profits for U.S. software companies in Brazil. The deputy U.S. Trade Representative noted that protection of intellectual property rights was vital to U.S. competitiveness in computer and computer-related industries. In the mid-1980s the International Intellectual Property Alliance estimated that U.S. software companies lost about $35 million per year from unauthorized duplication and distribution of software in Brazil. These losses were particularly disturbing because U.S. software companies viewed the Brazilian market as an important potential investment. The U.S. Department of Commerce estimated its size to be between $350 and $700 million. Since U.S. companies were estimated to hold a 70 percent share of the world software market, they were expected to be capable of attaining a comparable position in Brazil (U.S. House Committee on Energy and Commerce 1988; *Latin America Regional Reports Brazil* 1988; United Nations Centre on Transnational Corporations 1983).

Finally, the limitations on foreign investment imposed by the informatics policy were viewed as costly for U.S. firms. Between 1980 and 1984, the U.S. share of the Brazilian computer market dropped by 12 percent. In the product categories covered by the market reserve, that share dropped about 22 percent. U.S. government sources estimated that U.S. firms were losing between $340 and $450 million dollars in sales each year due to the market reserve policy. By the time the policy was scheduled to end in 1992, these firms were expected to lose a total of about $13 billion (U.S. House Committee on Energy and Commerce 1988; U.S. Trade Representative 1986).

While the above-listed concerns support the interests of U.S.-based transnational corporations in the Brazilian computer and software markets, the 301 case against Brazil was not initiated at the request of U.S. firms. Instead, for the first time, a U.S. President exercised his authority to initiate a 301 investigation. The major U.S. computer firms were told about the investigation before President Reagan announced it, but they did not participate in the decision to conduct it (Evans 1989a).

My interviews with executives at Brazilian subsidiaries of IBM and Unisys helped explain this lack of involvement by U.S. firms with the longest history of investment in the Brazilian computer market.[7] These executives described their reservations about the potential effects of the 301 investigation upon their relationship with the Brazilian government. They agreed with the U.S. government that the informatics policy should be changed. They had invested over sixty years, however, in Brazilian computer production. Moreover, they had managed to continue these profitable operations in a complex political climate, where policy goals of technological autonomy created tensions between foreign firms and the state informatics agency. Despite these problems, the firms developed a working relationship with the Brazilian government. They were concerned that a trade conflict might jeopardize that relationship and affect their position in the Brazilian market.

U.S. firms with a history of Brazilian computer production were not the driving force behind the 301 investigation.[8] Instead, the 301 case initially developed due to concerns by the U.S. government to promote high-technology exports to former Third World countries, an area where the United States had historically enjoyed a strong comparative advantage. This case presented an opportunity to respond to the U.S. decline in the international economy and potentially reduce its high trade deficit (Evans 1989a).[9]

These concerns were reflected in the initial demands made in the 301 case. The Reagan administration asked that the market reserve not be renewed after its scheduled expiration in 1992. It also requested clearer definitions of informatics products that were subject to import restrictions, in order to counteract what were perceived as "constantly expanding interpretations" applied by the Brazilian SEI (U.S. House Committee on Energy and Commerce 1988, 4).[10]

During the year after the 301 case was initiated, U.S.-based multinationals shaped the Reagan administration's demands upon the Brazilian government. These grew to address the firms' desires to loosen restrictions upon their Brazilian informatics operations. The Reagan administration also requested that the Brazilian government submit a software bill to the Brazilian Congress. It stipulated that the bill should include copyright protections, which would respond to firms' concerns about piracy in the Brazilian market (Evans 1989a; U.S. House Committee on Energy and Commerce 1988).

Once the 301 investigation had gotten underway and the demands on Brazil were developed, the administration's initiative enjoyed substantial support from U.S. firms in the computer, electronics, and communications sectors, as well as from members of Congress. This support was evident in congressional hearings on informatics trade problems with Brazil, held in July 1987 before the House Subcommittee on Commerce, Consumer Protection, and Competitiveness. Congressman Norman F. Lent, for example, testified that he "hoped the administration had decided to take a tough stance against blatantly unfair practices" (U.S. House Committee on Energy and Commerce 1988, 47). The Computer and Business Equipment Manufacturers Association commended the 301 investigation, primarily because of the lack of copyright protection for computer software (59). And James Johnson, a representative from Apple Computer, claimed that Brazilian firms simply copied foreign technology to create what they claimed were their own product developments. Johnson criticized the Brazilian policy for "protecting a pack of pirates who are stealing technology from the United States and other countries" (92). He estimated that

Apple had already lost between $200 and $250 million through sales of Apple clones in the Brazilian market, and warned that the impending release of the new Unitron Mac 512 clone could lead to much greater losses in the coming years (99).

A. G. W. Biddle, the president of the Computer and Communications Industry Association (CCIA), placed the Brazilian informatics case within a global context, as part of a larger problem of U.S. competitiveness with trading partners that pursued more protective industrial policies in their high-technology sectors. He noted the Brazilian market's extensive export potential for U.S. companies, as well as the bad precedent the Brazilian policy could set for other U.S. trading partners. CCIA was a national trade association of manufacturers and providers of computer, information processing, and telecommunications-related products and services. Its member companies had over $80 billion in annual revenues and employed over 800,000 people. The association had lodged complaints with the U.S. government since the late 1970s, urging action against Japanese and Korean policies to protect their computer markets. Biddle's testimony summarized his organization's position. He said, "We have to blow the whistle somewhere, and we would suggest that the Brazilian action is an appropriate message to developing countries that we can no longer stand by and be the patsy, leaving our markets wide open for the importation of their products, while our markets are foreclosed from their products by both tariff and nontariff trade barriers, and by reserve policies" (U.S. House Committee on Energy and Commerce 1988, 84).

The Section 301 investigation was thus commended as part of an overdue, broader effort to toughen U.S. trade policy in response to protectionist practices implemented since the late 1970s by major U.S. trading partners. In the words of CCIA president A. G. W. Biddle, this investigation signified the U.S. resolve that when these countries engaged in protectionism, "the mark goes down in cement, and not sand" (U.S. House Committee on Energy and Commerce 1988, 85). The Brazilian case was viewed as an example of the new U.S. government intolerance toward such restrictions upon the entrance of U.S. firms into foreign markets.

The Brazilian informatics case was part of a broader struggle to establish the political terms for U.S. firms to enter foreign markets for computers, software, semiconductors, and other high-tech products and services. It involved a number of key issues that characterized U.S. government concerns about the policies of its trading partners. These concerns extended beyond traditional trade issues, such as import restrictions, to include foreign investment and intellectual property. They reflected the growing U.S. government focus on computer manufacturing and software as key sectors affecting the U.S. ability to compete in processes of global economic restructuring.

CONCLUSION: HIGH-TECH TRADE WARS AND INTERNATIONAL ECONOMIC CONSTRAINTS

U.S. government efforts to gain "freer" access to the markets of its major trading partners were part of the broader rise of the discourse and practice of globalization. Globalization created structural constraints on former Third World governments as they sought to implement development policy, since they were pressured to open their markets to international trade and investment. Stallings (1992) argues that in the late 1980s, these constraints involved heavy pressure to adopt the so-called "structural reforms" of development strategies. Haggard (1992, 5) supports this view, noting that a consensus emerged in the development policy community, where this process of structural adjustment was identified with "liberalization" measures such as tariff reduction, privatization of state firms, export promotion, and deregulation of financial markets. These pressures to transform former Third World economic structures increased after George Bush won the U.S. presidential election in November 1988. As Stallings (1992, 86) puts it, "it became clear that the emphasis on structural change would not vary substantially."

Stallings (1992) emphasizes the importance of time period in shaping the international structural constraints faced by former Third World countries as they implemented development policy. During the 1980s, for example, international conditions became much more restrictive than they had been in the 1970s. She observes, "The world economy slowed, finance dried up, and an international ideological and organizational consensus emerged around the use of market mechanisms as the proper approach to development" (84–85). We now understand this "ideological and organizational consensus" as the globalization discourse, based on cultural values of free trade and objective market forces. The emphasis on structural reforms as the focus for development policy accompanied the rise of the globalization discourse, a narrative of power and knowledge that defined the nature of such policy.

The international constraints faced by former Third World governments vary depending upon when policies are implemented. Equally important, these constraints are shaped by the stage of the policy-making process. Stallings (1992) divides this process into three stages: decision making, implementation, and economic outcomes. She argues that international factors have the greatest influence during the first and last stages. Since the initial process of policy development generally involves a small group of people, led by the president and his or her closest advisors, Stallings views this group as particularly susceptible to pressure from international actors. In the case of Brazilian informatics, the policy was initially formulated in the late 1970s and early 1980s, when there was less international pressure to open markets in the former Third World. During the implementation stage, Stallings argues that international actors have less influence. Indeed, "powerful opposition forces can undermine policies they disagreed with in the first place. Perhaps more important, lack of state capacity can severely limit the ability to implement a program, especially one involving major structural change" (85). Finally, Stallings argues that international actors once again play a key role with respect to the economic outcomes of development policy. They exert powerful influences on broader market conditions that can either facilitate or undermine the effects of such policies.

Understanding international influences on former Third World development policy requires attention to the particular characteristics of the country involved as well as to the historical time period and the stage of the policy process. Stallings (1992) studied fifteen African, Asian, and Latin American countries during the 1980s. She found international influences to be most prevalent in countries where states had such low technical capacity that they depended on international assistance for basic activities like gathering statistics, developing economic policy, and occasionally even staffing ministries. Such countries included Ghana, Nigeria, Zambia,

Jamaica, Peru, and the Dominican Republic. International influence was least prevalent in countries with the political capacity to formulate and implement development policies, and where both trade and international finance were used to obtain foreign exchange. In these countries, the governments worked with private capital to strengthen the private sector and pursue international economic integration; they included Korea, Thailand, Chile, and Mexico. Finally, Brazil, Argentina, and the Philippines were "on the brink of self-sustaining growth but have yet to make it" (88). These were states with strong technical capacities, but they were plagued with problems arising from weak political institutions and personalistic political leadership. The decade of the 1980s was a time of transition for these countries, as authoritarian regimes underwent democratic reforms. Comments Stallings, "They have been more vulnerable to international pressure than the other strong state group because of their failure to fully develop their economies. But they can also resist, so policy tends to swing" (88).

The late 1980s and early 1990s were a time of many "swings" in Brazilian informatics policy, as the government struggled to implement a controversial development strategy in the face of international structural constraints. One of the most powerful of these constraints was a trade war with the U.S. government, in the wake of President Reagan's announcement of the 301 investigation. Brazilian state officials faced an increasingly complex series of pressures in their choices about informatics development. The U.S. government concerns raised in the investigation had to be taken into account in both domestic policy discussions and international negotiations over how to resolve the trade dispute. Chapter 4 analyzes how the implementation of development policy was shaped by international influences in the context of globalization, where U.S. concerns with economic decline and Brazilian efforts at industrial development converged in a high-tech trade war over informatics.

4 The Double Desire
Mediation and Resistance through Software Policy

ON SEPTEMBER 7, 1985, President Reagan announced the initiation of the 301 investigation of Brazilian informatics in his weekly radio address. This was the "first shot" in the high-tech trade war over Brazilian informatics. Brazilians speculated about whether the President had deliberately chosen that date for the announcement; it was Brazil's independence day, the equivalent of the United States' Fourth of July. Was this timing calculated to heighten the sting of the investigation and further reprimand Brazil for challenging the place of the United States in the global economic order? Or was it purely coincidental?

Five years after President Reagan's announcement, Brazilian industrialists and state officials continued to raise these questions in interviews about their roles in the political struggles over the informatics industry. These concerns revealed the political significance of the informatics law, which extended beyond its effects on economic development. The law was in many respects a symbol of Brazilian national identity. This symbolic power was partly due to the law's expressed purpose of promoting technological autonomy and national sovereignty through the growth of a local computer industry. In addition, the law was one of the first measures passed by the Brazilian Congress after two decades of military rule. It thus represented a kind of rebirth of Brazilian economic and political power in the transition from dictatorship to a more democratic system (Fregni 1990, interview; Manasterski 1990, interview; Calicchio 1990, interview; Costa Marques 1990, interview; Rocha, 1992, interview).

The 301 investigation of Brazilian informatics was not a straightforward investigation of a particular industrial policy. Rather, it was the beginning of a high-tech trade war between the Brazilian and U.S. governments. For many Brazilians, the investigation symbolized an attack on Brazilian economic and political sovereignty. It raised the specter of potential U.S. trade sanctions, and gave rise to geopolitical pressures that shaped the economic and political conditions for implementing the informatics policy. For their part, U.S. corporate representatives and government officials viewed the 301 case as a chance to defend U.S. global economic interests from "unfair" foreign trade.

This chapter traces the process of policy implementation in the wake of the 301 investigation, which involved complex political negotiation and compromise by Brazilian state officials. Throughout this process, these officials sought to balance conflicting demands from the U.S. government and local groups that supported continued protection of the Brazilian informatics market. They demonstrated a pragmatic concern to adapt the informatics policy to changing structural conditions and to de-escalate the high-tech trade war with the U.S. government. They walked a political tightrope, simultaneously pursuing two contradictory goals: mediating the trade war with the U.S. government and continuing to promote local informatics development. Eventually, this precarious balance was tipped by the combined weight of geopolitical and national forces.

THE DOUBLE DESIRE FOR SOFTWARE POLICY

By late 1986, Brazilian state officials were developing a twofold strategy to pursue these divergent goals. The strategy was based upon a tactical choice to focus on software policy. Software was the one area where U.S. demands coincided with Brazilian plans for informatics development on at least one fundamental point: both sides agreed that Brazil needed a software law. Strong disagreements about the content of software legislation, however, complicated its use as a mediation device.

The U.S. government wanted Brazil to pass a software law that included an author's copyright, largely to protect U.S. firms from software piracy. The International Intellectual Property Alliance estimated that in Brazil U.S. software companies were losing about $35 million per year from unauthorized duplication and distribution of software. In 1987 the Datalogica software company sold 4,000 copies of its software; however, corporate officials also discovered 3,500 unauthorized copies of the software that same year. Brasoft, the Brazilian distributors of Wordstar software, claimed that for each copy of the software program they sold in Brazil, seven illegal copies were available on the contraband market.[1] The Apple Computer Corporation complained that a Brazilian firm had copied its Macintosh; these machines were sold without internal operating systems to avoid breaking Brazilian patent laws. At the time of sale, buyers were given pirated copies of an operating system to run on their machines ("Mixed Reaction" 1988; United Nations Centre on Transnational Corporations 1983, 89; U.S. House Committee on Energy and Commerce 1988, 93, 102).

By contrast, the Brazilian government viewed the software sector as a great potential area for continued informatics development. The informatics policy had already fostered the emergence of a skilled professional labor force, which was the key resource required for the growth of a software industry. According to José Ezil Veiga da Rocha, who was Secretary of Informatics during this period, software policy was a logical tool to build upon this previous success in the area of human resources and thus deepen the process of informatics development. It was perceived as a distinct part of the informatics strategy that could address the unique conditions of the software market (1992 interview).

Thus, for different reasons, the Brazilian and U.S. governments both agreed that Brazil needed a software policy. This basic point of commonality created an opportunity for the Brazilian government to combine a response to U.S. concerns with its own efforts to promote informatics development. It developed a twofold strategy, using software policy as a bargaining chip to respond to U.S. demands as well as a mechanism for extending and adapting the informatics strategy. Mário Dias Ripper, former president of a Brazilian computer company, who participated extensively in the formation of the informatics policy, recognized this dual character of Brazil's software law. He viewed the law as responding to a "duplo desejo," or double desire: the U.S. desire to protect intellectual property and Brazil's desire to protect the development of a software industry (1990 interview). Former Secretary of Informatics Rocha described his efforts to build on these points of agreement in negotiations with U.S. trade officials: "We're not here to quarrel with the Americans. We're here to defend the interests of our country. If they happen to coincide with American interests, all the better" (1992 interview).

As Chapter 3 discussed, Stallings (1992) argues that international factors are particularly influential during the initial decision-making stage of policy making in the former Third World. She views this initial stage as shaped by a small group of people, led by the president and his or her closest advisors. International actors are more likely to be able to influence this small group than the range of interest groups that might participate in the subsequent process of policy implementation.

Stallings's (1992) conception of the decision-making stage of the policymaking process aptly describes the important role played by key government officials in attempting to deal with international influences on Brazilian informatics development. Indeed, the twofold software strategy was an effort to adapt the informatics policy to changing conditions in the international market. Rocha, one of the major state officials in charge of implementing the informatics policy, stressed the domestic and international legal concerns involved with developing a software policy in the mid-1980s. The question of software property rights was being discussed in various international bodies. He and other Brazilian government officials wanted the new software law to fit within that emerging international legal framework, so that Brazil would not be isolated from the rest of the world. In addition, they sought to formulate a law that would be reasonable from the point of view of domestic interests and contribute to the development of a local software industry (1992 interview).

These Brazilian government officials played central roles in the formation of the new software policy. This decision-making stage was fraught with tension, however, due to disagreements among a range of Brazilian groups about how the informatics policy should be crafted. Contrary to Stallings's (1992) depiction of the lack of influence by domestic forces on policy formation, the participation of disparate groups complicated the decision-making stage. Brazilian government officials struggled to craft a software law that balanced conflicting international and domestic concerns.

These tensions came to a head over an August 1986 ruling by the ministerial-level Conselho Nacional de Informática (National Informatics Council) (CONIN). The council approved a draft of software legislation proposed by Brazil's President Sarney that responded to U.S. demands by including an author's copyright. It also added controversial amendments, however, that made copyright protection for each software program contingent on its registration with SEI, the federal agency in charge of implementing the informatics policy. Under this draft legislation, users were required to renew their software registrations with SEI every three years. SEI officials would then monitor whether software distributors were complying with informatics policy requirements to invest in research and development, and thus contribute to the broader process of Brazilian technological and scientific development ("Veto" 1986; "Sarney" 1986; Maturo 1987a).

The software legislation was designed to adjust national development goals to changing conditions in the international market. Many members of CONIN viewed it as a legal foundation for a market reserve for software as well as a response to U.S. demands. While the draft legislation was part of the twofold software strategy, it was difficult to balance the strategy's divergent goals of mediating the 301 dispute and pursuing informatics development. These problems were evident in the contradictory pressures from domestic and foreign interests upon the Brazilian government.

These groups objected to the legislation proposed by CONIN for different reasons. The council's proposed legislation sparked conflicts with local groups that advocated continued protection of the local market from foreign competition and opposed concessions to U.S. demands. The MBI charged that "Brazil [was] being intimidated by the U.S. into revising the informatics law" ("Nationalists" 1986, 5). The MBI was a coalition of manufacturers and scientific and professional associations in the informatics industry. It was established in 1983 specifically to exert political influence over the formation of the national informatics law.

The role of the MBI illustrates the highly politicized nature of the decision-making process on software policy.[2] It also confirms Stallings's (1992) point about the importance of time period in shaping development policy. The software policy was formed at a time when groups such as the MBI had already organized to influence the direction of informatics policy. Conditions were ripe for a range of groups to participate in the decision-making process since they had already been involved in the formation of the broader informatics policy. The decision-making stage of the software policy was thus comparable, in many ways, to what Stallings views as the policy-implementation stage. This stage was not restricted to a small group of government officials since social groups had already mobilized during previous stages of implementing the informatics policy.

Domestic conflicts involving the MBI combined with international tensions. U.S. government officials pressured President Sarney to reject the CONIN amendments to the author's copyright provisions in the Brazilian software legislation. They argued that all software programs would be exposed to piracy unless they were registered with the SEI. The Reagan administration also criticized the three-year limit for registrations. It claimed that such a limit would create an uncertain environment, in which foreign products could be banned if similar programs were developed domestically.

The political complexity of the twofold software strategy was exemplified by these conflicts over the draft software legislation. Efforts by the Brazilian government to protect the national software industry prompted further pressures from the Reagan administration while also inciting opposition from domestic groups that supported more extensive protection of local firms from foreign competition. President Sarney vacillated in his attempt to pursue the software strategy's contradictory goals. Following U.S. objections he announced his intention to veto the amendments on the software registry. The next day, however, his advisors stated that the President might not veto the amendments if negotiations with the United States failed ("Veto" 1986; "Sarney" 1986).

There was little opportunity for extended debate over the draft software legislation during this period. On October 6, 1986, U.S. pressures escalated. Acting on recommendations from the U.S. Trade Representative, President Reagan announced that Brazil's informatics policies and practices were "unreasonable, and burden or restrict U.S. commerce" (U.S. House Committee on Energy and Commerce 1988, 4). A decision on the case was deferred for three months, largely to avoid making informatics an issue in Brazil's November congressional elections.

During those three months, the Brazilian government emphasized the mediation component of its twofold strategy as it formulated responses to key U.S. demands. The government agreed not to extend the market reserve beyond the informatics sector and reaffirmed the scheduled 1992 expiration date. It published a list of products that would not be covered by the market reserve regulations. The Brazilian government also promised to modify administrative procedures for the informatics law, to shorten the waiting period for import licenses, and to establish an ad hoc group to review problems identified by U.S. computer firms.

During the fall of 1986, informatics policy decisions were based primarily on the goal of mediating conflicts with the U.S. government and adapting to new conditions posed by the threat of trade sanctions. This emphasis on mediation, however, did not represent complete capitulation to foreign interests. Brazilian state officials continued to explore ways for software policy to address the particular conditions of the local market. President Sarney submitted a draft of legislation to the Brazilian Congress in December that included the copyright protection demanded by the U.S. government, as well as the controversial amendments from CONIN (U.S. House Committee on Energy and Commerce 1988; Riding 1987).

The Brazilian government's efforts at mediation brought effective short-term results. On December 30, 1986, President Reagan suspended the parts of the 301 investigation pertaining to the market reserve policy and the administration of the informatics law. He delayed a decision on investment issues in order to assess Brazil's response to firms that wished to upgrade their Brazilian facilities. He also delayed a decision on software since the Brazilian Congress would not convene until February 1987 and did not plan to consider regular legislation until the new constitution had been drafted. The U.S. government wanted time to study the draft software legislation; specifically, it wanted to assess whether the legislation provided adequate copyright protection. The deadline for the two countries to reach an agreement on intellectual property rights and informatics investment policy was extended for six months, from December 31, 1986, to July 1, 1987 (U.S. House Committee on Energy and Commerce 1988, 4–5).

Brazil's responses to U.S. demands won it a temporary respite from the threat of trade sanctions. As the Brazilian Congress discussed the software legislation during 1987, the U.S. government continued to make its concerns felt through steady correspondence. It emphasized that President Reagan would make a decision about the investigation on June 30 and was extremely concerned about the software legislation (Dantas 1987a). The lower house of the Brazilian legislature approved the proposed legislation just in time to meet the deadline in late June. Congresswoman Cristina Tavares, a strong supporter of both the informatics law and the vote on the software legislation, summarized the approach to the legislation at that time: "We weren't able to resist the American pressures and we had to make a concession with the author's copyright" (Dantas 1987b, 6).

The software law was thus initially formulated as part of a short-term political strategy, a first step toward satisfying the "double desires" of the Brazilian and U.S. governments. The Brazilian government's immediate goal was to mitigate the threat of sanctions by complying with Reagan administration demands for conformity with international norms and copyright rules. It also retained its long-term objective of protecting local software development. The proposed legislation embraced the principle of functional equivalency, barring imports of software similar to that already produced within the country. This principle was designed to extend the market reserve to software by protecting locally developed programs from competition by similar foreign software. In addition, the proposed legislation maintained the controversial provisions that required software to be registered by SEI in order to be sold on the Brazilian market. The registration was valid for three years, and its renewal depended on an evaluation to demonstrate the local distributor's investment in research and development (Maturo 1987a).

The Brazilian government drafted the software legislation as a pragmatic political response to the threat of U.S. trade sanctions. The deputy U.S. Trade Representative testified that passage of the software legislation "represented significant progress in the informatics dispute" (U.S. House Committee on Energy and Commerce 1988, 5). This legal action was decisive in prompting President Reagan to suspend the intellectual property rights portion of the 301 case on July 1, 1987, and to monitor the copyright bill's progress in the Brazilian Senate. With respect to investment issues,

President Reagan decided that more time was required to monitor the implementation of the informatics law. Concerns remained about whether the Brazilian government would allow greater administrative flexibility in this process, such as allowing firms to upgrade their existing investments. The issue of retaliations thus remained open for potential future action (U.S. House Committee on Energy and Commerce 1988, 5–6; Dantas 1987b).

The decision to suspend the threat of sanctions, and particularly to suspend the software portion of the 301 investigation, brought mixed reactions from U.S. firms and legislators. In the hearings on informatics trade problems with Brazil discussed above, Congressman Norman F. Lent acknowledged that the Brazilian software legislation addressed some concerns about the author's copyright. However, he objected to its inclusion of the concept of market reserve, viewing it as detrimental to multinational firms operating in Brazil. Overall, he judged that suspending the 301 case "raises as many questions as it resolves." In his view, the United States was not "acting decisively" and would be "seen as a paper tiger unwilling to pursue a vigorous and aggressive trade policy" (U.S. House Commitee on Energy and Commerce 1988, 48).

A. G. W. Biddle, president of the Computer and Communications Industry Association (CCIA), supported this position. He called for the Reagan administration to be more aggressive in ensuring that the Brazilian informatics policy was dismantled. He argued that little progress had been made after more than eighteen months of high-level negotiations, the exchange of several letters, and a visit to the United States by Brazilian President Sarney (U.S. House Commitee on Energy and Commerce 1988, 89–91).

In response to these critiques, Michael B. Smith, the deputy U.S. Trade Representative, explained that the decision to suspend the 301 case had been strongly influenced by discussions with U.S. firms: "We consulted very, very closely with U.S. industry, particularly when it got to the notion of . . . should we be taking, if you will, more decisive actions—and you can read between the lines as to what that means—and our industry counseled us repeatedly to be cautious in this area, that things such as sanctions or retaliation could be counterproductive. We had to weigh this very, very carefully" (U.S. House Commitee on Energy and Commerce 1988, 48–49). A number of industry representatives voiced support for the decision to suspend the 301 case. William A. Maxwell, the director of the International Issues Group of the Computer and Business Equipment Manufacturers Association (CBEMA), viewed the decision as a way to acknowledge both that progress had been made and that much more remained to be done. He described the Brazilian software legislation as a "very substantial advance in providing full copyright protection for software" (60) and emphasized the importance of recognizing and rewarding that action. "Given Brazil's influence," he commented, "we cannot overemphasize the global significance of Brazil's move to bring their law into conformance with international norms" (60).

The representative of the American Electronics Association (AEA), William A. Burck, who also served as the assistant general counsel for the International Data General Corporation, supported this position. The AEA has 3,000 members representing various segments of the electronics industry, including semiconductors, computers, telecommunications, and software. The AEA representative noted that thirty-five member companies had formed a Brazil work group to meet with Brazilian industry associations and consult with U.S. trade negotiators. These firms supported the Reagan administration's decision to suspend action in the 301 case as a way to recognize the importance of the software legislation newly passed by the Brazilian Congress, both for the Brazilian market and as a model for other countries. He described this law as "an important precedent to the rest of the Third World" with respect to intellectual property protection, as well as market access (U.S. House Committee on Energy and Commerce 1988, 71–72).

A representative of the Computer Software and Services Industry Association (ADAPSO), Ronald J. Palenski, also joined in commending the ruling on software. This U.S. industry association represents companies that are primarily involved with software development for mainframe, mini, and microcomputers, as well as programming and other computer services (U.S. House Committee on Energy and Commerce 1988, 102–4).

The CBEMA, AEA, and ADAPSO representatives all noted that substantial concerns remained about several aspects of the Brazilian informatics policy: Would the software legislation pass the Brazilian Senate? Would its provisions for marketing software prove discriminatory or damaging to U.S. industry? Would the informatics policy be institutionalized in the new constitution so that the market reserve would fail to expire in 1992? Would opportunities develop for investment in informatics? And would the administration of the informatics policy become more flexible? They viewed continued problems in these areas as grounds to consider retaliatory measures against the Brazilian government in the future (U.S. House Committee on Energy and Commerce 1988, 69–70, 75, 77, 83). They cautioned, however, that such measures might hinder the larger goal of developing trade relations with Brazil as a strategically important country with major market potential for U.S. computer exports. The CBEMA representative, William A. Maxwell, summarized this support for the "suspend and monitor" approach: "Retaliation could prove to be a two-edged sword, with the potential to inflict damage on the U.S. as well as on Brazil. And it is a weapon that, in this case, we can probably use only once. . . . We must not throw away the opportunity to make additional gains . . . by moving precipitously toward trade retaliation" (70).

U.S. industry representatives thus largely applauded the Reagan administration's decision to suspend the intellectual property portion of the 301 case and to continue monitoring the software bill as it moved through the Brazilian Senate. The U.S government attempted to balance the goals of presenting a tough stance against protectionism as an example for its trading partners and of maintaining favorable economic relations with Brazil over the long term. It recognized trade retaliation as a potentially dangerous action that might undermine the main objective of gaining access to the substantial Brazilian market for U.S. computer firms. Retaliation remained an option for the future, if the Brazilian government failed to make sufficient changes in its informatics policy.

THE POLITICAL STRUGGLE INTENSIFIES

With the immediate threat of U.S. sanctions lifted, the Brazilian government's political strategy shifted to emphasize national development. This intensified the political struggle within Brazil, which focused on the proposed software legislation presented to the Senate in late June. There was widespread criticism of the legislation by people from a broad range of political and ideological positions. Extensive debates occurred in the Senate, reflecting four general perspectives about how best to promote the development of a domestic software industry.

First, the MBI and SEI supported the market reserve approach to informatics development and wanted to extend it to the area of software. They viewed the Brazilian market as part of the national patrimony, in which trade and production could promote national technological and industrial development. They devised the concept of functional equivalency as the central legal mechanism to implement the market reserve strategy in software. They required foreign companies to register their software with the SEI before marketing it in Brazil. Government officials had to verify that the software did not duplicate any existing, nationally produced program (Mourão 1992, interview; Aquino 1987; Herédia 1987c).

Senator Roberto Campos represented a second, and strongly dissenting, perspective. He voiced the strongest opposition to the software legislation from within the Senate itself. A longstanding opponent of the informatics policy and known for his support of U.S. interests, Campos proposed over fifteen amendments to the draft software legislation. He objected both to what he viewed as a general increase in government intervention into the rights of computer users and to the particular role of the SEI. He argued that the proposed law would create a new market reserve that would be "arbitrarily administered" under the "diabolical power" of the SEI. He noted that this power had even become alarming to "nationalist associations" of software firms, which opposed the legislation in the version passed by the House (Herédia 1987a; Dantas 1987c).

Senator Campos's criticism of the software legislation was part of his ongoing opposition to the concept of the market reserve in Brazilian informatics policy. He shared the concerns of U.S. firms and congressional representatives about restrictions on foreign investment in Brazil under a market reserve policy. His position also resonated with other groups in Brazil who viewed certain provisions of the draft legislation as unnecessary government obstacles to the marketing of software in Brazil. An editorial in a major newspaper, *O Estado de São Paulo,* declared that Brazil had entered the era of the "electronic gulag." There was growing discomfort in

Brazil with the power of SEI officials to make such decisions and to exert so much influence over informatics development (Chaves 1988, 206).

Many of these concerns were shared by what might be called the "loyal opposition," which formed a third perspective within the debate over the software legislation. Senators who traditionally defended the informatics policy joined in the critique of the version of the software law passed by the House. Congresswoman Cristina Tavares, one of the informatics policy's most loyal defenders, qualified her support for the software legislation, saying, "The policy isn't good, but it's what we need" (Herédia 1987b, 7).

This strand of criticism was largely due to the complexity of the process of evaluating imported software according to the criterion of functional equivalency. Even within the SEI, some officials agreed with some of Senator Campos's arguments (Dantas 1987c). They wondered how the SEI should interpret and apply the law in making decisions such as whether it was appropriate to buy or license a certain type of software. The SEI needed verifiable measures to judge whether programs were functionally equivalent, based upon technical support and advice from universities and other research centers (Maturo 1987c).

Finally, an unusual coalition of groups from the informatics sector also opposed the proposed software legislation. These groups included the Sociedade dos Usuários de Computadores e Equipamentos Subsidiários (So-ciety of Computer and Subsidiary Equipment Users) (SUCESU); the Associação de Empresas Brasileiras de Software e Serviços de Informática (Association of Brazilian Informatics Software and Services Firms) (ASSESPRO); and the Associação Brasileira de Empresas de Software (Brazilian Association of Software Firms) (ABES). ASSESPRO was constituted primarily by the owners of large companies that offered services like data processing to other firms but did not produce their own software. Its members also included some national software producers and distributors of foreign software. ASSESPRO and ABES had an acrimonious history; ABES was established in 1987 by firms that had originally belonged to ASSESPRO but rejected its position supporting import controls for software. They did agree, however, on the need for a law to control the access of foreign software to the Brazilian market as a way to promote the development of a local industry. SUCESU was formed in 1974 as an association of the major computer users in Brazil, primarily to negotiate with IBM as the leading provider of informatics equipment. All three groups shared a history of opposition to the informatics law because of its prohibitions of certain imports and restrictions on the distribution of foreign products (Calicchio 1990, interview).

As software users and providers, these groups had different reasons for supporting a common position on the software legislation. SUCESU consistently sought to attain the best possible machines at the lowest price, and the group opposed the informatics law because it blocked Brazilian users' access to the most advanced products. It viewed the software legislation as an opportunity, however, to broaden access to both foreign and domestic software. For their part, the software associations viewed the legislation as a way to monitor imports sufficiently to protect local software producers without unduly hampering distributors of foreign software.

These groups were able to cooperate, largely because of their united opposition to the concept of functional equivalency as a basis for instituting import controls. Along with the other critics mentioned, they viewed these criteria as virtually impossible to apply, due to the often-subtle differences between software programs (Serro 1987b; Maturo 1987c; Pereira de Lucena 1990).

These shared criticisms of the concept of functional equivalency led the users' society and software associations, in cooperation with Senator Campos, to formulate a proposal to amend the proposed software legislation. They recommended, as an alternative, monitoring imports through a tax on foreign software. Programs that were comparable to an existing national product would be taxed more highly, up to a maximum of 200 percent of their value. To encourage imports, taxes could be reduced for programs without similar national products. Tax revenues would go into an incentive fund for national production of computer programs, which would contribute to the broader effort to develop human resources in the software sector (Maturo 1987b; Serro 1987b).

The MBI and officials in the SEI opposed the taxation amendment. Calling the plan "illusory," MBI representatives argued that regulations under GATT required foreign products to receive the same treatment as local ones once they entered the country. SEI officials emphasized that such discrimination between foreign and local products was unconstitutional in Brazil. Concerns to uphold both Brazilian law and international trade agreements thus led these groups to oppose the taxation amendment (Mourão 1992, interview; Aquino 1987; Herédia 1987c).

The range of conflicts over the software legislation led to months of negotiation in the Senate before the draft legislation came up for a vote. No one appeared to be interested in pushing the legislation through the Senate with the same speed as had been applied in the House. Minister of Science and Technology Renato Archer thought it would be a tactical error to press for a vote until an agreement was reached with the leaders of the parties in the Senate and the other concerned industry associations.

A solution was eventually reached by the end of October 1987. Negotiators from the users' society and software associations, the SEI, and the MBI finally accepted both taxation and functional equivalency as means to monitor imports of foreign software. The concept of functional equivalency approved in the legislation was very different from the original proposal made by the SEI and the MBI. Struggles among the groups involved in the negotiations, combined with pressures from the Reagan administration, led the concept to be defined very strictly. Under this definition, two products would practically have to be clones in order to be viewed as equivalents, rather than simply serve the same purpose for computer users. Negotiations and revisions continued until late November, involving discussions between Senator Campos and other Senate leaders. The Senate finally approved the legislation in early December 1987 (Mourão 1992, interview; Dantas 1987c, 1987d; Herédia 1987f, 1987h, 1987j; Serro 1987a).

The conflicts over the software legislation in the Senate reveal the short-term, strategic nature of the consensus previously developed in the House. The latter's passage of the legislation represented a first stage in the Brazilian government's response to the threat of U.S. trade sanctions. After the legislation went to the Senate, a second stage of political struggle began. Internal debates intensified as divergent groups defended differing approaches to the regulation of the software sector. These groups shaped the final content of the software legislation and defined the concept of functional equivalency, which became a focal point of debate in the negotiations. These debates took place in the context of U.S. pressures on Brazil both to pass a software law and to eliminate the market reserve approach to informatics development that the concept of functional equivalency represented. These pressures continued to weigh on Brazilian government officials in their decisions about how to implement the informatics law.

DILEMMAS OF DOMESTIC SOFTWARE DEVELOPMENT

The political negotiation over the software legislation served two purposes for the Brazilian government. In the House, the legislation was an effective vehicle both to mediate the relationship with the United States and to respond to the immediate threat of trade sanctions. In the Senate, the legislation became the focus of domestic political struggles to craft a national development policy for the software sector. Although no one was totally satisfied with the legislation finally approved by the Senate, negotiators felt a sense of accomplishment because they had worked through their differences to develop an acceptable compromise. This accomplishment was overshadowed by a series of other events, however, which made it impossible to balance the divergent goals within the twofold software strategy. The choices about which of these goals to pursue reveal two further sets of constraints that limited the options for political action by Brazilian state officials.

In addition to the pressures from the 301 investigation by the U.S. government, the international software market presented a second set of conditions that affected the implementation of the informatics policy. Certain aspects of the informatics law created problems for Brazilian firms in the context of changing software technologies and products. The law required that all computers sold in Brazil include an operating-system license. It also contained protectionist provisions barring imports of products similar to those produced within the country by national firms.

The effects of these policies are exemplified by the case of the Scopus Company, which was established in the mid-1970s as the first private Brazilian company in the informatics sector. Scopus invested extensive financial and human resources to develop Sisne, an operating system compatible with MS-DOS. Scopus registered the first version of Sisne in late 1983, and continued to develop new versions that offered capabilities similar to those in the latest versions of MS-DOS available on the market (*Data News* 1987a; Herédia 1987e).

The development of Sisne was an impressive achievement that reflected the proficiency of Brazilian engineers. It also demonstrated the challenges involved with seeking technological autonomy in an international software market characterized by rapid technological change and the rise of MS-DOS as an international standard. In December 1986, six Brazilian computer manufacturers asked the SEI to approve licenses for version 3.2 of Microsoft's MS-DOS operating system. The debates over Brazil's software legislation were thus accompanied by discussions about how to respond to this particular licensing request. The U.S. government and Microsoft Corporation joined the Brazilian manufacturers in pressing for a positive licensing decision (Herédia 1987d).

The Brazilian firms' request to license MS-DOS reveals key disadvantages of both product-development incentives and the mandatory operating-system policy as part of a larger informatics development strategy in Brazil.

One drawback was that efforts at local product development were prone to problems with marketing. It was difficult to justify the time and financial resources involved if the benefits were measured strictly in terms of short-term profits. Critics of the policy argued that the Brazilian government was providing incentives for local firms to "reinvent the wheel" instead of acknowledging the technical superiority of foreign products and facilitating access to them. By contrast, policy supporters contended that the knowledge gained through the product-development process was invaluable for building Brazil's long-term capacity to compete in the world market.

The case of Sisne suggests three major sources of marketing problems. Most importantly, MS-DOS had become an international standard in the industry. Firms viewed it as a better investment since it would serve as a foundation for future developments in the international market. Second, firms were reluctant to license Sisne because it was more expensive than MS-DOS. And finally, many other Brazilian computer manufacturers did not want to buy their operating systems from a competitor. For example, the director of Polymax noted that his firm had about 11 percent of the

Brazilian market; Itautec, Microtec, and Scopus were the main competitors. He expressed his willingness to negotiate about using Sisne, but only if the software was utilized cooperatively. Different firms could then invest in its development and gain equal advantages (Fujii 1987d; 1990 interview with Ivan da Costa Marques, former president of Cobra).

The preference for MS-DOS exemplifies the more general difficulty of developing local products in a market where foreign technologies and products set international standards. In 1990 interviews, Edson Fregni and Josef Manasterski, the engineers who ran Scopus, and Ivan da Costa Marques, the former president of Cobra, emphasized the powerful incentives to use foreign products. Although some Brazilian firms benefited from the protection they received from the informatics policy, others viewed access to foreign technologies and capital as an advantage that might provide them a competitive edge. These firms attempted to bolster their market positions through covert relationships with foreign capital or by copying foreign products.

As firms pursued competitive advantages, the mandatory operating-system policy contributed to a second major problem, that of piracy. This problem arose from the effects of the operating-system policy within the broader context of the informatics policy, which lacked provisions to protect intellectual property. The requirement to provide operating systems with each computer sold in Brazil actually created incentives for piracy, which were not counterbalanced by a system of protective rules such as an author's copyright. Product-development incentives increased the availability of local products that were perceived as inferior for various reasons. Within this policy environment, several Brazilian firms opted to copy Microsoft's operating system rather than license either MS-DOS or Sisne. In March 1987, the president of Microsoft went to Brazil for talks with officials from the SEI and the Ministério da Ciência e Tecnologia (Ministry of Science and Technology) (MCT). He accused a number of Brazilian firms of illegally copying MS-DOS, and the firms paid fines as compensation (Costa Marques 1990; Herédia 1987d).[3]

The interactions with Microsoft increased pressure on the Brazilian government to license MS-DOS. The licensing request posed a serious dilemma for the SEI because the firms were asking to use a foreign operating system when a compatible local system was on the market. Granting the request would undermine Scopus, one of the few firms that engaged in the kind of product development that the informatics law was designed to promote.

In addition to developing Sisne, Scopus was engaged in cooperative activities with other Brazilian firms that supported development policy goals. In May 1987, Scopus made an agreement with the state computer-manufacturing firm, Cobra. Cobra had invested $30 million to develop SOX, a Unix-like operating system for supermicro computers of thirty-two bits. Scopus and Cobra agreed to license each other's software as part of a strategy for local technological development. By September of that year, Itautec, a major Brazilian computer manufacturer, reached an accord with Cobra and Scopus to develop and market basic and support software.

The agreement with Itautec was consistent with a key objective of the informatics policy: to develop local capacities for joint projects, and to maximize the benefits of investments in local skills, technologies, and products. Created by Itaú, Brazil's second-largest bank, Itautec had been the third-largest local computer firm since 1984 (Evans 1986, 802). It originally supported the licensing of MS-DOS, so the accord signaled the firm's readiness to develop local arrangements for software development rather than rely on foreign systems. At a time when firms like Scopus and Cobra were having problems garnering local support for their products, the accord represented the kind of cooperation between national firms that was needed for the informatics policy to be successful (Fujii 1987a; *Data News* 1987c).

Considerable pressures were thus created for the SEI not to license MS-DOS, and instead to support local firms that were pursuing fundamental policy objectives. Licensing the foreign operating system would have undermined Scopus's extensive investments and sent a message that local product development would not be protected by state policy. It would also have decreased the opportunities to pursue the accord between Scopus, Cobra, and Itautec. Fernando Calicchio, the secretary-general of the MBI, emphasized that there was much more at stake than simply importing a software program. For state officials and organizations in the informatics sector, the decision involved "whether [Brazil] can try to find a way to develop its own software . . . whether a national product was possible to export, or whether we'd always have to import" (1990 interview). The vice-president of Scopus summed up the potential effects of such a decision: "If SEI allows licensing of MS-DOS, the next day Scopus will totally change its mode of business operations . . . the decision would represent a change of direction in the informatics policy itself" (Mahlmeister 1987, 43).

FACING SANCTIONS: RESISTANCE AND CAPITULATION

Brazilian state officials were keenly aware of the political complexity of the MS-DOS decision. The Secretary of Informatics at that time was convinced that Brazil needed to change its informatics law to adjust to the new international reality of MS-DOS as an international standard on the software market. Conditions had changed radically since the law was passed; the development of open systems made it increasingly impractical for manufacturers to design proprietary operating systems to compete with industry standards. After analyzing these changes, the Secretary concluded that Brazil should develop a new set of policies that were more open to foreign products.

The process of making such a transition was fraught with conflict, particularly in the context of the trade dispute with the U.S. government. Time was required to phase out the old policy and to minimize the losses to firms like Scopus that had complied with the existing law. Rocha described a conversation with the Minister of Science and Technology about how to change the rules restricting imports of operating systems similar to national products: "We can't just do away with this, because we are the ones who obligated these people to invest. But neither can we freeze the process, because it is a new reality. At the time that we established this rule, we didn't perceive this" (1992 interview).

In deciding how to implement the informatics policy in the MS-DOS case, Brazilian officials struggled to adjust development policy to shifting market conditions. They viewed their original goal of technological autonomy as impractical in a rapidly changing global economy. Their overriding concerns were legal and pragmatic, focusing on how to make a transition to a new set of policies with minimal damage to firms that had followed the existing laws. Such an adaptation was also difficult in the context of pressures from the U.S. government and Microsoft.

The Secretary of Informatics, the Minister of Science and Technology, and other Brazilian negotiators proposed that existing rules be maintained on operating systems compatible with MS-DOS 3.2. Firms in Brazil would then be required to use Brazilian products like Sisne that were similar to MS-DOS up to the 3.2 version. They suggested that from that point on, they would begin to modify Brazilian laws to adjust to the new reality of MS-DOS as an international standard. There would be a transition to new laws allowing more openness to foreign products, beginning with the software legislation then under consideration by the Brazilian legislature. The negotiators pointed out that even the concept of functional equivalency, which was viewed as a protectionist measure, could end up benefiting foreign firms. Restricting imports only of products similar to those produced within the country would create opportunities to import newly developed foreign products. Since foreign software firms would develop new versions of their products more rapidly than Brazilian firms would, those imports would be permitted under the new law. Thus, denial of the licensing request for MS-DOS 3.2 would not preclude future licensing of newer versions of that operating system, or other new software.

After making their case at the bargaining table, Brazilian state officials denied the licensing request for MS-DOS 3.2 in September 1987. They based their decision on article 22 of the National Informatics Law, which barred foreign products from the market if there was a Brazilian counterpart. The Secretaría Especial de Informática argued that Scopus was already manufacturing software similar to MS-DOS version 3.2. The import of Microsoft's competing program would thus have undermined the operations of a local firm, making it difficult to retain its market position (Rocha 1992, interview; Herédia 1987d).

The decision to deny licensing was made by a few key Brazilian government officials, including the Secretary of Informatics, the Minister of Science and Technology, and the President. The restricted participation by a few top officials fits Stallings's (1992) description of the decision-making stage of the policy-making process rather than the implementation stage. As discussed above, a range of groups rallied to influence the developing software policy. Several local firms pressured the government to make exceptions to policy regulations by licensing MS-DOS. The choice to deny licensing was a difficult one, since it was likely to provoke trade sanctions from the U.S. government. International influences on development policy thus came to a head during the process of implementing that policy, contradicting Stallings's argument that international influences lessen during the policy-implementation stage. However, this unfolding of events is consistent with her emphasis on the importance of timing in shaping the international constraints upon former Third World development policy.

Rocha described the decision to deny the licensing of MS-DOS as part of a "jogo de risco," a dangerous game of chance, where the risks of international sanctions were weighed against the potential negative impacts on Brazilian firms. Over the course of the negotiations, Brazilian state officials determined the price they were willing to pay to make a point about the importance of complying with existing law. In the end, they denied the licensing of MS-DOS because this was the only decision consistent with existing Brazilian law. Any other ruling would have undermined the firms whose activities were currently protected under the informatics policy and whose investments had been made with the expectation of that protection (1992 interview).

Once Brazilian negotiators determined the price they were willing to pay to uphold the informatics law, they paid it almost immediately. The MS-DOS ruling provoked conflicts with foreign capital and the U.S. government. Microsoft argued that Scopus had pirated its software. It requested the U.S. government to impose sanctions against Brazil, arguing that retaliation was necessary for its alleged loss of $50 to $100 million in sales (Riding 1987; *Latin America Regional Reports Brazil* 1987, 4–5). In late November 1987, U.S. trade officials announced the imposition of $105 million of sanctions on Brazilian exports.

The criteria used to target specific firms for sanctions reflect the Reagan administration's strategy for changing Brazil's informatics policy. The U.S. government sanctioned firms that were 100 percent Brazilian owned and used primary materials from Brazil. They also targeted firms with labor-intensive products so that any future problems with unemployment might influence workers to oppose the informatics law. Finally, they sought to minimize any damage from the sanctions to U.S. firms and consumers.

President Reagan argued that by restricting the import of MS-DOS, the Brazilian government effectively banned U.S. companies from Brazil's computer market. He expressed his willingness to lift the sanctions, however, if the action were reversed. He contended that the U.S. government had been quite patient with Brazilian nationalism. His administration delayed retaliatory measures twice to avoid potential negative effects upon Brazil's delicate debt negotiations with international banks (Fujii 1987c; Herédia 1987h; Riding 1987; *Latin America Regional Reports Brazil* 1987).

U.S. trade sanctions gave rise to a nationalist response by supporters of the informatics law in Brazil. They favored a diplomatic strategy that did not openly yield to U.S. government pressure, and defended Brazil's right to protect its industry and firms from foreign competition. Finance Minister Bresser Pereira exemplified such an approach when he stated, "Brazil will continue to follow the economic policy that it considers best for the country" (Farnsworth 1987, A1).

The Brazilian response eventually focused upon three legislative actions. First, 68 out of 89 members of the congressional commission drafting the new constitution voted to include one of the main principles underlying the informatics law. They approved an article stating that Brazil's internal market was part of the national patrimony and should be organized to promote socioeconomic development, as well as technological and cultural autonomy. This action laid the legal groundwork for other sectors to implement nationalist development strategies with constitutional guarantees. Second, the congressional commission approved an amendment that identified technological research on national, regional, and local problems as the duty of the Brazilian government. Even legislators who were not involved in the informatics policy expressed support for Brazil's right to use state policy to promote technological development. Finally, the Brazilian Senate granted urgent priority to consideration of a proposal by Senator Severo Gomes, a strong supporter of the informatics law. The proposal included suspension of profits for firms whose countries practiced trade retaliations against Brazil (Fujii 1987b; Herédia 1987k).

In part, the strength of the nationalist response was due to the timing of the sanctions, coming after months of hard negotiations over the software legislation in the Brazilian Senate. Although passage of a software law was one of the main points raised by the U.S. government for negotiation with Brazil, the Reagan administration imposed sanctions just as the legislation was nearing approval. The timing contributed to the impression of many Brazilians that the U.S. government was making Brazil a scapegoat for its own domestic problems. They viewed trade retaliations as a political strategy to divert attention from the U.S. trade deficit and lack of competitiveness with Japan (Herédia 1987l; Fujii 1987b; Dantas 1987a).

Informatics policy supporters thus advocated specific legislative actions as part of a government response to U.S. trade sanctions. Brazil's positioning in the world market, however, made it possible for sanctions to create considerable pressures on the Brazilian government (Rocha 1992, interview; Fujii 1987a; Herédia 1987d; Lemos 1987). The imposition of sanctions created a third set of constraints on the Brazilian government from economic sectors with longstanding export relationships with the United States.

Exporters dependent on trade with the United States argued that Brazil was jeopardizing vital export markets for the sake of the informatics industry. As Brazil's major trading partner, the United States was expected to take about 60 percent of Brazil's exports in 1987. Sanctions were proposed on sixty-six Brazilian exports. Brazil's major concerns involved aircraft produced by Embraer, refined petroleum products, steel, and vehicles. Renato Archer, former Minister of Science and Technology, noted the importance of the sanctions' effects on morale, since Brazil prides itself on exporting planes and shoes to the United States (1992 interview). Auto parts was one of the sectors with the highest exports to the United States. Pedro Eberhardt, president of the Sindicato da Indústria de Autopeças (Auto Parts Industry Union), stated that the "negotiation of the market reserve is the only way for the Brazilian government to avoid an even greater impasse" (Lemos 1987, 6). Abram Szajman, president of the Federação de Comércio do Estado de São Paulo (Commercial Federation of the State of São Paulo), argued that without a negotiated solution, Brazil would be isolated in the world market (6).

Representatives from other sectors agreed, largely because of their dependence on trade with the United States. These sectors included footwear, with 80 percent of output exported to the United States; orange juice, with 56 percent exported; and iron and steel, with 47 percent exported. Members of the ceramic and furniture industries also blamed their impending export problems on the informatics law. A range of industry representatives lobbied Brazilian state officials to negotiate with the U.S. government and to stop jeopardizing export markets for the sake of the informatics strategy. They were joined by the Associação de Comércio Exterior do Brasil (Brazilian Association of Foreign Trade) (AEB) and the Departamento de Comércio Exterior (Department of Foreign Trade) of the powerful Federação das Industrias do Estado de São Paulo (Federation of Industries of the State of São Paulo) (FIESP) (Fujii 1987b; Herédia 1987g, 1987h; Lemos 1987; "Mixed Reaction" 1988).

Even before the official sanctions were announced, representatives from the shoe industry asked for a meeting with the Minister of Science and Technology. The Minister told them that Brazil was open to dialogue with the United States and that it was studying ways to respond. In a later series of high-level meetings with government officials, local business executives warned that lucrative markets built up over many years could be lost in the effort to protect Brazil's computer and software industries. They criticized the government for letting the trade dispute reach a crisis, by consciously taking actions that the United States had warned were subject to reprisals. One senior government official described the exporters' concerns: "They're aware of the political complexity of the problem, but they've also made it clear to us how much is at stake. . . . They obviously want us to show maximum flexibility" (Riding 1987, D1).

RESPONDING TO LOCAL CAPITAL

The U.S. sanctions thus introduced a third set of challenges for the Brazilian government as it sought to implement the informatics policy. Brazil's position in the global economy, and particularly its trade dependency on the United States, made it imperative to respond not only to changing international market conditions and the pressures from the 301 investigation but also to domestic exporters affected by trade sanctions. Government officials weighed the goal of promoting national informatics development against the need to maintain key export relationships between the United States and local capital. Implementing the informatics policy thus involved confronting pressures not only from a powerful foreign state but from local capitalists whose dependent trade relationships made them extremely vulnerable to sanctions. The Sarney administration's strategy changed as the interests of the U.S. government and Microsoft converged with those of local exporters. The sanctions thus created a new configuration of interests, where segments of local capital with dependent trade relationships supported U.S. government demands.

The Brazilian government finally responded to these contradictory pressures by making concessions in the informatics field. U.S. and Brazilian officials held a new round of talks in late 1987 and January 1988. U.S. negotiators reiterated their demand to license MS-DOS, and also asked that two articles in the new software law be vetoed by President Sarney. The first defined the concept of functional equivalency, and restricted imports of foreign software to programs that did not have a Brazilian counterpart. The second article instituted a taxation system for foreign software to generate funds for local software development.

After these meetings, President Sarney vetoed the article in the new software law requiring a tax on foreign software, finding it unconstitutional. More importantly, the ministerial-level CONIN announced its decision to authorize sale of the MS-DOS 3.3 program. The council presented its decision as a technical one, and not as a response to the threat of U.S. trade sanctions. It used the principle of functional equivalency as the legal guideline for ruling that Sisne was not equivalent to the latest version of MS-DOS (*Latin America Regional Reports Brazil* 1988).

Indeed, Brazilian officials depicted themselves as autonomous decision makers as they described their negotiations. They did not publicly admit that pressures from U.S. trade sanctions had influenced their decision to license MS-DOS. The decision was nevertheless a victory for the U.S. government, and a reflection of the structural constraints upon the Brazilian state. One of President Sarney's informatics advisors underscored the lack of any technical foundation for such a ruling. The latest version of MS-DOS was so similar to its predecessor that it offered insignificant new capabilities.[4] Scopus's operating system was completely comparable, so Brazil had no technical need to import from Microsoft (1990 interview with former informatics advisor to President Sarney; Herédia 1987h, 1987m; Evans 1989a; Dantas 1987f). The president of Scopus, Edson Fregni, explained the significance of this decision: "The United States won. . . . In practice, this means the end of the market reserve policy in the area of software" (Riding 1988).

TOWARD THE END OF THE MARKET RESERVE

Fregni and other supporters of the market reserve approach saw the MS-DOS decision as a clear defeat for Brazil; however, U.S. multinationals doing business in the country objected to the software law approved by President Sarney. They complained that the concept of functional equivalency and the process of registering foreign software at the Secretaría Especial de Informática were cumbersome obstacles to their Brazilian operations. Despite these continuing reservations about Brazil's informatics policy, the Reagan administration suspended trade sanctions against Brazil in late February 1988.

As the concept of functional equivalency was implemented, concerns about its hindering the entrance of foreign firms into Brazil's software market proved to be largely unfounded. As discussed above, the concept was defined so strictly that two programs had to be virtually identical in order to be judged equivalent. As a result, Brazilian software technicians and engineers found themselves engaged in a time-consuming process of examining each foreign software program. This did little to protect local software producers. According to the chief of the Divisão de Programas de Computador e Serviços Técnicos of the DEPIN, approximately 10,000 foreign software programs were registered in Brazil by 1992. Fewer than thirty were denied market entry because of the existence of a national equivalent (Mourão 1992, interview).

The National Informatics Law passed in 1984 provided for eight years of market protection in the computer industry, to end in October 1992. When Fernando Collor took office as Brazil's President in March 1990, his economic team hastened the process of dismantling the informatics regulations, including those pertaining to software. These changes were part of a broader neoliberal economic program to open Brazilian markets, as Chapter 5 discusses.

Software continued to play a distinct role in the Brazilian informatics market during the transition to a neoliberal economic regime. Many local businesspeople viewed the software sector as one of their most viable options for continuing involvement in the informatics industry as the market increasingly opened to foreign competition. Edson Fregni and Josef Manasterski, the engineers who once ran Scopus, founded a new firm that specialized in artificial intelligence. One of the top technical specialists at the state computer manufacturing firm became a partner in a firm devoted to software applications and solutions. Skills honed through years of work in product development could now be applied in market niches requiring specialized attention to customer needs. The ability to apply research and technical skills to solve a myriad of customer problems became a strategic competitive asset for firms in the emerging computer market. These abilities were perhaps the most valuable legacy of the market reserve, as firms negotiated the next uncertain phase in the trajectory of Brazilian informatics development—the transition to a market more open to foreign competition (Moraes 1992, interview; Campos 1992, interview; Gomes 1992, interview; Araujo 1992, interview; Sousa 1992, interview; Guaranys 1992, interview; Calicchio 1992, interview; Nunes 1992, interview; Fregni 1992, interview; Manasterski 1992, interview).[5]

CONCLUSION

The high-tech trade war over Brazilian informatics can help us understand the international structural constraints on development and development policy in the former Third World, in the context of globalization. As Chapter 1 discusses, Sassen (1999) critiques theorists who view globalization as an inexorable process of economic expansion, a "zero-sum game" whereby national states lose power whenever the global economy wins. She argues that states actively struggle against global capital and foreign states to retain control of national development. Globalization thus involves an economic and political battle by national governments against foreign governments, multinational corporations and banks, multilateral financial institutions, and international bureaucratic organizations that seek to open markets for global capital. As a nationalist development strategy, the Brazilian informatics policy opposed neoliberal efforts to "de-nationalize" individual markets by breaking down so-called "barriers to trade." By seeking to control the development of critical high-technology computer and software industries on a national level, the informatics policy thus posed a threat to what McMichael (2000b, 11) calls "the market as a de-nationalizing movement."

The Brazilian government struggled against three major international structural constraints as it implemented the informatics policy in the mid-to-late 1980s. The 301 investigation by the U.S. government, the structure of the international software market, and the imposition of trade sanctions created successive rounds of pressures on the Brazilian government. They made it virtually impossible to maintain the informatics strategy, despite the flexible political judgment of Brazilian negotiators and their willingness to adapt to Reagan administration demands.

The 301 investigation precipitated a high-tech trade war that presented a significant challenge to the Brazilian government, as it sought to implement the informatics policy after 1985. The investigation was part of a larger effort by the U.S. government to gain access to the high-technology markets of its trading partners. As Chapter 3 discusses, U.S. congressional representatives and business executives supported the 301 investigation as a way to show U.S. trading partners that "protectionism" would no longer be tolerated. In this context, high-technology development strategies are likely to spark conflicts with the U.S. government, especially if they contradict the principles of free trade.

The international market creates both economic opportunities and constraints on efforts to implement development policy in former Third World countries. In high-technology industries like computer manufacturing and software, technologies and products change so rapidly that it is difficult to predict the effects of policy choices. In the Brazilian informatics case, unforeseen changes in the international market had differing consequences during the early and later periods of the industry's development. In the mid-to-late 1970s, the informatics policy was successful largely due to a fortuitous circumstance that facilitated informatics development. Designed to protect the lower end of the computer market, then consisting only of minicomputers, the informatics policy ended up applying to the more lucrative personal computer market as well. If the Digital Equipment Corporation (DEC) or IBM had been interested in manufacturing their early minicomputer models in Brazil during the early 1970s, they could have established a market presence that would have made growth by

Brazilian-owned firms much more difficult. The emergence of mass-produced microchips also facilitated the development of the earliest Brazilian computers, since cheap components were readily available on the international market. The initial development of the informatics industry thus benefited significantly from favorable conditions in the international market (Langer 1989; Evans 1986).

In the mid-to-late 1980s, the effects of the international market were reversed. Unforeseen negative consequences arose from changes in product and technology markets. The rise of MS-DOS as an international standard made existing Brazilian regulations to promote the development of local operating systems impractical. The need to adjust the informatics policy to meet this new reality posed problems for state officials, who felt obliged to minimize the damage to firms that had invested in product development under the earlier legal regime. Their decision to uphold existing law while making a transition to more open policies incited trade sanctions from the U.S. government.

Using keen political judgment and negotiating skills, Brazilian state officials pursued a twofold software strategy in the face of both these types of constraints. The imposition of trade sanctions introduced a third set of factors that proved insurmountable by political action. Brazil's dependence on exports to foreign markets was the key element that limited the possibilities for state action in the Brazilian informatics case. This trade dependence made Brazilian export sectors extremely vulnerable to U.S. trade sanctions. It created a convergence of interests between domestic exporters and the U.S. government that eventually provoked concessions on the informatics policy.

Brazil's dependency on exports to foreign markets thus constituted the third and decisive set of constraints on the implementation of the informatics policy during the high-tech trade war. The influence of these factors underscores how prospects for both informatics development and political action were affected by Brazil's history of dependency. Brazil's experience also underscores the importance of examining current patterns of development in historical context. Past patterns of foreign investment and trade relationships often place strong limits on what can be accomplished through development strategies.

The legacy of dependency persists in the context of globalization and the rise of neoliberalism. Indeed, a history of dependency facilitates the process of denationalization that Sassen (1999) and McMichael (2000b) identify as a key part of globalization. Although informatics represented a new sector targeted for industrial development, political strategies to transform dependency were constrained by familiar forces. Brazilian state officials and industrialists acquired a range of new skills in developing an informatics industry and in negotiating over the political terms for its continued growth. Brazilian negotiators were adept in their efforts to manage ties with international capital and to adjust their development strategy to changing market conditions. However, these strategies were eventually subjected to a powerful array of structural constraints that made it virtually impossible to assert national control over informatics development. With its history of dependency on trade and foreign investment, the Brazilian government could not counteract neoliberal pressures to open the informatics market. The high-tech trade war with the U.S. government was a geopolitical force that catalyzed domestic support for a neoliberal regime. This combination of international and domestic constraints created conditions for neoliberalism to denationalize the Brazilian informatics market.

The weight of this legacy of dependence on foreign trade and investment underscores the importance of historical context in shaping processes of development and development policy making. Indeed, the processes of decision making and implementing software policy were influenced by groups like the MBI, SUCESU, ASSESPRO, and ABES, with a history of organizing around the broader informatics policy, and by the complex international and domestic conditions that led the U.S. government to pursue a trade war with Brazil. Stallings's (1992) argument that international influences would be greater during policy decision making than during policy implementation did not hold in this case. A range of Brazilian groups mobilized to influence the development of the informatics policy, and actively engaged in the decision-making process for software policy as well. By contrast, critical developments during the policy-implementation process forced a few key Brazilian government officials to make tough decisions that risked trade sanctions by the U.S. government.

These events suggest the need for greater emphasis on how changing conditions of local politics influence the process of making and implementing development policy. General models of the policy-making process suggest some issues to consider in evaluating local conditions; however, local actors are negotiating a complex and dynamic array of international and domestic factors that may not fit such models. The Brazilian informatics case suggests that it may be more useful to identify the major international and domestic forces at work, highlighting the interplay between structural constraints and actors' efforts to negotiate them. In the Brazilian informatics case, examining this interplay allows us to understand when and why international influence was successfully brought to bear, as well as the reasons why particular interest groups or government officials engaged in the process of policy making and implementation.

International structural constraints had a profound influence on the implementation of development policy during the high-tech trade war between Brazil and the United States. The Brazilian state, however, was continually active in responding to those constraints. Government officials struggled to implement the policy throughout a complex series of events, opposing efforts by the U.S. government to "denationalize" the Brazilian market. This oppositional stance was transformed by the election of Fernando Collor on a neoliberal economic platform in 1989. Paradoxically, however, the Brazilian government continued to play an active role in facilitating that process of denationalization, by constructing an "open" market.

5 From Technological Autonomy to Neoliberalism
Constructing an Open Market

THE EARLY 1990S was a turbulent time in Brazilian informatics. Brazilian concessions to international and domestic pressures in the MS-DOS case, and the suspension of U.S. trade sanctions, marked an end to the high-tech trade war with the United States. These events also signaled the beginning of the end of Brazil's informatics policy. When Fernando Collor became President of Brazil in March 1990, he implemented a series of neoliberal reforms that transformed market conditions in informatics. These included granting permission for technological joint ventures; opening the market to imports; and, in October 1992, approving the end of the market reserve, on the timetable originally set by the 1984 informatics law (Nunes 1992; Tigre 1993).

The process of constructing an open market had begun, raising a myriad of questions about the future of the informatics industry. Executives in multinational corporations like IBM and Unisys were optimistic; these policy changes fit their beliefs in the free market as the best way to promote industrial development. However, many local entrepreneurs and other informatics policy supporters were concerned that years of work to build the industry would be threatened by the rapid pace of deregulation. The goals of the major industry association, ABICOMP, shifted from developing Brazilian technological capacity to promoting national production by foreign and local companies. Protecting national productive capacity, whether financed by foreign or by local capital, began to take precedence over the earlier emphasis on growth of locally owned segments of the industry.

This chapter examines the transition to an open market in informatics, as the Brazilian government implemented a new policy framed within a neoliberal discourse that emphasized reducing the role of the state and opening the market to foreign trade and investment. This was a radical transformation of industrial policy that, combined with the economic recession then in progress, created volatile economic and political conditions in informatics. As one observer noted, "The recession by itself would be a big problem. The informatics policy by itself would be a big problem. But the change in the informatics policy in the context of a recession, these are two explosive factors" (Nunes 1992, interview). State, foreign, and local capital struggled to develop new strategies to adapt to these unpredictable circumstances. Informatics firms wrestled with questions about the viability of their operations, encountering unexpected conflicts and opportunities in the process.

EXPECTATIONS FOR THE TRANSITION PERIOD

As discussed in previous chapters, the 1984 informatics law was articulated within an oppositional, nationalist discourse infused with cultural values of technological development and national sovereignty. It was designed to promote the development of local firms in the informatics field. Through the market reserve and other measures, state officials established differing conditions for local and foreign firms to operate in the Brazilian market. They limited the strategies of foreign firms by prohibiting joint ventures and restricting the use of foreign technology. From 1976 until 1990, the Brazilian informatics policy fostered an environment where the differing interests of local and foreign firms were emphasized, and where little collaboration occurred between them.

When President Collor took office in 1990, he implemented a new economic policy, articulated within a neoliberal discourse that supported cultural values of free trade and the objective laws of the market. In informatics and other sectors, policies focused on opening markets to foreign investment, technology, and trade. A major change in the discourse of economic policy thus involved a transformation in the economic and political conditions in Brazil. This shift was the expected outcome of a presidential campaign in which neoliberal, free-market reform was the centerpiece of the Collor candidacy. The Collor government dissolved the SEI, the government agency that had been in charge of implementing the informatics policy. In its place, it created the Departamento de Política de Informática e Automação (Department of Informatics and Automation Policy) (DEPIN) to implement changes in the informatics industry as the previous policy was dismantled and replaced by the neoliberal regime.

The shift to a neoliberal discourse in Brazilian economic policy fits with Sassen's (1999) description of the dynamics of globalization, where national states develop and implement policies to adapt to the interests of global capital. A process of "incipient denationalizing" (160) thus occurs, where governments enact neoliberal policies that facilitate global capitalist activities within their national territories. In the Brazilian case, bureaucratic changes accompanying the shift from the SEI to the DEPIN put new people in charge of implementing the informatics policy and gave the neoliberal informatics discourse a concrete organizational form. Indeed, the neoliberal discourse defined policy "implementation" as a process of dismantling existing regulations and opening the market to foreign trade and investment. The development of a neoliberal discourse and practice for economic policy thus raised questions about whether such an "incipient denationalization" process would occur.

A high-ranking official within DEPIN, who did not wish to be identified, discussed his concerns about the transition to an open market in the following terms: "The tendency when you open the market is to have assemblers and importers. And this makes it very complicated to have an industrial policy, because industrial policy is made for industry and not for merchants. To the extent that there is no industry, it is more difficult" (1992 interview).

Artur Pereira Nunes, who worked at the SEI in the 1980s and later became a leading member of ABICOMP, expressed similar fears that the Brazilian computer industry would lose productive capacity and become dominated by distributors and retailers. Ironically, although the U.S. government had pressured Brazil to open its informatics markets, this change was viewed as benefiting Japanese producers more than American ones. Nunes stated that if the government did not seek to retain manufacturing capabilities, "four years from now . . . everyone will become distributors of products, and most probably, Japanese products" (1992 interview).

Some business and government officials believed that the problems associated with opening the market might be eased if the transition occurred more gradually or in a different form. They supported the basic direction of Collor's industrial policy, but questioned the timing and some of the details of its execution. The unnamed DEPIN official referred to above described the challenges to the Collor government in implementing the shift to an open market: "The question is basically one of opportunity, of timing . . . of when to do this, of the form in which to do this. . . . The discourse of this government is cohesive; in reality it is this for which the country needs to strive. But it is the form in which it is being done that is problematic" (1992 interview).

The transition to a neoliberal policy regime in Brazilian informatics was initially viewed as a clear victory for three main constituencies. First, it was perceived as a boon to global capital, whose activities had been restricted under the market reserve. Second, Brazilian computer users had complained about their lack of access to high-quality foreign computer products and about the high prices of Brazilian computers. Finally, the policy change was viewed as supporting Brazilian computer firms that wanted to distribute foreign products. By contrast, the transition to an open-market regime was perceived as a loss for local industrialists who had supported earlier policy goals of developing local products and technologies and had sought to become independent producers contributing to the development of a national computer industry.

Foreign and local firms had very different expectations about how the end of the market reserve would affect their business operations. There was widespread support among foreign multinationals for opening the Brazilian informatics market. Multinationals had faced policy restrictions on their Brazilian activities since 1976. While they had developed working relationships with the Brazilian government and maintained profitable operations under the market reserve, they never approved of the informatics policy. Fernando de Moraes, a senior executive at IBM's Brazilian subsidiary, described the firm's relationship with the Brazilian government as that of "a son with a father who does not like him. But he is economically and psychologically dependent on the father." Despite these tensions, he added, "The relationship with particular people was very good" (1992 interview).

In this and other interviews during the summer of 1992, executives at IBM and Unisys expressed enthusiasm about the changes occurring in Brazil and particularly about the prospects for increased joint ventures, imports, and investments in previously restricted segments of the Brazilian informatics market. By contrast, executives at Brazilian-owned firms emphasized their concerns about how they would fare under the changing market conditions. Even those who supported the shift to the open market wondered how they would compete with imports and whether or not they could maintain a viable business in the face of greater competition (Moraes 1992, interview; Campos 1992, interview; Gomes 1992, interview; Araujo 1992, interview; Sousa 1992, interview; Velloso 1992, interview; Guaranys 1992, interview; Fregni 1992, interview). A supporter of the former informatics policy viewed the transition to an open market as an unqualified success for foreign firms, largely because of the dominance of the neoliberal discourse in shaping both official and popular conceptions of economic policy:

A common discourse exists; practically all the multinationals here use the discourse of "free trade." They succeeded . . . because . . . if you talk with the president, he speaks the discourse of free trade. If you talk with the doorman at the elevator, he speaks the discourse of free trade. This is something that not one political party in Brazil has achieved. Not the Brazilian church, not the political parties have achieved this uniformity, this unity of thought. (Calicchio 1992, interview)

This informatics industry activist emphasized what Escobar (1995) calls the "hegemonic effect" of economics as a cultural discourse. In this case, neoliberalism was widely accepted as a "normal" description of reality. Everyone from the doorman to the President used the same language, accepting free trade as the most rational approach to economic policy. A key part of the shift to a neoliberal economic regime thus involved the rise of neoliberalism as a cultural discourse with the power to define reality, truth, and normalcy both for government officials and for people in the street.

Supporters of the 1984 informatics strategy were concerned that the new neoliberal economic policy would mean losing the professional employment base developed under the market reserve. For example, José Rubens Doria Porto, former Secretary of Informatics, discussed his fears about potential declines in informatics employment. He noted that in the 1980s, graduates of the major engineering and professional schools easily found jobs in the informatics industry. Work was plentiful in the areas of software, hardware, communications, and other fields linked to informatics. This situation changed dramatically, however, with the transition to an open market: "In these last few years, people who were at the end of their courses were desperate about finding employment. And they do not have it. This remains with people. This brands people. This is going to have an effect in the future. I think this is one more error that was committed in the American assessment" of the situation (Porto 1992, interview).

In the former Secretary's view, the U.S. government lacked an understanding of the effects of opening the market on professional employment, and may also have overestimated the potential for U.S. firms to compete with firms from Japan and other countries that would enter the Brazilian market once the informatics policy was dismantled.

Critics of Collor's neoliberal policies were particularly concerned about the speed and extent of the reforms. According to José Guaranys, ABICOMP's main negotiator with the government, the Collor administration saw the informatics industry as a "strange beast." The government was ideologically opposed to the industry because it had developed under state protection (1992 interview). In a similar vein, a former informatics advisor to President Sarney compared the Collor government's opening of the informatics market to people burning down a house without first looking inside, simply because they did not like the people who had built it (Henrique 1992, interview). He described a striking image of the local informatics industry, constructed painstakingly over a period of decades, going up in flames.

This image characterized struggles in the Brazilian informatics industry over the next ten years. Many industrialists who had supported the informatics strategy remained committed to the process of informatics development. They were not willing to give up on years of hard work to build the industry. Instead, they devised new ways to work within the changed political and economic context. As Guaranys stated, "I think it is possible to defend this industry. Because it is a respectable industry that generates a lot of employment . . . I do not know how much will be here in three years, but I think we can still preserve an industrial force" (1992 interview).

Edson Fregni, the former president of Scopus, emphasized the importance of professional skills and other industrial capacities as a legacy of the informatics policy. He described such capacities as the "eggs" left behind by the "serpent of the market reserve" (1990 interview). During the volatile period between 1990 and 1992, this legacy became apparent in curious and unpredictable ways. The fragile, yet fertile, offspring of the informatics policy provided resources for the struggle to preserve what remained of the local industry. They generated surprises for both national and foreign firms, contradicting many of these firms' original expectations, and gave rise to complex efforts to cope with the vicissitudes of the transition period.

LEGACY OF THE MARKET RESERVE: SURPRISES FOR LOCAL AND FOREIGN CAPITAL

Despite their general optimism, foreign firms faced many problems and uncertainties in the transition to an open market. As discussions progressed about the new industrial policy and controls over imports were dismantled, many multinationals expected marked increases in sales. After all, Brazilian users had complained about their lack of access to the highest-quality equipment, bemoaning the high prices of Brazilian computers relative to prices paid in the United States or Europe. They dreamed of buying foreign products that were viewed as synonymous with quality and advanced technology. Many of these users were firms that viewed access to top-of-the-line equipment as essential to their business operations. Both foreign and local firms expected that as soon as foreign products were available in Brazil, national-brand computers and contraband machines would become much less popular.

These expectations began eroding, however, as soon as the new machines began to arrive on the market. While national-brand machines continued to sell, the more expensive foreign equipment sold only a few units. Brazilian manufacturers, and particularly their new foreign partners, began to conclude that the Brazilian market was not as large as they had imagined; nor was there a great demand for the more expensive and better-known foreign products (Dantas 1992j).

A representative of one multinational lamented that sales that used to take a maximum of three months had begun to take more than a year. Clients seemed overwhelmed by the variety of options that had become available. They had money to buy equipment, and they were not delaying purchases with the expectation that prices would fall after the market opened completely. They were simply unsure what choices to make now that their options had grown so extensively (Dantas, 1992l). Another manufacturer remarked, "We didn't expect that the user would buy so little." He described the disappointment of foreign firms that entered joint ventures in Brazil expecting strong consumer demand for their products: "Nobody enters a joint venture expecting to sell 100 machines. The firms provided resources and so far, they are getting ridiculous results" (Dantas 1992j).

Why did Brazilian consumers not buy famous-brand computers in the quantities that both foreign and local firms expected? These "ridiculous results" can be understood in the context of the history of the market reserve, which created opportunities for the development of local capital. Despite users' complaints about price and quality, local firms under the market reserve developed products that met the needs of many Brazilian users. These computers were priced lower than many of the foreign machines that entered the market after 1991. Indeed, Brazilian informatics industry analysts suggested that the only clear reason for weak sales of foreign machines was their price. Beginning late in 1991, high-quality brands like IBM, Compaq, NCR, and others entered the market through joint ventures and licensing accords. Their products were expensive even in the United States and Europe, where customers were used to paying more for high-quality equipment. The majority of Brazilian users appeared to choose their machines according to the price, however, particularly in difficult economic times. Users were more reticent than expected, and continued to buy national-brand computers like Itautec, SID, and Scopus that were well-known in Brazil (Dantas 1992j).

IBM's efforts to market its PS/2 model exemplified the problems faced by foreign capital in the area of price competitiveness. The PS/2 represented an important strategic shift for IBM in its attempt to move beyond mainframes and tap the burgeoning personal computer market. In Brazil the mainframe market consisted of about 1,500 organizations, all of which had machines; there was thus virtually no potential for growth in this market. The market for personal computers, however, was estimated to be about 10 million, representing considerable potential for the expansion of IBM's customer base (Campos 1992).

The PS/2 was introduced in Brazil through MC&A Personal Systems, a joint venture where IBM held 49 percent ownership in a partnership with the Brazilian firm SID to assemble and sell the new line of machines. MC&A encountered problems with marketing the PS/2, primarily because the prices were considered high. The firm responded to these problems by changing its strategy; IBM created an office in charge of marketing the PS/2 in an effort to make the equipment more competitive. MC&A reduced the price of the PS/2 three times, decreasing the price about 25 percent from its original level. The director of marketing at MC&A was optimistic about the PS/2's commercial success after the price reductions; a total of about 1,500 machines were installed in twenty large firms. The director of Computerware, one of the major retail stores selling the PS/2, viewed the price reductions as the key to improving the PS/2's performance in Brazil. After selling 150 PS/2 machines in the first five months of 1992, he expected to sell a total of 1,000 machines by the end of the year. The commercial director of Sacco, a retail store distributing the PS/2 in the São Paulo market, also viewed the reduced price as a good impetus for improved sales. His firm had increased sales in the months since the last price reduction, despite the unfavorable economic conditions (Neto 1992).

These problems with sales of famous-brand computers puzzled national as well as foreign firms. Brazilian companies had prepared themselves to suffer great losses in the competition with foreign brands and were surprised to encounter the opposite (Dantas 1992j). According to an experienced Brazilian manufacturer, these unexpected results were due largely to advantages that Brazilian computer manufacturers had developed under the market reserve, such as responsiveness to the needs of customers. The manufacturer emphasized that foreign products might not be tailored as closely to the needs of Brazilian business users:

> While nobody has a machine it is very easy to . . . say that there are going to be low prices and they are going to sell some thousand units . . . [but] at the moment that they have to pay taxes and face a series of small problems, these firms begin to . . . see that peripheral X or Y isn't going to integrate as perfectly as they had hoped, that they lack a fundamental connector and that it will be necessary to transfer many specialized technicians to solve innumerable problems that eventually arise. (Dantas 1992k, 4)

At the discursive level, the change to an open-market informatics policy was a victory for foreign capital and local firms that wanted to distribute foreign products. This shift to a neoliberal informatics policy discourse occurred in a historical context, however, where local firms had been protected under the market reserve. The state had created opportunities for the development of local capital that provided ongoing advantages during the transition to an open market. A number of these firms had developed as independent producers of good-quality computers that were designed to meet the needs of Brazilian users. With the transition to an open-market policy, these firms retained the expertise they had accrued in serving the Brazilian market. Sergio Velloso, a manager of international operations at Itautec, described the importance of the legacy of the market reserve for local firms during the transition period: "The reserve was fundamental. Without it, we would not have had the technological cooperation, the formation of all these resources, the investment in research and development that was required by the law. The firms were required to industrialize, do projects, nationalize the industry. It created a series of contractors and subcontractors, distributors, that would not have existed" (1992 interview).

Despite complaints about the price and quality of Brazilian computers, many Brazilian consumers continued to buy locally made machines after the market was opened to imports. Paradoxically, it was foreign firms that had problems with the prices of their products during the transition period. These unexpected results were the catalyst for new alliances between local and foreign firms, as they adapted their business strategies during the uncertain process of constructing an open market.

FROM OPPOSITION TO PARTNERSHIP:
SHIFTING RELATIONSHIPS BETWEEN LOCAL
AND FOREIGN CAPITAL

The Collor government's shift to neoliberalism occurred within a broader context of globalization during the 1980s. Evans (1995, 183–84) analyzed informatics development as part of a "new internationalization" in the global economy, based upon new kinds of alliances between local and foreign capital. These alliances involved joint ventures and other kinds of business partnerships, as well as technology and licensing agreements. Under the old form of internationalization, foreign multinationals invested in former Third World countries by establishing wholly owned subsidiaries that often dominated the market and operated independently of local firms. These subsidiaries imported goods to supply local markets and exported a limited range of products. Under the new internationalization, local firms increasingly provided links between multinational firms and local users; they assembled components into final products, integrated imported hardware into systems, and drew upon a range of international products to develop solutions to the problems of local users.

Dependence on imports was one of the hallmarks of the old internationalization, where former Third World countries lacked local productive capacity. Under the new internationalization, however, local firms took a more active role in adapting and applying imported technologies and products to formulate solutions for local users. Equally important, local firms engaged in a growing range of export activities that sometimes included sophisticated products like Korean semiconductors and PC clones, or Indian software. Under the old internationalization, local firms exported minor components, or assembled and packaged imported components for re-export. The new internationalization involved a transformation in the export capacities of local firms in some former Third World countries. Local Brazilian firms did not engage extensively in exports of sophisticated products; however, there was an increasing mutual need for alliances on the part of local and foreign capital. These firms worked together in a growing variety of manufacturing and export activities (Evans 1995, 183–84).

The shift to a neoliberal regime in Brazilian informatics can help us understand the changing relationships and alliances among local and foreign capital and the state that emerged in the context of globalization. The neoliberal globalization discourse viewed international market expansion as an inexorable force that would dominate local markets, particularly in the former Third World. It was considered futile for the state to oppose the rule of global capital, which expanded according to objective economic laws. As authors such as Sassen (1999) have argued, however, the process of globalization is much more complex than these deterministic scenarios portray. Pressures toward "incipient denationalization" were exerted through international structural constraints, such as the trade war with the U.S. government, and through domestic shifts, such as the Collor government's adoption of a neoliberal economic policy. These pressures were countered, however, by both local and foreign firms that engaged in an array of strategies to maintain their business operations.

The trend toward increasing alliances between local and foreign capital was evident in the business strategies that firms used to adapt to the vicissitudes of the transition period in the early 1990s. A general pattern emerged whereby Brazilian firms attempted to gain access to external sources of components and technologies. They developed a range of ways to forge links with foreign suppliers that could provide access to competitive products and technologies.

These new approaches entailed strategies to operate efficiently within the new institutional framework based on free-trade principles. They involved a shift away from the model encouraged by the 1984 informatics policy, where the largest Brazilian computer manufacturers participated actively in commercial and technical-support activities, as well as production. By contrast, during the transition to an open market, firms concentrated their resources in particular parts of the productive chain, such as research and development, manufacturing, or marketing. This "targeting" approach allowed firms to focus on their areas of strength. They developed more specialized niches and engaged in a broader range of alliances.

The major divisions and alliances in the informatics sector were no longer defined by differences between local and foreign firms, but by differences between *strategies*. Under current conditions of globalization, the growing alliances between local and foreign capital meant that strategies often focused on constructing the relationships among local firms, multinational firms, and local users. These strategies also involved efforts to compete within the existing framework of a neoliberal policy regime.

For example, some firms decided to specialize in production. They concentrated their efforts on manufacturing and shifted their commercial and support activities to third parties like distributors, retailers, and marketing partnerships. This "production strategy" involved a range of production activities that linked manufacturers in new ways to the global market, such as integrating imported hardware into systems designed to meet the needs of local users.

Other firms pursued a "distribution strategy." They reduced their production and development operations to become distributors of foreign products, or to focus their activities on marketing and customer services. Again, these "distributors" participated in global markets in new ways, often by drawing upon a variety of international products to formulate solutions for local users. New networks of relationships were formed among local firms, multinational firms, and local users as firms with different strategies concentrated their activities in these more specialized market niches (*Data News* 1992a; Velloso 1992, interview; Fritsch 1992, 148–51).

These strategies emerged in the context of globalization, as local firms increasingly served as links between local users and multinational corporations. The choice of strategy often depended upon the local firm's bargaining power and comparative advantages as it negotiated with foreign partners. After joint ventures became legal under the new informatics law, such partnerships became the major way for new firms to enter the informatics market. In 1990 and 1991, more than ten major joint ventures were formed. Foreign firms were attracted by the financial health of Brazilian companies, as well as their marketing contacts, distribution networks, and close relationships with Brazilian users. The connections that Brazilian firms had fostered under the market reserve represented valuable resources for foreign companies seeking to enter or expand in the Brazilian market. Indeed, Evans (1979) highlighted local capital's role in marketing as a key to its relationships with global capital.

The Brazilian informatics market thus experienced an infusion of new players, as well as popular brands, sophisticated technologies, and high-quality equipment (Dantas 1992a; Tigre 1992; Rocha 1992). Brazilian firms went through profound changes as they restructured their operations to adapt to their new foreign partners and their increasing links to global markets, as well as to the new political conditions involved with the transition to an open market.

For example, Itautec, a major Brazilian computer manufacturer, was established in the 1970s to develop automation systems for Brazil's second-largest bank, Itaú. By 1984 Itautec had developed into the third-largest local firm in Brazil (Evans 1986, 802). As the firm grew, Itautec's products became increasingly diversified. At one time under the market reserve, the firm made over 150 different informatics products, ranging from data communications systems to personal computers and banking automation systems.

With the transition to an open market, Itautec developed new strategies that emphasized retaining its production activities. As Itautec executive Sergio Velloso told me in 1992, "We have an industrial capacity that we do not want to lose. We do not just want to distribute. But we want to link our industrial capacity with distribution." In its strongest area, banking automation, Itautec focused on its expertise in solutions and applications. It continued to do its own research and development to meet the specialized needs of its customers without forming partnerships with foreign firms. In the personal computer field, Itautec had competed with local firms in the context of the market reserve. Its managers recognized, however, that the transition to an open market would require new kinds of partnerships to keep the firm competitive. Itautec developed a production strategy that linked its local production capacity and familiar Brazilian brand name with well-known foreign brands. Its position in the Brazilian market as a well-established computer manufacturer made it an attractive partner for foreign firms seeking to expand their informatics activities during the transition period. Itautec formed a partnership with Microsoft for an operating system to sell with the Itautec brand of computers. It also developed a partnership with IBM to produce the IBM S400 supermini computer in Brazil at Itautec facilities (Velloso 1992, interview).

Such emerging relationships between local and foreign capital were made possible largely by the earlier market-reserve policy, which had fostered the development of local firms. Under the reserve, local firms developed experience with technology, production, marketing, and distribution. The government was open to their interests and strategies, and provided resources to encourage their growth. Although state support for local firms was dismantled under the Collor government, local industrialists' knowledge of the market and the industry was a valuable asset as they developed new alliances with foreign firms during the transition period.

According to Velloso, Brazilian companies negotiated from a position of strength with their potential foreign partners. He stated, "Brazilian firms are capable of sitting down at the same table [with foreign firms], and discussing, knowing what they are talking about. They may not have the most advanced level of technology, but they know what it is, and they know how to discuss from a very strong position. And they have a very strong structure already behind them. They have distribution, they have an image, a national brand in Itautec. In Brazil, it's a very well known brand, as are SID and Microtec. These national firms have a strong chance to negotiate with possible partners" (1992 interview).

Brazilian firms' experiences as independent producers thus gave them extensive resources to draw upon as they formulated new relationships with foreign firms. Their network of contacts in Brazil's various regional markets, and their knowledge of customers' particular needs, made them especially valuable to foreign firms attempting to enter the country for the first time. Local producers of well-known Brazilian brands also enjoyed considerable loyalty from customers who decided to stay with less expensive, familiar local brands rather than pay more for a foreign product (Velloso 1992, interview).

The transition to an open market thus involved shifting relationships between local and foreign capital characteristic of current conditions of globalization. New alliances developed based on partnership rather than opposition between local and foreign firms. Velloso described these changes in the following terms: "All the [local] firms that are representing foreign companies, Microtec and Digital, SID and NCR, Elebra and Digital, Edisa and Hewlett-Packard—they have all entered partnerships at one moment or another, and distribution in some cases. These alliances are really changing the scenario. Our philosophy is changing, too, to adjust" (1992 interview).

As firms developed strategies to focus either on distribution or production, they faced problems with economic recession, contraband, and the lack of a clear industrial policy to guide the transition to an open market. They discussed the need for policies to stabilize economic conditions and support their business strategies. The formation of distribution and production strategies thus occurred simultaneously with efforts to develop particular policies for the informatics sector and to negotiate with the government to implement them. Struggles emerged between firms engaged in different strategies or that supported differing policy proposals. The process of constructing an open market continued, as firms negotiated with each other to shape the political and economic conditions of the transition period. Together they developed further ways to pressure the state to create market conditions that would be conducive to their operations.

THE POLITICS OF TRANSITION, 1990–1992: DEBATES OVER A NEW INDUSTRIAL POLICY

Evans (1995) views the new internationalization as a key reason for the shift to a neoliberal regime in Brazilian informatics in the early 1990s. The growing importance of alliances between local and foreign capital meant that local firms relied less on state support and "became potential recruits to the campaign to make the establishment of 'openness' the overriding aim of state involvement" (219). Despite the importance of state action to the ongoing development of the informatics industry, it became politically unfeasible to continue state involvement without the support of local business groups.

Local firms' support for the transition to an open market, however, was more complex and varied than Evans (1995) describes. The nature of their support depended primarily upon the strategies these firms engaged in to construct their relationships with foreign capital and local users. These strategies formed the basis for alliances and conflicts between firms, whether they were local or foreign, in business independently, or forming partnerships with other firms.

Struggles emerged over policies to guide the transition to an open market in informatics. The basic framework for the Collor government's neoliberal informatics strategy was codified into law in October 1991, when the Brazilian Congress passed a new informatics law. The law was firmly entrenched within neoliberal discourse, as it replaced prior goals of fostering local technological capacities with new objectives to stimulate competition between imported and local products. It provided for the complete liberalization of imports after October 1992 and eliminated restrictions on production in informatics. It included measures to stimulate informatics investment after the October expiration of the market reserve, providing "fiscal incentives" to reduce the Impôsto sobre Produtos Industrializados (Tax on Industrialized Products) (IPI), which firms paid on goods produced within Brazil. These incentives reduced the firms' taxes on those goods by up to 15 percent of the cost of the final output. Despite its general neoliberal orientation, the 1991 informatics law included a provision reminiscent of 1984 policy goals to promote the development of local scientific, technical, and productive capacity in informatics. In exchange for offering fiscal incentives, the government required informatics firms to invest at least 5 percent of their gross revenues in research and development activities, 2 percent of which would involve cooperation with universities, research institutes, or programs that the government identified as priorities for informatics development (Ministério da Ciência e Tecnologia 1999). Consistent with its neoliberal policy orientation, the Collor regime also redefined the concept of the national firm that established distinct rules for treatment of Brazilian and foreign companies under the old informatics regime (Nunes 1992; Tigre 1993).

In the spring and summer of 1992, informatics industry representatives and Brazilian government officials negotiated extensively over industrial policy. In interviews during this period, executives from local and foreign firms expressed their eagerness for the government to define a policy for the sector more clearly, or at least to implement existing policies. The prospect of further changes in October, when the market reserve was officially scheduled to expire, created great uncertainty and volatility in the market. Some industrialists questioned the wisdom of opening up the market. They accepted that this would occur, however, and were anxious to clarify the terms for the transition. Local and foreign firms agreed that a new open-market policy should be implemented as soon as possible, rather than waiting until the original October deadline (Moraes 1992, interview; Campos 1992, interview; Gomes 1992, interview; Araujo 1992, interview; Sousa 1992, interview; Velloso 1992, interview; Guaranys 1992, interview; Nunes 1992, interview; Calicchio 1992, interview; Guaranys 1992; Tigre 1992).

General agreement that a policy framework was needed, and acceptance that a neoliberal regime had the broadest political support, did not mean that all local firms supported openness as the overriding objective of state involvement. Indeed, difficult discussions occurred over the specific measures to be included in the new industrial policy for informatics. Struggles emerged between firms adhering to different business strategies, and these developed into conflicts over what kind of state involvement was most appropriate for the sector. The major arguments focused upon the appropriate levels for tariffs on imports.

As discussed above, firms following the "production strategy" sought to maintain production in Brazil and to avoid becoming mere distributors of foreign products. This strategy emerged as local firms sought to build on previous goals of the market reserve, which had encouraged Brazilian firms to become independent producers and to minimize reliance on foreign capital and technology. These computer manufacturers often integrated imported hardware or components to develop systems and solutions. They sought to maintain maximum independence from foreign capital and to focus on meeting the needs of local users through their own productive capacities. Their activities thus depended largely on whether tariffs on components remained low enough to make production operations viable. Many firms recommended a tariff of about 10 percent on components. "Only in this way will it be possible to continue producing locally. With the existing taxes, the only viable place to have an industry is [the free-trade zone in] Manaus," stated one manufacturer (Dantas 1992c).

Firms engaged in a production strategy supported the principle of open markets only to a limited extent. As noted above, they were concerned about losing the national productive capacity that had developed under the market reserve. Artur Pereira Nunes, a representative from ABICOMP, called the transition to an open market "a whole process of deindustrialization" (1992 interview). This characterization is consistent with Sassen's (1999) and McMichael's (2000b) arguments that globalization involves the possibility for denationalization. Despite their own fears about deindustrialization, advocates of the production strategy argued that demand for informatics in the Brazilian market was substantial. This demand meant that some firms would continue producing; unfortunately, from their perspective, foreign firms would be more competitive in this area. Nunes described the situation this way:

> The process of deactivation of multinational factories is not going to be as violent, as rapid as that of national firms . . . Brazil imports close to one billion dollars of informatics goods per year, [even] with the national industry. . . . But the total market is $6 billion. So if you stop producing you are going to have to satisfy a $6 billion market with imports . . . if everyone stops producing. So some will continue producing. (1992 interview)

Supporters of the production strategy generally took a pragmatic approach to the neoliberal policy. They accepted it as the dominant economic discourse at the time and sought to work within it to establish the best possible conditions to pursue their production activities. They tended to take a more optimistic view of how local products would fare in the open market, and defended their strategy by arguing that the Brazilian market was too large to be supplied completely through imports. With Brazil's balance-of-payments problems, only firms that were producing could justify importing parts and components. In policy debates, these firms supported higher tariffs on finished products to give them a better chance of competing with distributors of foreign goods. ABICOMP represented their position in policy debates (Dantas 1992d; Velloso 1992, interview).

By contrast, firms following the distribution strategy focused on distribution of foreign products rather than local production. They supported the neoliberal discourse to varying degrees and for different reasons. The most wholehearted support for the transition to a neoliberal regime came from foreign firms like IBM and Digital, which could import well-known brand equipment and distribute it in the Brazilian market. Many local firms that engaged in a distribution strategy, however, held more qualified support for neoliberalism. They adopted this strategy as a pragmatic reaction to the uncertain political conditions in the market. They viewed distribution of imported products as the best chance to conduct a viable business operation in the current context. Equally important, they were pessimistic about the government's promises to revitalize industrial policy for informatics, which they viewed as indispensable for the industry's continued development. With no repression of contraband products, and with government incentives for imports to the free-trade zone in Manaus, they saw little choice but to forsake production activities and focus on distribution.

Both foreign and local firms that engaged in the distribution strategy tended to support lower tariffs. Low tariffs would allow them to minimize the costs involved with importing foreign products and keep prices on those goods as low as possible. In negotiations over the proposal to be brought to the Brazilian government, a group of these firms proposed that tariffs be reduced to 10 percent on finished products and eliminated completely for components.

Conflicts thus arose between proponents of the production and distribution strategies. ABICOMP and other adherents of the production strategy sought to maintain production activities in Brazil, fearing that an open market would erode these capacities and transform Brazilian high-tech companies into mere distributors and assemblers of foreign products. Critics accused local firms engaged in the distribution strategy of a range of things, from opportunism to fear of competition. Some saw them as choosing the easiest and most profitable option to remain in the Brazilian informatics market (Dantas 1992f; Guaranys 1992, interview; Calicchio 1992, interview; Nunes 1992, interview; Velloso 1992, interview; Henrique 1992, interview).

Such charges were leveled against Edisa, a Brazilian firm that formed a joint venture with Hewlett-Packard in 1990 and publicly supported the total opening of the market to foreign products. The firm also advocated reliance on tariff policy as the sole mechanism of industrial protection. Edisa did not endorse ABICOMP's proposal to maintain the tariff on imports of finished products at 50 percent until 1992. Instead, Edisa proposed an initial tariff of 40 percent for finished products, with a lower levy on imported components, as a way to encourage local industrialization.

Edisa supported a neoliberal approach to industrial policy, one generally viewed as more favorable to firms that were shifting from production into distribution of foreign products. The company could be viewed as one of Evans's (1995) "recruits" to openness, its stance prompted by increasing alliances under the new internationalization. Edisa's president qualified the firm's support for the neoliberal regime, however, by distinguishing Edisa from other firms that had abandoned manufacturing altogether and transformed themselves into distributors of imported products. Some of these firms had supported a stronger neoliberal approach to industrial policy by proposing that tariffs on finished products be lowered to 15 percent. The company president commented, "Edisa is going to work in accordance with the existing economic rules. If we find it impossible to industrialize, Edisa will become a retailer. That is not what we want, but we have a level of protection that makes it possible to maintain our industrial activity. I am going to make a decision to close activity in sector A, B or C to the extent that it is more profitable to import" (Dantas 1992f, 3).

Edisa's adherence to the neoliberal discourse, and its focus on distribution rather than production, thus shifted in response to state policy. The firm calculated which activities were most profitable under a given policy, and also sought to influence the process of policy formation.

COMMON CHALLENGES FOR LOCAL AND FOREIGN CAPITAL

Considerable differences thus existed between firms engaged in production and distribution strategies during the transition to an open market. In many ways, however, the uncertainties of this period created new incentives for foreign and local firms to work together. Firms faced a series of common challenges as they sought to develop strategies to adjust to the changing economic and political environment. These problems plagued efforts to implement *any* business strategy. Uncertainties about market conditions, and about the specific policy framework to address them, made it difficult to develop strategies for either production or distribution. And the prevalence of contraband activity presented a serious obstacle for all informatics firms that sought to engage in legal business activity.

The volatile policy environment after 1990 aggravated existing problems with illegal trade as the market was flooded with contraband. (Under the market reserve, restrictions on imports and high prices for Brazilian computers created incentives to distribute contraband products.) Manufacturers estimated that contraband machines accounted for between 50 and 70 percent of the market, and expected that percentage to grow before the end of the market reserve in October 1992.

The prevalence of contraband equipment created severe problems for both foreign and local informatics firms. It was virtually impossible to compete by operating a legal business when the competition was selling contraband products at markedly lower prices. For example, virtually unknown firms won a series of bidding competitions to sell computer equipment to state companies. The winning informatics firms offered equipment for as little as a quarter of the prices quoted by better-known companies. According to one industry observer, the only way these firms could offer such low prices was to deal in contraband. Some firms took advantage of a loosening of vigilance in the transition period preceding the opening of the market to assemble a "mix" of legal and contraband components, and thus offer equipment at very competitive prices (Dantas 1992b, 1992e; Ferreira 1992; Giurlani 1992).

During discussions over informatics policy, the need to combat contraband helped bridge the conflicts between firms engaged in either production or distribution strategies. All agreed on a fundamental point: it was virtually impossible to compete against contraband, as well as equipment produced in Brazil's free-trade zone in Manaus. These shared concerns created incentives for firms to put their differences aside and forge a unified policy proposal to present to the Brazilian government. Past conflicts eased as firms strove to combat the presence of contraband in the Brazilian market. They pressured the Brazilian government to construct the "open" informatics market in a particular way, by being more effective in restricting contraband activities and by stabilizing general macroeconomic conditions. Sergio Velloso described discussions between the computer industry association, ABICOMP, and government officials over contraband. ABICOMP representatives argued that contraband "should interest the government, because it has millions of dollars of equipment, too. If we have a local sector, and are to compete with imports, [contraband] should have to pay taxes too. They have to play by the same rules, so it is equal for everyone. It is easier to compete that way. You need a tariff structure that goes against products coming in without paying anything. We need to have it be legal, or it is too difficult" (1992 interview).

Apple Computer's representative in the Brazilian market proposed one way to address the contraband problem. He argued that with the current 50 percent tariff on imports, the actual rate was 25 percent since only half of the suppliers paid the tariff; the rest engaged in contraband and paid nothing. If the official tariff were reduced to 30 percent, the effective rate would be 15 percent and contraband would continue to be strong. But if the tariff were lowered to 20 percent, contraband would die out; users would prefer to pay 10 percent more for their computers in order to receive a product with a warranty from a firm in the formal market (Dantas 1992e).

The president of the Brazilian computer firm Medidata made a similar proposal. He estimated that contraband firms composed 70 percent of the market. With a tariff of 20 percent for finished products, 10 percent for subcomponents, 5 percent for components similar to those already manufactured in the country, and no tariffs on components not manufactured in Brazil, firms would be better prepared to compete with both foreign products and contraband (Giurlani 1992).

The transition to a neoliberal policy regime thus created conditions for shifting alliances between foreign and local capital, and between firms pursuing production and distribution strategies. They joined together to pressure the government. Government efforts to minimize the state's regulatory role had the contradictory effect of contributing to political struggles for increased government action. Foreign capital's position changed from broad support for a free-trade regime to pressure on the government to be more active in particular ways, such as in fighting contraband.

Local and foreign firms thus formed political as well as economic alliances. They struggled to adjust to their changing environment during the transition period and pressured the state to construct an open informatics market that would be stabilized by a clearer macroeconomic strategy. Through these pressures, the firms sought to forge an alliance similar to what Evans (1979) called a "triple alliance" among local and foreign capital and the state. Evans describes this as "a complex alliance between elite local capital, international capital, and state capital. . . . The result is not a monolith. Each of the partners comes at industrialization with different strengths, and their interests vary accordingly" (11). Equally important, Evans notes, "the triple alliance must be a political alliance as well as an economic one" (272). In the transition to an open market in Brazilian informatics, local and foreign firms pursuing production and distribution strategies found common ground and forged an alliance to pressure the state. This "double alliance" between firms with divergent interests then sought to create a political alliance with the state over the content of industrial policy. While the triple alliance these firms attempted to develop did not involve a partnership with state capital of the kind Evans describes, it did involve a complex political alliance over the direction of economic development.

The most striking example of this new double alliance occurred when foreign firms were allowed to join ABICOMP, the major informatics-industry association that had traditionally been open only to Brazilian-owned companies. ABICOMP was a key organization involved in the development and passage of the market reserve in 1984, as well as in the defense of the reserve as it came under increasing attack during the late 1980s. Its commitment to the values of national sovereignty and technological autonomy led it to a conflictual stance toward foreign capital. It viewed foreign firms as the beneficiaries of Brazil's dependence on imports and foreign productive capacities (Calicchio 1990, interview).

With the transition to an open market, ABICOMP adjusted its strategy to fit the new political and economic environment. Its goals shifted from defending technological autonomy to preserving informatics production capacity within Brazil by whatever firms would engage in it. José Guaranys explained why the association, and the government, changed the focus on technological autonomy:

The technological question in a country like Brazil depends on heavy investments, and on a stable regulatory environment that clearly pursues that objective. These rules existed under the previous policy. The objective of this new policy is different, it is price and quality. To have products that are competitive in the sense that they are modern technologically, and with prices lower each time. Many times when you want to develop technologically, you will have a product that is not the latest, but you learned while you were doing the project. So our new phase of the policy has a new objective. The government made the necessary alliances to establish this modernity, because not just the government but the society had started to demand price and quality, prices and the latest products. (1992 interview)

ABICOMP took a pragmatic stance toward the dismantling of the informatics policy. Since the 1984 informatics law included provisions for the policy to end in 1992, the end of the market reserve was anticipated even before the rise of Collor's neoliberal regime. ABICOMP adapted its strategy to promote informatics development as strongly as possible, in the context of the Collor government's rapid actions to dismantle the market reserve before the October 1992 deadline. This change transformed ABICOMP's conflictual stance toward foreign firms and made alliance building a top priority. Guaranys described this shift in objectives and its ramifications for relationships between local and foreign informatics firms:

The technological question was . . . abandoned, at least temporarily. And at the time that the objective became national production, it interested us that the objectives between the firms with national and foreign capital [changed so that] the conflicts ceased to exist. Because producing in the country interested foreign firms as well. . . . For this reason, ABICOMP . . . opened its membership to incorporate the Brazilian firms with foreign capital. (1992 interview)

Again, the ABICOMP negotiator's words echo Evans's (1979, 11–12) description of the triple alliance: "As in any economy, there are differences among sectors of industry. In addition, goals vary among the branches of the state apparatus. Over and above the differences, however, is the consensus that all members of the alliance will benefit from the accumulation of industrial capital within Brazil." The alliance that emerged in Brazilian informatics is more aptly characterized as a double alliance between firms pursuing production and distribution strategies. This double alliance was based on the same goal, however, as Evans's triple alliance: uniting firms with divergent interests to promote national production. These double and triple alliances differed with respect to the actors involved while sharing common goals and the complex task of unifying divergent interests.

With the development of this double alliance in 1991 and 1992, a sea change thus occurred in the relationship between foreign and local capital in the informatics sector. This transformation led to the entrance of IBM, Digital, Unisys, NCR, and Xerox into ABICOMP during this period. These emerging political ties became increasingly attractive as firms formed joint ventures and engaged in other kinds of economic cooperation. Velloso described it as a process whereby firms that once perceived each other as adversaries became increasingly linked to one another and needed to develop an understanding. He explained, "Firms proceeded to create ties that brought them to a cooperative action, and gave them more patience to reach a consensus . . . all this flexibility in the formation of partnerships and alliances facilitated the development of a consensus. . . . So things changed. Now it is impossible to remain in the market in an isolated way" (1992 interview). The formation of economic alliances supported the development of common positions on political questions to be taken to the government, and firms developed more harmonious relationships.

These emerging economic and political alliances between local and foreign capital raise interesting questions about the meaning of "denationalization" in the context of globalization. Sassen (1999) and McMichael (2000b) suggest that this denationalization process emerges as global capital expands into local markets, and as national governance systems become oriented toward the interests of global capital. This process challenges the ability of states to define and implement national development goals that contradict neoliberal pressures favoring global capital. Denationalization thus involves a growing orientation of national economic and political activity toward global economic interests and toward neoliberal efforts to break down national regulations of trade and development.

The Collor government's neoliberal economic strategy was based on such an orientation toward the interests of global capital, and it emphasized creating economic conditions of denationalization during the transition to an open market. At the same time, however, firms and industry associations such as ABICOMP with a history of defending national production redefined the meaning of that production in the context of globalization. They viewed any firm that sought to produce within Brazil as contributing to hard-won gains in informatics development and as counteracting what they saw as a tendency to deindustrialize under Collor's neoliberal regime. In their struggle to defend informatics production, these firms and industry associations constructed a new definition of national production that was not based upon the location of a firm's corporate headquarters. Instead this definition was rooted in the nature of a firm's strategy for operating in the Brazilian market. Brazilian-based firms such as Edisa, which devised a distribution rather than a production strategy, were viewed as contributing to the process of denationalization.

In the Brazilian informatics case, denationalization thus had a complex meaning. On the macro level, it was similar to Sassen's (1999) and McMichael's (2000b) conception of a growing orientation of national economic and political conditions toward the interests of global capital. On the micro level, however, the meaning of denationalization was constructed by local firms and industry associations as they struggled to forge a political strategy to navigate the uncertainties of the transition period. Like the partners in Evans's (1979) triple alliance, they found common ground in their interests in preserving national productive capacities. In a context where macro-level denationalization involved shifting economic and political conditions toward the interests of global capital, this double alliance redefined the meaning of denationalization at the micro level.

The Brazilian case suggests that denationalization can best be understood within its particular national context as a socially constructed process that occurs at both the macro and micro levels. Globalization is not a predetermined unfolding of objective economic laws that sets into motion universal consequences such as denationalization. As Sassen (1999) and McMichael (2000b) argue, there is a tendency or movement in the direction of denationalization. This tendency is shaped, however, by local economic and political struggles. It is contingent and flexible, changing in response to local conditions. Some of the most important of these conditions involve the emerging relationships among local and foreign capital and the state.

PRESSURING THE STATE

Contemporary conditions of globalization in Brazilian informatics thus fostered new political alliances between local and foreign capital, in addition to developing new kinds of economic ties. As we have seen, major divisions emerged between firms with different strategies to construct the relationships among local firms, multinational firms, and local users. These divisions supplanted earlier tensions between local and foreign firms, divisions that were eventually bridged through a process of extensive negotiation, as firms with divergent strategies developed ways to address their common concerns.

After months of intensive debate, informatics firms following both production and distribution strategies reached consensus on a tariff policy proposal. Velloso described the negotiations leading up to this agreement: "It was much discussed, not just between foreign and local, but within local firms themselves, because each one changed position. Not all local firms are producers. Some are distributors, and they do not want to produce. This was complicated, but what was interesting was that the position that was taken was a consensus of the whole industry" (1992 interview).

In April 1992 representatives from ABICOMP presented the tariff policy proposal to the government. They recommended that tariffs for components be fixed at 20 percent, while those for finished products would be 50 percent in 1992 and 1993, and 40 percent in 1994. This policy was designed to encourage local production by setting lower tariff levels for components and higher levels for finished products. If firms wanted to import informatics products and distribute them, they would pay higher taxes than firms that were importing components to use in manufacturing operations. The firms asked the government to reduce taxes on the industry and institute a crackdown on contraband (Guaranys 1992, interview).

The tariff policy proposal represented an industry-wide agreement about what the government should do to promote the development of the informatics industry during the transition to an open market. Firms pursuing very different strategies, emphasizing either production or distribution, wrestled with the question of how to establish the minimum tariff protection the industry needed to remain competitive. They sought to contribute to the development of an industrial policy that protected the industrial base in informatics from premature exposure to the international market. Velloso described the significance and intent of the proposal: "This was a very difficult discussion, [for example] between a local firm and a firm like Digital, which could just distribute, so why should it defend a higher tax? But in the end, all the positions were discussed and agreed upon by all these firms. . . . Even a year ago, you would not have imagined all these firms sitting down together at the same table, talking about an industrial policy" (1992 interview).

Government officials eventually responded to ABICOMP's proposals by pushing for a more drastic reduction in tariffs in a shorter period of time. This change was designed to anticipate the end of the market reserve in July instead of October. In exchange, the government offered to take stronger action to deal with contraband. The firms in ABICOMP accepted these proposals.

By early May 1992, government and industry representatives reached an accord to end the market reserve. The agreement included provisions to define a tariff policy for the informatics sector within sixty days, reduce taxes on the industry, and combat contraband. The import-tariffs reduction program was developed as a major part of the government's effort to liberalize the informatics sector. It was designed to reduce tariffs on imports in the period between July 1992 and December 1994. As Table 5.1 shows, tariffs on imports of finished goods, assembled and disassembled printed-circuit boards, modules, and semiconductors were scheduled to be reduced by up to 50 percent during that period. The tariff-reduction program differed from ABICOMP's proposal in two main respects. First, ABICOMP had proposed that tariffs on finished goods remain at 50 percent during 1992 and 1993, and drop to 40 percent in 1994. The government's tariff-reduction program lowered the tariff on finished goods to 40 percent at an earlier date, in October 1992, and it further reduced that tariff to 35 percent in July 1993. Second, ABICOMP had proposed that tariffs on components be fixed at 20 percent. In the tariff-reduction program adopted by the government, tariffs on "critical inputs" that were not manufactured in Brazil were scheduled to be eliminated entirely by October 1992. Critical components were defined as those having significant effects upon production costs, such as microprocessors (Nunes 1992; Tigre 1993).

The tariff-reduction program thus lowered tariffs on both final products and components more drastically and more quickly than ABICOMP had proposed. Many firms were relieved, however, that an accord with the

TABLE 5.1 Import-Tariffs Reduction Program Adopted by the Brazilian Government, 1992

Class of Imports	Import Tariffs (%)		
	Before 7/92	10/92–7/93	7/93–12/94
Final goods	50	40	35
Printed-circuit boards (assembled)	50	35	30
Modules, subassemblies	35–50	25–30	20–30
Semiconductors	40	20	15
Boards (disassembled)	30	20	15
Critical inputs (not manufactured in Brazil)	30–50	0	0

SOURCE: Paulo Bastos Tigre, "Brazil's IT Sector—The Profile in 1992" (paper presented at "The Future of Information Technology in Brazil" conference, University of California, Berkeley, January 1993).

government had been achieved. The uncertainty of the transition period made it difficult for them to gauge market conditions or maintain their business activities. Having a policy in place, even one with which firms might disagree, was viewed as vital to restore some stability to the market and allow firms to develop business strategies. These firms did not want to wait until the original October deadline to end the market reserve and clarify the new policies to guide the transition to an open market (Dantas 1992g, 1992h, 1992i; Velloso 1992, interview).

The new provisions did not, however, take effect as scheduled. As Jessop (1990a) argues, the state does not always act as a unified political force. In this period of the development of Brazilian informatics, the state did not implement *any* policy consistently. Evans (1995) argues persuasively that the Brazilian state should have promoted the continued development of informatics through what he calls "high-tech husbandry"; however, the state had no commitment to such a course of action. And although government officials publicly discussed their commitment to establishing a neoliberal policy regime, they failed to implement the agreements they negotiated to ease the transition to such a regime in the informatics sector.

By the end of June 1992, industry and government representatives were at an impasse. After accepting the tariff reductions and revised timetable for their implementation, firms were anxious because these policies had yet to be implemented. Guaranys described his concerns over whether the agreement with the government would ever be put into practice:

> During the negotiations ... what we were able to achieve was, in reality, a group of mechanisms that still indicate that it is worth producing in the country. But it could be that over a longer period of time, like a few years, these instruments would not be implemented, or would be in a phase of implementation. Now it is June, there are only three months left, and we have not managed yet. First you need the law, then you need to implement it with the [government]. We still have not been able to implement the fiscal incentives planned in the law. It is a great concern of ours. (1992 interview)

Informatics firms also criticized the Collor government for failing to establish macroeconomic stability as a precondition for its program of trade liberalization. The lack of coordination of general economic health and more specific plans for trade liberalization left industrialists wary and uncertain about whether they could engage in investment or become competitive in the international market.

In an effort to smooth relations with the business community, the government established a series of councils to meet and negotiate with industrialists from specific sectors about their policy concerns. The government subsequently canceled these meetings, however, claiming to have lost confidence in industrialists when they raised prices during the Eco92 environmental conference in Rio. Velloso described the tenuous nature of negotiations with the government: "So we are at an impasse, waiting to see if we can meet [with the government]. If we do not, it will be a shock to the business sector because we have accepted these tariffs, and they are supposed to be put in place. But on the other hand, economic stability was lacking. Inflation was high, interest rates were high, the economic and fiscal reforms that were so necessary did not occur, and it does not look like they will" (1992 interview).

Firms continued to struggle with uncertainty about which measures would guide the transition to an open market and when they would take effect. The process of constructing an open market continued, characterized by a complex interplay of struggles between the state and capital. Although the state initiated a shift in the principles underlying the informatics policy, it failed to devise a unified way to put those principles into practice. Local and foreign firms, by contrast, developed a unique and effective double alliance to defend their newfound common interest in retaining a Brazilian informatics industry.

CONCLUSION: DISCOVERING THE EGGS OF THE SERPENT

The transition to an open market in Brazilian informatics echoes earlier lessons about the importance of a tenacious but flexible political response to the power of structural constraints. In the aftermath of the high-tech trade war with the U.S. government, geopolitical pressures eased and domestic problems took center stage. Export dependency continued to create general problems of recession and economic instability. The terrain of struggle shifted from mediating the trade dispute to implementing the transition to an open market.

This transition was fraught with conflicts and surprises. Virtually everyone expected the local industry to be dismantled along with the policy that had protected it. The industry that remained, however, became the focus for political struggle by local and foreign firms alike. They developed ingenious, unanticipated forms of political action in the wake of trade conflict and the rise of Collor's neoliberal regime.

During the transition period, the structure of the international market continued to pose constraints and opportunities for informatics development. As Sassen (1999, 159) argues, "global processes materialize in national territories," fostering alliances between foreign and local capital as local firms play a growing role in linking multinational firms with local users. Firms viewed these alliances as the key to their competitive ability in the changing economic and political environment. In the wake of the trade war with the United States and the rapid dismantling of the market reserve, local firms feared that they would completely lose their market position. They responded by seeking out new alliances with foreign companies. For their part, foreign firms discovered that they needed local firms more than they had anticipated, as a way to make connections to Brazilian users.

The ability of local firms to enter strong partnerships with foreign ones was a valuable legacy of the informatics policy. The policy's support for local informatics development laid a foundation for new forms of collaboration with foreign firms once it had been defeated. Novel forms of economic alliances arose during the turbulent transition to a neoliberal economic regime. These alliances thus emerged within and were shaped by the historical context of the informatics development strategy.

With the growth of these new economic partnerships, the basis for conflict between firms in the informatics industry shifted. Whereas tensions had previously arisen between foreign and local firms, current conflicts involved firms engaged in different economic strategies. This change was also rooted in the new political conditions for informatics development, where the Collor government dismantled protections for local firms and opened the market to foreign competition. Foreign and local firms developed "production" and "distribution" strategies to build upon their strengths and confront the uncertainties of the transition period. Conflicts arose between firms engaged in these divergent strategies. The divisions between foreign and local firms continued to blur, as they joined together to advocate informatics policy proposals to benefit their chosen economic strategies.

By transforming the informatics policy regime, the transition to an open market created the conditions for unprecedented political alliances between local and foreign firms in the industry. Although some local and foreign firms developed economic partnerships even under the old informatics policy, the volatility of the transition period prompted them to forge new political alliances. Finding common ground in their desire to maintain a competitive industry and their vulnerability to the uncertainties of the transition process, they engaged in intensive negotiations. Through a long and difficult process, these firms finally overcame their differences and forged a double alliance, presenting a unified proposal to the Brazilian government.

The government's inability to implement the accords it negotiated with industry representatives sheds some light on the dilemmas of the neoliberal state in the context of globalization. For the Brazilian state, the transition from a protected to an open market posed a quandary with respect to its role in economic policy. The underlying values of the neoliberal regime provided broad guidelines for state action. They dictated that the state should disengage from its extensive involvement in informatics policy so that market forces could operate smoothly. It became difficult to implement this new regime, however, because of the political aspects of constructing an open market and the particular problems associated with economic development in the former Third World. Making the transition from a protected to an open market required state action to dismantle existing policies and formulate new ones, and to establish the terms for new forms of foreign investment, joint ventures, technology transfers, and imports. Conditions of dependency on foreign trade, investment, and debt financing meant that the economy was wracked by recession and instability that complicated any form of state action.

The Brazilian state faced what Kahler (1990, 55) argues is a fundamental challenge for states that seek to implement "orthodox" (neoliberal) economic policies. He notes, "Orthodoxy has not dealt successfully with the paradox of using the state—its only instrument—to change policy in a less statist direction." What Kahler calls the "orthodox paradox" aptly describes the Collor regime's relationship to the informatics industry. Its neoliberal economic strategy called for it to disengage from its earlier involvement in the informatics sector by dismantling the market reserve. In principle, the state's role was to allow the invisible hand of the market to take over. However, implementing the shift to a neoliberal regime required state action to create the economic and political conditions for an "open" market. The state was caught in Kahler's orthodox paradox, experiencing increasing pressures from local and foreign capital to act even though its overall goal was to reduce its role in economic policy making.

These struggles over policies to guide the transition period reveal the political nature of markets, even those that profess to be open. In the Brazilian informatics case, "openness" was constructed through political struggle and debate, and it was regulated through policies that established the conditions for trade, investment, and other economic activities to occur. The transition to a neoliberal policy regime involved grappling with volatile economic conditions and engaging in struggles to develop a new policy framework. The Brazilian state, however, failed to put the agreements it negotiated into practice.

Despite the vacillation of the state and the decline in the informatics sector, possibilities remained for Brazilian informatics development. Guaranys described the difficulties of making a transition to an open market, as well as his optimism for the future:

> The transition from the old policy to the new was very turbulent. The new economic team was very young and inexperienced, the country was in recession, the businessmen did not know exactly what was happening. This transition from 1990 to 1992 is now reaching an end. If it works, certainly our industry will not be as nationalized as it was in the past. There will be less participation, but it will not be a totally denationalized industry. . . . if we are able to implement what is still missing in terms of regulation, we will have a Brazilian informatics industry. (1992 interview)

The optimism expressed by this skillful Brazilian negotiator resonates with questions about the nature of "denationalization" in the context of globalization. In Sassen's (1999) terms, how are global processes "embedded" or "materialized" in local conditions? This study suggests that the answer to this question lies with local struggles and contingencies as they encounter international structural constraints. For those who fought for decades to develop a Brazilian informatics industry, and who viewed that industry as central for Brazil's position in a globalizing economy, the possibility of having a national industry hinged on national production. These longtime advocates of Brazilian informatics development reshaped their definition of nationality to include any firm that produced within Brazil. Indeed, the process of redefining what it meant to have a national industry played a vital role in the broader struggle to forge economic and political alliances to fight for such an industry. Discursive strategies were inextricably linked to economic and political ones, as the definition of the issues at stake helped create conditions for firms to shift their perceptions of their economic interests, and to develop economic and political alliances to support those interests.

The political commitment and skill of industry representatives were powerful resources in the struggle to retain a national industry. In addition to forming new kinds of economic and political alliances, foreign and local firms wrestled with tough policy questions and finally overcame their disparate interests to forge an industry-wide agreement. These political skills, and the political will to press the government to implement the hard-won accords, made the double alliance of local and foreign capital a potent political force. The ability to overcome differences and fight for a common position was an invaluable asset with which to confront the vicissitudes of the transition period.

In many ways, the transition to an open market marked the end of the Brazilian informatics strategy and the ascendancy of a neoliberal regime. This transition, however, occurred within a historical context where that strategy had promoted Brazilian informatics development. As Edson Fregni, the former president of Scopus, wisely noted, the market reserve was like a serpent that left many "eggs" behind, and these continued to influence the development of the industry in subtle and complex ways (1990 interview). The economic, political, and technological knowledge developed by local firms under the market reserve prepared them to forge economic and political alliances with foreign firms, and to struggle to preserve Brazil's productive capacity in the "master industry of late-twentieth-century development" (Evans 1995, 95). Foreign multinationals and the U.S. government consistently criticized the Brazilian informatics strategy for unfairly restricting the activities of foreign firms. In the early 1990s, however, foreign firms pursued alliances with Brazilian companies to help them face the challenging task of constructing an open market. Those partnerships represented another substantial and, for some, unexpected legacy of the Brazilian informatics strategy.

6 Incipient Denationalization
Brazilian Informatics in 2001

ON 11 JANUARY 2001, Brazilian President Fernando Henrique Cardoso signed a new Brazilian informatics law. At a signing ceremony that received much attention in the Brazilian business press, he made a speech that revealed some of the legacies of the Brazilian informatics strategy. He began by warning that he was going to speak about something that "some almost consider heresy." Some of his remarks resonated with the nationalist discourse of the 1984 informatics policy, with its cultural values of developing national scientific and productive capacities to promote national sovereignty. For example, President Cardoso noted that the future of any nation will be based upon its capacity to define conditions for the creation and development of new technologies, particularly in the area of informatics and telecommunications. He remarked, "If we do not become capable of creating conditions for production of electrical and electronic components, we will create a serious problem for our future" (*Valor* 2001b). President Cardoso called for Brazil to develop an industrial policy "that is not, pure and simple, what we did in the past, because now, conditions are different.... We need to define it in a way that is more adequate to the times of today" (quoted in *Gazeta Mercantil* 2001). He announced that he would launch an "ambitious program" for the country to advance in the areas of informatics and automation. Citing the example of India, whose annual software exports are valued at $6 billion, Cardoso remarked, "India is poor, after all, with an immense population, larger than our own, it has difficulties equal to ours, but it is exporting software.... Why don't we do the same thing?" The

President then answered his own question, vowing, "We are going to do this" (*Valor* 2001b).

President Cardoso's remarks at the signing of the 2001 informatics law hinted at continuing tensions over Brazilian informatics development. President Cardoso was serving a second term in office, following President Collor's impeachment for corruption in 1992. This speech was the first time, however, that he had emphasized the idea of developing an industrial policy. He suggested that members of his own administration would consider such a position "heresy"; Finance Minister Pedro Malan and his economic team, for example, had consistently opposed the idea. By contrast, Minister of Health José Serra and Minister of Development Alcides Tápias were more supportive. President Cardoso clearly indicated his desire for a more active governmental role in informatics development. He did so in a defensive way, however, carefully distancing himself from the 1984 informatics law (*Valor* 2001b). This cautious articulation of support for industrial policy reflected the tensions involved with such a position in a climate of neoliberal globalization.

Indeed, the 2001 informatics law was decidedly neoliberal, containing incentives for global capital to enter the Brazilian market. A slightly modified version of the 1991 informatics law, the new statute was designed to remain in effect for eight years. It provided fiscal incentives for firms to invest in informatics by reducing the Tax on Industrialized Products (IPI) in decreasing amounts until 2009, when the law would expire. In return for these tax breaks, firms were required to invest in research and development, again in decreasing amounts, until 2009. The specific provisions for tax breaks and corresponding corporate investments varied according to the region of Brazil in which informatics investments were made (see Tables 6.1 and 6.2) (Presidencia da República 2001).

These provisions in the informatics law were shaped by regional tensions over Brazilian informatics development. The 2001 informatics legislation was embroiled in fifteen months of congressional negotiation, much of it fraught with regional conflict. Beginning when the 1991 informatics law was scheduled to expire in October 1999, the Brazilian Congress kept that law in force as it discussed provisions for a new informatics law. Each month Congress enacted provisional measures to renew the system of tax

TABLE 6.1 Schedule of Reductions in the Impôsto sobre Produtos Industrializados (Tax on Industrialized Products) for Corporate Investors, by Region, 2001–2009 (%)

Year	2001	2002	2003	2004	2005	2006	2007	2008	2009
North	100	100	100	95	90	85	85	85	85
Northeast	100	100	100	95	90	85	85	85	85
Central West	100	100	100	95	90	85	85	85	85
South	95	90	85	80	75	70	70	70	70
Southeast	95	90	85	80	75	70	70	70	70

SOURCE: Presidência da República, "Sancionada Lei de Informática—11.01.01" (Brasília: Presidência da República, 2001).

TABLE 6.2 Corporate Investments in Research and Development Required for Reduction in the Impôsto sobre Produtos Industrializados (Tax on Industrialized Products) for Corporate Investors, by Region, 2001–2009 (% of Gross Revenues)

Year	2001	2002	2003	2004	2005	2006	2007	2008	2009
North	5	4.85	4.6	4.35	4.1	3.85	3.85	3.85	3.85
Northeast	5	4.85	4.6	4.35	4.1	3.85	3.85	3.85	3.85
Central West	5	4.85	4.6	4.35	4.1	3.85	3.85	3.85	3.85
South	4.75	4.5	4.25	4	3.75	3.5	3.5	3.5	3.5
Southeast	4.75	4.5	4.25	4	3.75	3.5	3.5	3.5	3.5

SOURCE: Presidência da República, "Sancionada Lei de Informática—11.01.01" (Brasília: Presidência da República, 2001).

breaks for informatics investment provided by the 1991 law (Manzoni 2000; Queiroz 2000b). During these congressional negotiations, struggles arose involving representatives from the Amazon region, the southeastern state of São Paulo, and the federal government.

The Amazonian representatives supported neoliberal incentives designed to reduce what firms considered "barriers" to investment. They sought to attract those firms to the free-trade zone in Manaus, in the northern state of Amazonas. In early 1999, the Superintendência da Zona

Franca de Manaus (Superintendency of the Free-Trade Zone of Manaus) (SUFRAMA) gave firms importing components for cell phones and computer monitors an 88 percent reduction in the import tax (*Valor* 2001a). For example, Philips received approval for a project to manufacture digital cellular phones with an 88 percent reduction in the import tax; so did NG Industrial, a joint venture between Nokia and the Brazilian firm Gradiente (Manzoni 2000).

In the Amazon region, there was general political disapproval of any restrictions on corporate activities, such as those included in the 1991 informatics law and preserved in the new informatics legislation under consideration in Congress. Virtually the only restrictions in these laws was the requirement discussed above, for informatics firms to invest a certain percentage of their gross revenues in research and development in return for reductions in the IPI. Opposition to this requirement arose in early 2000, when Samsung challenged it in a regional court in Manaus. Samsung's lawyers argued that the requirement violated the principle of equality before the law since it applied only to firms producing informatics goods. The court accepted this argument, and Samsung won the case. The court then waived the requirement for Samsung to invest 5 percent of its gross revenues in research and development in order to receive an exemption from the IPI (Farias 2000).

The Samsung case supported the efforts of congressional representatives from Manaus to preserve incentives for corporate investment in the region. These representatives supported a development strategy that granted firms free rein, with virtually no expectation of corporate contribution to the local economy aside from their investment. Indeed, this was more of an "antistrategy" since it sought to attract the maximum corporate investment by removing all policy requirements. For this reason I characterize this strategy as "radical neoliberalism." This strategy created conditions for dramatic increases in cell phone and video monitor production in the free-trade zone of Manaus. For example, as Table 6.3 shows, production of cell phones in Manaus rose 205 percent between January 1999 and May 2000 (Manzoni 2000; Queiroz 2000d).

Radical neoliberal incentives for corporate investment thus contributed to large increases in the production of cell phones and computer monitors

TABLE 6.3 Manufacture of Cell Phones, Computer Monitors, and PCs in Manaus (units)

Product	1999	January–May 2000	Change (%)
Cell phones	806,000	2.4 billion	205
Monitors	85,000	803,000	844
PCs	36,000	25,000	−30.56

SOURCE: Ralphe Manzoni, "Disputas regionais emperram lei de TI," *Computerworld*, 27 July 2000.

in the free-trade zone of Manaus. Equally important, however, they also fostered a heavy reliance on imported components. As is discussed below, components imports had become the major contributor to a large trade deficit in the informatics sector by the late 1990s. As discussions over the proposed new law continued in the Brazilian Congress, manufacturers of cell phones and computer monitors in Manaus took advantage of the opportunity to pay lower taxes (Manzoni 2000; Queiroz 2000b, 2000d). Secretary of Informatics and Automation Policy Vanda Scartezini warned that these corporate activities undermined the prospects for informatics development. He expressed concern about the delay in passing the law "because the major interests injured by this delay are the states of the North, Northeast and Central West. This is because the firms, while this new law is not voted upon, do not comply with the requirement to invest in research and development in these regions. That which could be an important infusion of resources in the sector . . . is not occurring" (Queiroz 2000e).

Conflicts over the strategies to promote informatics development came to a head during negotiations over the new informatics law. On one side, representatives from the North, Northeast, and Central Western states supported the radical neoliberal strategy to attract foreign investment by dramatically cutting the import tax and exempting firms from the informatics policy's requirement to invest in research and development. They viewed this strategy as vital for development in their region, providing extra incentives for firms to invest in an area that lacked São Paulo's scientific and industrial infrastructure. They did not share Secretary Scartezini's concern that they were undermining investment in research and development. On the other side were the powerful industrialists and politicians from São Paulo state, the most highly industrialized region of Brazil. Indeed, some informatics industry experts view São Paulo state, with its urban industrial powerhouses of São Paulo and Campinas, as the only region in South America with an adequate infrastructure for investments in high-technology sectors such as informatics. They rank São Paulo state as one of only eleven such regions in the world, four of which are in the United States (Jimenez 2001; *Panorama Brasil* 2001). Representatives from all parts of Brazil knew that if policy conditions were equal throughout the country, most informatics firms would choose to locate near the networks of services and marketing connections provided in São Paulo's cosmopolitan urban economy.

In an effort to counteract the radical neoliberal strategy, representatives from São Paulo state and the federal government proposed to include cell phones and computer monitors in the definition of informatics goods. Such a definition would make these products subject to the system of tax breaks and corresponding requirements for research and development investment defined by the 1991 informatics law. It would undermine the radical neoliberal strategy embraced by SUFRAMA. Representatives from Amazonia thus opposed the proposal to define cell phones and computer monitors as informatics goods. They argued that it could mean the end of the free-trade zone of Manaus (Manzoni 2000; Queiroz 2000b, 2000d).

After a series of negotiations, however, the Amazonian representatives eventually agreed to define cellular phones and computer monitors as informatics goods. The federal government prevailed, arguing that equality before the law was a key principle for the new informatics policy. From the Cardoso regime's view, basing the law upon this principle would help to establish a needed equilibrium among all regions of the country. As discussions over the new law continued, federal government representatives insisted that participants respect the accord over the definition of informatics goods to avoid regional instability (Queiroz 2000c). They also supported a neoliberal strategy geared toward attracting foreign investment to Brazil. Their strategy was based on the knowledge that most firms would prefer to locate in highly industrialized São Paulo. Corporate and political representatives from São Paulo state weighed in heavily to support this more moderate neoliberal approach. Secretary Scartezini summed up the federal government's position, articulating its goal of attracting foreign investment and acknowledging São Paulo's attractiveness for such investment: "Investors need to have equally balanced options and, obviously, the balance occurs as a function of some comparative advantages in relation to each region, because a region with few resources, like the Northeast, certainly has comparative disadvantages in relation to the South, which is more developed" (Queiroz 2000e, 1–2).

By promoting what it called "balance" and "regional stability," as well as the principle of "equality before the law," the Cardoso government established political and discursive conditions to further the globalization process. The President, and key government officials such as Secretary Scartezini, advocated a neoliberal strategy of allowing foreign investors free choice in their decisions about where to invest in the Brazilian market. They described this strategy as contributing to the national interest by promoting the values of stability and equilibrium. They thus articulated a policy discourse that defined the national interest as consistent with the interests of global capital. After a series of negotiations, they eventually agreed upon a definition of informatics goods that favored the interests of global capital, as well as Brazilian firms located in the most industrialized region of the country. The Brazilian government thus contributed to conditions of incipient denationalization (Sassen 1999), in which the state uses industrial policy to create political conditions conducive to investment by global capital.

Indeed, attracting foreign investment to Brazil was the overarching theme in discussions of the 2001 informatics law. As negotiations over the new law continued, Brazilian informatics industry analysts and executives, as well as members of the Cardoso government, were concerned that the delay was creating uncertainty for investors (Queiroz 2000e). They believed that the government needed to clarify the policy environment. For example, the director of Dell, Fernando Loureiro, stated, "The government must signal that the incentives will not end and that it plans to revise the provisional measures until the approval of the new legislation" (Manzoni 2000, 2). As occurred in 1992 when the Collor government dismantled the informatics policy and began constructing an open market, the lack of a clear policy made it difficult for firms to formulate their business strategies.

The protracted negotiations over the new informatics law finally came to an end in December 2000, with its approval by the Brazilian Congress (*Valor* 2001b). In furthering the conditions of incipient denationalization (Sassen 1999), the new law represented another policy defeat for the Amazon region. Before he signed it, President Cardoso vetoed article 10 of the proposed law. Written by Senator Paulo Souto from the northeastern state of Bahia, this article would have restricted new investments in states that had received 50 percent of the informatics sector's investments during the preceding two years. The only state that fit this criterion was São Paulo. Senator Souto argued that article 10 would promote the spread of industry throughout Brazil, rather than continuing to concentrate it in São Paulo (*Valor* 2001a; *Panorama Brasil* 2001). The governor of Amazonas criticized the President's veto as serving to undermine the comparative advantage of the free-trade zone of Manaus, and threatened to challenge the informatics law in the courts (*Gazeta Mercantil* 2001). In response, President Cardoso denied that his veto was an act against the free-trade zone of Manaus. Rather, he argued that production in the free-trade zone needed to be done "within the national context" (*Valor* 2001a).

Here President Cardoso used the term "national context" to define the national interest in terms of the interests of global capital. His plan was for Brazil's industrial policy to facilitate foreign investment. Indeed, multinational corporations and national informatics firms overwhelmingly supported the veto of article 10 as opening the door for informatics investments in Brazil as a whole, and particularly in São Paulo. The vice-president of the Associação Brasileira da Indústria Elétrica e Eletrônica (Brazilian Association of Electrical and Electronics Industries) (ABINEE), Brazil's major industry association in informatics, stated, "The veto of article 10 will be important for all of Brazil. The new firms that will install plants in the country will have the freedom to choose in which region to build their factories" (*Panorama Brasil* 2001). He argued that Brazil could not afford to lose potential foreign investments. In his view, the new law provided needed political stability for the informatics sector and allowed foreign firms to pursue their interests in the Brazilian market. These firms had been wary of investing while the law was under discussion due to the uncertain policy environment. ABINEE's vice-president explained, "The lack of definition of how the local market functions confused so many new firms that studied how to enter the country" (*IT Web* 2001). With the signing of the 2001 informatics law, informatics industry executives and government officials predicted between $320 and $400 million in new investments in components, cellular phones, and other areas. José Anibal, the Secretary of Science and Technology for São Paulo state, expected $200 million of those investments to go to his state alone. As one of the major proponents of the new informatics law, Anibal expected at least five big informatics producers to proceed immediately with investment plans. For example, soon after the signing of the new informatics law, Hewlett-Packard announced its decision to pursue new production projects worth $40 million, including a server manufacturing plant in the Barueri region of São Paulo state, where the company already had a plant. Hewlett-Packard representatives also disclosed that they were considering installing a plant to produce personal computers for corporate use. Gilberto Galan, director of corporate affairs for Hewlett-Packard's Brazilian subsidiary, stated, "Certainly new projects, that were on the back burner for many firms, will now be moved to the front" (*Gazeta Mercantil* 2001). He added, "Now we can signal stability in the future scenario for our headquarters" (Jimenez and Akikusa 2001).

The signing of the new informatics law was thus a signal for some firms to begin to reveal their investment plans, and for others to hint at possible future decisions. The regional manager of 3Com do Brasil said that the incentives in the new law would make it possible for the firm to invest at least $100 million to install a plant in Brazil, one to produce high-speed Internet equipment targeted to the Brazilian market as well as to the regional South American trading bloc of Mercosul (Jimenez and Akikusa 2001). Luis Cornetta, the director of corporate affairs for Motorola's Brazilian subsidiary, remarked that the new informatics law signaled the redefinition of the Brazilian industrial model. Intel and three unnamed competitors were also rumored to be considering opening plants in Brazil to serve the Latin American market (*Panorama Brasil* 2001; *Canal Web* 2001a; *Jornal de Comércio* 2001b; *Gazeta Mercantil* 2001).

Brazilian government officials viewed foreign investment as the key to the informatics sector's future development. They considered this investment vital to boost local production and decrease Brazil's trade deficit, particularly in the areas of electronics and informatics components and semiconductors (*Panorama Brasil* 2001). Indeed, the Brazilian informatics sector had become heavily dependent on imports by the end of the 1990s. It exported $289 million worth of goods in 1999 and imported $993 million, with a negative balance of $703 million. In 2000, informatics exports rose to $317 million; they were accompanied, however, by over $1 billion worth of imports, leading to a considerably larger deficit of $942 million (Associação Brasileira da Indústria Elétrica e Eletrônica 2001).

Import dependency was particularly acute in the area of components, making them the major factor in the informatics trade deficit. Brazil imported $605 million worth of informatics components in 1999, and $791 million in 2000 (Associação Brasileira da Indústria Elétrica e Eletrônica 2001). Cell phones were the leading example of import dependency in informatics: fully 100 percent of the components to manufacture the phones in Brazil were imported, although close to 88 percent of the phones were exported (*Canal Web* 2001a).

In discussing his reasons for vetoing article 10 of the 2001 informatics legislation, President Cardoso emphasized the importance of fostering component production to support recent investments in Brazil's telecommunications sector. Minister of Science and Technology Ronaldo Sardenberg viewed consolidation of a policy for components production and for stabilizing the balance of payments in informatics as key challenges following the signing of the new informatics law. Minister of Development Alcides Tápias noted, "We needed to approve this law to know what conditions to offer the firms that want to produce here" (*Gazeta Mercantil* 2001). He predicted large investments in components plants near factories producing finished informatics products, primarily in São Paulo (*Gazeta Mercantil* 2001; *Valor* 2001b; *Canal Web* 2001a). A representative of Multek, a Brazilian manufacturer of components for telephones, electronics, informatics, and automation, echoed this optimism about prospects for Brazilian components production. He argued that conditions could be created in the medium to long term to lower components imports by close to 40 percent. He called for the development of economies of scale, arguing that Brazilian firms could eventually export components (*Gazeta Mercantil* 2001). Toward this end, the Ministério do Desenvolvimento, Indústria e Comércio (Ministry of Development, Industry, and Commerce) created a working group to develop a policy to attract components manufacturers to Brazil (Queiroz 2001).

The Brazilian government clearly recognized the need to promote components production to reduce the problem of dependency on imports in that area. This recognition, however, was not reflected in any systematic government policy. Indeed, the informatics law of 2001 included no provisions to address the problem of import dependency in components or other products. Nor did it address the question of export promotion, which was vital for Brazil to begin reducing its trade deficit in informatics (Manzoni 1999a, 2000).

In his pledge to launch an "ambitious program" to develop national capacities to generate new informatics technologies, to reduce the deficit by cutting reliance on imported components, and to export high-technology products like software, President Cardoso identified essential elements of an informatics policy for Brazil in 2001. Unfortunately, however, these elements were completely absent from the 2001 informatics law. The law, like the 1991 informatics policy before it, remained grounded in the neoliberal discourse of relying on open markets and foreign investment to promote informatics development. Indeed, the policy's most notable success appeared to be in calming the foreign investors who worried that their freedom to enter the Brazilian market might be compromised.

Despite this emphasis on attracting foreign investment, the Brazilian informatics sector had established a considerable industrial base. The industry, which had developed under the informatics laws of 1976 and 1984, continued to grow concurrently with neoliberal efforts to construct an open market. As Table 6.4 shows, the total number of informatics firms grew substantially between 1991 and 1997. Between 1991 and 1998, the informatics sector employed about 100,000 workers, of whom 35 to 40 percent had college or graduate degrees (Ministério da Ciência e Tecnologia 1999). As this chapter emphasizes, however, growth in the informatics industry was accompanied by a burgeoning trade deficit. Brazil's depend-

TABLE 6.4 Firms in the Brazilian Informatics Industry, 1991–1997

Segments	Total Number of Firms						
	1991	1992	1993	1994	1995	1996	1997
Total hardware industry	206	206	218	228	231	286	271
Data processing	77	77	87	110	116	139	123
Teleinformatics	51	51	55	52	55	70	77
Industrial automation	42	42	48	46	43	59	50
Microelectronics	16	16	14	11	11	9	8
Digital instrumentation	20	20	14	9	6	9	13
Total software industry	106	106	107	153	133	130	176
Total technical services	108	108	105	100	116	99	75
Private	87	87	85	79	90	74	53
Public	21	21	20	21	26	25	22
Federal	4	4	4	4	4	4	4
State	14	14	14	13	18	17	14
Municipal	3	3	2	4	4	4	4
Total informatics sector	420	420	430	481	480	515	522

SOURCE: Ministério da Ciência e Tecnologia, *Panorama do setor de informática*. Available from http://www.mct.gov.br/temas/info/Dsi/panorama/panorama.htm. Accessed 9 January 2001.

ence on foreign investment and imports was apparent, and industrialists and industry analysts joined President Cardoso in lamenting the trade deficit and calling for foreign firms to shift operations into the country. This situation confirmed the fears expressed to me by an official from DEPIN in a 1992 interview. Then he had warned that "the tendency when you open the market is to have assemblers and importers." Nine years later, as the rising numbers of Brazilian informatics firms were accompanied by a rising trade deficit, those fears had largely been realized.

In 2001 heavy dependence on imports and foreign investment characterized conditions of neoliberal globalization in Brazil. Under these conditions, President Cardoso framed his call for an industrial policy in informatics with a veiled apology for committing "heresy." He drew upon the legacy of nationalist discourse from the 1984 informatics policy while simultaneously acknowledging that such a discourse was widely discredited in the neoliberal climate of 2001.

In this climate, the Brazilian informatics sector experienced incipient denationalization (Sassen 1999), as the state used industrial policy to create conditions conducive for global capital. As Sassen argues, the state established "the mechanisms necessary to accommodate the rights of global capital in what [were] still national territories under the exclusive control of their states" (159). Similar to earlier periods of Brazilian informatics development, the state played a vital role in constructing market conditions. It did not lose its political sovereignty during this period of incipient denationalization. As Krasner (1999) argues, the state retained the authority and legitimacy to govern its territory. Both global and national capital went to the Brazilian state for help, pressuring it to pass an informatics law in order to stabilize conditions for investment. As occurred in the construction of an open market in the early 1990s, these pressures from capital combined with interests within the state during a complex process of negotiations. Throughout this process, the state played an active role in developing an industrial policy to shape the political and economic conditions for investment. The state participated in creating the economic, political, and discursive conditions for informatics development, and for neoliberal globalization itself.

The Cardoso government was thus a key actor in the process of constructing an open market that was begun by the Collor regime. It resolved regional tensions that arose during negotiations over the new informatics law to guarantee global capital full access to the Brazilian market. The informatics policy, once a nationalist force to resist the interests of global capital, was transformed into a mechanism to accommodate those interests. In the process, the Brazilian state assured foreign investors that neoliberalism reigned in Brazil, and that the invisible hand of the free market protected their freedom to invest anywhere from the Amazon to São Paulo's industrial heartland.

7 Neoliberal Globalization and Beyond
Protest, Celebration, and Alternatives to Development

THE BRAZILIAN INFORMATICS case was a cardinal example of high-tech development politics in the context of globalization. It involved a series of complex political processes, from the implementation of a nationalist development policy in the face of a high-tech trade war with the U.S. government, to the transition to a neoliberal economic regime. This case provides insights into the nature of international influences on development policy in the former Third World, and into the nature of the globalization process itself. Equally important, it suggests prospects for states and social groups to shape the globalization process, and to respond to the structural pressures created by neoliberalism. Recent examples of such responses illuminate possibilities to create alternatives to neoliberal globalization and development.

THE NATURE OF GLOBALIZATION

By combining the analytical tools of political economy and poststructuralism, I conceptualize globalization as a process with discursive, economic, and political dimensions. As Chapter 1 discussed, globalization is a discourse, a narrative of power and knowledge, constructed through a process of political struggle that defines particular actors as qualified to speak the truth in particular institutional contexts. Drawing upon Foucault's (1978) work on discourse and Gibson-Graham's (1996) analysis of the globalization script, I identify key assumptions in the dominant discourse on globalization, which articulates certain ideas as normal, objective representations of reality. The dominant discourse on globalization is linked to the discourses of neoliberalism and neoclassical economics; all these discourses view the economy as based on objective laws that determine the conditions for market operations. Globalization is thus understood as the inevitable expansion of international economic activities, which will benefit all nations if allowed to function freely.

In the 1980s a neoliberal globalization discourse arose that justified the interests of global capital in entering international markets for trade and investment. This discourse was inextricably linked to economic and political pressures to transform nationalist development policies and expand free trade. Foucault (1978, 100) argues that "it is in discourse that power and knowledge are joined together." By defining the market as driven by objective underlying laws, the neoliberal globalization discourse supported the interests of global capital and First World governments. In the 1970s and 1980s, multinational corporations and First World governments sought to create an international agreement to open markets for digital trade and communication, as well as services. In the mid-1980s, the U.S. government constructed a definition of "unfair" trade that allowed it to defend its declining economic position in telecommunications and other high-technology sectors. After unsatisfactory efforts at political negotiation, the U.S. government decided to pursue its dispute with Brazil and other key trading partners under Section 301 of the U.S. Trade Act (U.S. House Committee on Energy and Commerce 1988). This act provided the legal, or discursive, framework to justify a high-tech trade war with the Brazilian government over its informatics policy. By 1990 President Collor's neoliberal economic regime defined rules to open the Brazilian market to foreign trade and investment, and dismantled the existing informatics policy that had sought to exert national control over informatics development. In 2001 President Cardoso extended this neoliberal strategy, as a new informatics law promoted the interests of global capital in entering the Brazilian market.

Future studies could fruitfully trace the discursive dimensions of globalization to examine how national laws, regional and international trade agreements, and other legal systems are structured to favor the interests of global capital and First World governments. Studies of the neoliberal globalization discourse could thus explore the effects of that discourse on the interests of global capital as well as on First and former Third World governments. Equally important, they could identify the connections between the discursive and economic dimensions of globalization.

Escobar (1995) highlights those connections in his study of the development discourse, which has many elements in common with the globalization discourse. Both are based upon neoclassical economic assumptions that production, the market, labor, and development are objective material entities whose "reality" can be quantified and analyzed. By contrast, Escobar's poststructuralist perspective provides a way to conceptualize development and globalization as cultural discourses rooted in values like rationality that have arisen during the course of capitalist development. These values have shaped the ways that modern people understand themselves and their social world as linked to the process of production. What appear to be primarily economic trends, such as globalization and neoliberalism, are cultural forms that create particular kinds of people who view production and economics as defining features of social life and personal identity.

Conceptualizing globalization as a discourse thus allows it to be understood as a cultural form, rooted in values peculiar to the modern period. These values include the acceptance of the economy as an objective material entity. Once the economy is viewed in such terms, it becomes easier to accept neoliberal assumptions about free trade as the most rational way to support international market operations.

Conceptualizing globalization as a cultural discourse does not mean, however, that globalization can be understood entirely in discursive or cultural terms. Indeed, the economic dimension of globalization is equally important for understanding the nature of the globalization process. As Escobar (1995) notes, forms of production are imbued with cultural values and closely linked to discursive representations; the discourse of production (or globalization, neoliberalism, development), however, can be distinguished from the particular form of production for analytical purposes.

Sassen (1999) understands the economic dimension of globalization by highlighting the dynamics of international economic expansion and what she calls the "materialization" of global processes within national boundaries. In the 1970s and 1980s, technological change in microelectronics and telecommunications facilitated this expansion. As Chapter 2 discussed, these changes made it possible for multinationals to engage in new forms of digital trade, particularly in the area of services. The expansion of economic activity on a global scale, however, is not a monolithic, objective process whereby global capital dominates national markets. The workings of global capital within national borders are shaped by the historical context of capitalist development, and particularly by the conditions of local capital in a given industry. As we saw in Chapter 5, Brazilian computer firms were in strong positions to form partnerships with global capital during the transition to a neoliberal regime, due to the marketing and production capacities they had developed under the market reserve. In the Brazilian case, the economic dimension of globalization involved complex relationships between local and global capital, shaped by the capacities of local firms with respect to foreign ones.

This study thus supports the arguments of world systems theorists like Wallerstein (1999) and Arrighi (1999), who view globalization as part of the historical process of capitalist development. The dominant globalization discourse portrays globalization as a ground-breaking, novel development introducing unprecedented levels of international economic integration. These world systems theorists, as well as political economists such as Hirst and Thompson (1999), argue that the current globalization of production needs to be understood in the historical context of the development of capitalism as a global economic system over the past 500 years.

A key element in the rise of capitalism as a world economic system has been the economic and political domination of colonies by the colonial powers. This colonial legacy has taken a particular form under current conditions of globalization, which Sassen (1999) describes as the "incipient denationalizing" of economic activities. As global economic activities "materialize" within national borders, questions arise about whether national economies will become dominated by global capital. The Brazilian informatics case suggests that this possibility emerges through such economic changes as increasing foreign investment and the development of alliances between local and foreign firms. In Brazil the prospect of denationalization was also powerfully at stake in the political and discursive struggles that took place as local firms negotiated with each other, foreign firms, and with the state in the transition from a nationalist to a neoliberal economic policy. Activists who had fought to develop an informatics strategy that protected the development of local firms changed their political and economic priorities to emphasize the protection of any industrial production within Brazil. For them, the national origin of the firm no longer determined whether that firm could contribute to national production. Instead, they viewed a firm's decision to produce within the country as paramount. The definition of nationalization shifted through a process of political negotiation, where negotiators for the industry association forged a new policy discourse to use in their dealings with the government and with each other.

The Brazilian case suggests that denationalization in the context of globalization cannot be understood as an objective economic condition, one that can be quantified by counting the numbers of firms with home offices in particular countries. Rather, like globalization itself, denationalization is a socially constructed phenomenon shaped through political and discursive struggle. In the Brazilian informatics case, globalization involved contradictory tendencies toward nationalization and denationalization. As Brazilian firms formed economic and political alliances with foreign ones, they strengthened the prospects for continuing national production. At the same time, however, this national production was "denationalized" in the sense that it was carried out by foreign as well as local capital. By 2001, although the number of firms in the informatics sector had grown, so had the industry's dependence on imports, particularly in the area of components. By opening the market to foreign trade and investment, the transition to a neoliberal economic policy thus contributed to the overall process of denationalization during the 1990s.

This study shows that the economic dimension of globalization is inextricably linked to the political and discursive dimensions. Economic conditions are created in conjunction with discursive and political processes and relationships, particularly between local and foreign capital and the state. By asking whether denationalization will occur as global capital expands into national markets, Sassen (1999) highlights the political implications of the globalization of economic activities. As we saw in Chapter 1, former

Third World governments raised similar concerns about denationalization in the 1970s. They feared a new form of information dependency, based upon their relative shortage of technologies, skills, research facilities, and industries involved with computer manufacturing and software. The Brazilian government sought to counteract this new form of dependency when it decided to promote the national development of computer and software industries, or informatics. Chapter 2 examined how former Third World governments resisted the prospect of denationalization, seeking to retain control over conditions for digital trade and communication by upholding their national telecommunications laws. Conflicts over information trade politics continued as former Third World governments opposed the definition of transborder data flows as trade in data services, as well as the inclusion of services trade under GATT. The U.S. government, other First World governments, and their multinational corporate allies won these successive episodes of confrontation over information trade politics. They succeeded in establishing GATT as an international agreement governing services trade, and set the stage for the WTO to continue GATT's support for a global neoliberal trade regime.

Equally important, the Brazilian informatics policy was a key example of a nationalist strategy to oppose the control of a former Third World market by global capital. As we saw in Chapter 4, this policy was implemented through a complex process of political negotiation and compromise. Brazilian government officials sought to balance contradictory pressures to develop and implement a nationalist development policy and to mediate a trade war with the U.S. government. After that nationalist strategy was dismantled in 1990, the Collor and Cardoso governments used state policy to create conditions conducive to investment by global capital, thereby contributing to incipient denationalization (Sassen 1999).

The centrality of political struggle in the globalization process makes it imperative to examine the political dimensions of globalization and their relationship to the economic and discursive dimensions. The political dimensions studied here involved struggles over the dominant, neoliberal version of the globalization discourse. The question of whether national states would lose political sovereignty in the context of globalization was an underlying tension in these struggles. Krasner (1999) argues that globalization creates new challenges to the sovereign ability of states to control economic activities within and across their borders, although it does not reduce their authority to govern their territories. Such new challenges were evident in Chapter 2, which discussed the fears of former Third World governments that they would lose control over the emerging opportunities for digital trade and communication if their national telecommunications laws were undermined. These laws allowed governments to control market access by multinationals that sought to use their telecommunications infrastructures to engage in digital trade, and thus gave the governments leverage in establishing conditions for such trade to occur. Successive episodes of confrontation over information trade politics posed similar challenges for former Third World governments, which consistently sought to bolster their control over conditions for digital trade, including trade in services. In the high-tech trade war with the U.S. government, the Brazilian government struggled to implement a nationalist strategy designed to promote domestic development of an informatics industry. This trade war posed a series of challenges to the Brazilian government's effort to control conditions for national development and eventually led to capitulation to U.S. demands. Paradoxically, as we saw in Chapter 5, the transition to a neoliberal economic policy posed challenges to the Brazilian government's control over national economic development. Economic recession and the myriad economic and political uncertainties of the transition period meant that the Brazilian government was unable to implement the neoliberal policies in a coherent, consistent way. Globalization thus posed challenges to the state's ability to control national economic activities, whether or not economic policy conformed to neoliberal dictates of open markets.

In addition to these challenges to state control over economic activity, the political dimension of globalization involves a complex process of struggle to forge the conditions of globalization itself. Indeed, political struggles shaped economic and discursive practices in national and international arenas. In the 1970s and 1980s, First and former Third World governments and multinational corporations engaged in protracted negotiations over the political agreements governing digital trade and communication, as well as trade in services. The resulting agreements were key parts in the development of a neoliberal discourse that promoted "free" trade in services, and created economic and political conditions in which former Third World governments were pressured to change existing trade policies and open their markets to global capital. These struggles over neoliberalism dovetailed with U.S. trade policy debates in the 1980s. During this period, U.S. trade policy was also forged through a political process of debate over problems with U.S. economic competitiveness, and which policy approach provided the best response to U.S. decline with respect to its major trading partners. When U.S. government officials made the political choice to pursue bilateral trade disputes under Section 301, this created economic as well as political conditions for the high-tech trade war over Brazilian informatics. In response, Brazilian government officials engaged in adept forms of political action to mediate the international structural constraints resulting from the trade war with the United States and from Brazil's history of dependence on foreign trade and investment.

Following Brazil's capitulation to U.S. demands and the rise of President Collor's neoliberal economic policy, foreign and local firms in Brazil organized new economic and political alliances. Through a complex process of political struggle, they redefined the political and economic issues at stake in the transition to a neoliberal regime, developing a strategy designed to protect "national" production by any firm that would engage in it. This peculiar and unprecedented alliance within the informatics industry pressured the government to implement economic policies, while the government failed to implement any policy in a consistent or unified way. By 2001, however, facilitating investment by global capital emerged as a guiding theme for state development policy. Brazil's 2001 informatics law fostered neoliberal globalization, as the state used industrial policy to promote the interests of global capital in entering the Brazilian market.

The political, economic, and discursive dimensions of globalization were thus linked in a complex combination of struggles, creating the conditions of globalization in a fluid and uncertain process. As Gibson-Graham (1996) argues, globalization is like a script without a fixed sequence or conclusion, where the characters interact in response to each other's cues. This process involves political struggles to defend or oppose particular strategies to shape conditions for economic development. These strategies often take the form of policy discourses, such as national or international trade agreements or development policy. Neither economic, political, nor discursive practices are predetermined by objective laws, since they are forged through a process of interaction and struggle that combines all of these dimensions at once. It is possible, however, to make analytical distinctions to highlight the economic, political, and discursive dimensions of globalization and the ways they interact. Such distinctions help to clarify the multidimensional nature of the globalization process.

The case study of high-tech trade wars over Brazilian informatics provides some important guidelines to understand the globalization process. Indeed, this process formed the broader context for struggles over informatics development to occur. It was one of the major international structural constraints faced by former Third World governments as they sought to implement development policy. Understanding these constraints represents a second set of lessons from this study.

INTERNATIONAL STRUCTURAL CONSTRAINTS ON FORMER THIRD WORLD DEVELOPMENT POLICY

In the 1980s the rise of a neoliberal discourse on trade and development created economic, political, and discursive conditions that constrained the implementation of national development policies in the former Third World. From a political economy perspective, Haggard and Kaufman (1992) and Stallings (1992) emphasize that by the mid-1980s, a consensus had emerged in the development policy community that eradicating trade regulations and privatizing state companies was the optimum approach to development. Poststructuralism can be used to understand this consensus as part of a neoliberal discourse that defines certain economic "truths"; for example, free trade allows the objective laws of the economy to function most smoothly. The neoliberal discourse defined state economic policies as an impediment both to the operation of market laws and to the process of development itself. The neoliberal discourse was often interwoven with the globalization discourse since the smooth operation of market laws was understood to produce an inexorable international expansion of trade and production. The neoliberal globalization discourse became the focus for struggles over international trade policy, such as whether to include services trade under GATT.

The neoliberal globalization discourse, which initially developed in the 1970s and became more prominent by the mid-1980s, thus constituted a constraint on development policy in the former Third World. Governments that sought to control national development faced pressures from international bodies such as GATT to open their markets. When the U.S. government instigated a trade war over Brazilian informatics, it escalated the pressures of the neoliberal globalization discourse into a bilateral trade dispute. This trade war constituted a second international structural constraint that the Brazilian government had to contend with in implementing its informatics development policy. The trade war created a set of consequences, primarily in the form of trade sanctions, that increased the pressure on the Brazilian government to open its markets to global capital. As Chapter 4 discussed, Brazil was especially vulnerable to trade sanctions because of its history of dependence on foreign trade and investment. This dependency represented a third constraint on the Brazilian government as it struggled to implement the informatics policy. This process was particularly difficult because of the structure of the international market in computers and software, which was shifting rapidly with the rise of international standards like MS-DOS. Brazilian government officials knew that they needed to transform the informatics law to adapt to changing international market conditions. They had decided, however, to postpone those changes in order to uphold existing Brazilian law and protect the firms that had complied with it. When Brazilian exporters with longstanding business relationships with U.S. firms pressured the Brazilian government, it became untenable to defend the nationalist informatics policy. Brazilian government officials capitulated in the face of four sets of international structural constraints: the neoliberal globalization discourse, the trade war with the United States, the structure of the international computer and software markets, and the history of dependence on foreign trade and investment. As Chapter 6 discussed, the informatics law of 2001 highlights the ongoing importance of Brazil's dependence on foreign trade and investment in shaping current economic, political, and discursive conditions of globalization. In the 1990s, the growth of the Brazilian informatics industry was marked by a striking trade deficit that arose primarily from dependence on components imports. Equally important, President Cardoso's call for an ambitious program for informatics development was largely reduced to creating conditions for global capital to invest in the Brazilian market.

The Brazilian informatics case highlights the influence of international structural constraints on the implementation of development policy in the former Third World. This complex combination of constraints, however, came into play in a way that was shaped by the particular economic and political conditions in Brazil, the United States, and the global political economy. It is important to understand the details of these conditions in order to interpret the effects of structural constraints. Other studies might use a similar approach by examining whether these structural constraints came into play in a particular case, and if so, how they combined with each other and were shaped by the specific historical context. This study does not provide grounds to assume that the same constraints will affect development policy in all former Third World countries, or that these constraints will operate in a consistent, predictable way. As Stallings (1992) emphasizes, the nature and effects of such constraints depends upon the historical time period and the characteristics of the country involved.

Struggles over information trade politics in the 1970s and 1980s, and the U.S.-Brazilian trade war over informatics in the mid-to-late 1980s, support Stallings's (1992) argument that timing plays an important role in shaping the international constraints on development policy in the former Third World. Pressures from the neoliberal globalization discourse emerged in the 1970s and came to a head in the late 1980s. Thus the Brazilian informatics case fits Stallings's view of the late 1980s as a time when former Third World countries were pressured by international constraints to open their markets to global trade and investment. The Brazilian experience contradicts, however, Stallings's argument that international constraints will have a greater influence on development policy in the former Third World during the stage of initial decision making than during policy implementation. Brazil's informatics policy was initially formulated during the 1970s, when there were fewer international pressures. The software law was formed during the trade war with the U.S. government, however. It was developed as a strategy both to mediate that trade conflict and to extend the nationalist approach to informatics development into the software sector. Indeed, international pressures were most intense during the implementation of the informatics law during the trade war. Since the software law was still under negotiation in the Brazilian legislature, Brazilian government officials struggled to implement the existing informatics policy during this period. The U.S. government threatened trade sanctions if Brazilian negotiators did not change the policy, and those negotiators faced difficult choices between complying with national laws or confronting trade sanctions.

Again, the Brazilian informatics case highlights the importance of considering a complex combination of historical conditions, including international structural constraints and local political struggles to mitigate those constraints. It is difficult to identify a model of when international constraints can be expected to influence development policy, or of the precise nature of those effects. Indeed, Stallings's (1992) model was inadequate to capture the changing configuration of structural constraints and local struggles that characterized the implementation of Brazil's informatics policy. A more fruitful approach would identify the international structural constraints at play at a particular time, and the ways that local political struggles responded to and shaped those constraints. The clearest lesson that emerges from this study is about the importance of political struggle, by the state and capital and potentially by other groups, in the implementation of development policy as well as in shaping the conditions for development itself. These struggles are contingent and uncertain processes that unfold as actors shape the economic, political, and discursive conditions of development in the context of globalization.

This study views globalization and development as forged through political struggle, as former Third World governments confront neoliberalism, their own history of dependence on foreign trade and investment, and other international structural constraints. To what end, however, are these struggles waged? What are the possibilities of opposing and transforming these constraints? And equally importantly, are there alternatives to globalization and development as they have been conceived within the neoliberal discourse?

ALTERNATIVES TO GLOBALIZATION, NEOLIBERALISM, AND DEVELOPMENT

As Chapter 1 discussed, Escobar (1995) raises similar questions about the effects of efforts to "develop" the former Third World. He views many such efforts as "costly gestures ... ways of producing change without transforming the nature of the discourse as a whole" (216). These "costly gestures" amount to an "empty defense of development" that reproduces the same fundamental dynamics of power and oppression in the former Third World, perhaps under the guise of a different policy, governmental organization, or political administration. Here Escobar exemplifies not only the poststructuralist perspective but the postdevelopment perspective as well. Post-developmentalists reject the entire paradigm of development as a dead end for the former Third World, a game they cannot win because it has been designed according to rules set by multinational corporations, First World governments, and multilateral institutions like the World Bank and the International Monetary Fund (Rahnema and Bawtree 1997). In this vein, Escobar (1995) argues, "The empty defense of development must be left to the bureaucrats of the development apparatus and those who support it, such as the military and (not all of) the corporations. It is up to us, however, to make sure that the life span of the bureaucrats and the experts as producers and enforcers of costly gestures is limited" (217).

Was the Brazilian informatics policy such an "empty defense of development," a "costly gesture"? From the postdevelopment perspective, this strategy sought to promote national development of key high-technology sectors like computers and software. It was a nationalist strategy supported by a coalition of groups, including the military, scientists, engineers, and technicians. They sought to transform Brazil's dependency on foreign investment and trade, and its position in the international division of labor, by fostering local industrial growth. In other words, this strategy was designed to gain greater national control over the development process rather than to transform the process itself. This strategy ultimately became untenable due to the combination of international and domestic pressures that arose during the trade war with the U.S. government. Postdevelopment theorists might conclude that such strategies are futile attempts to gain greater control for former Third World governments in a "development game" that is stacked against them. The legacy of the informatics strategy continued in significant, unexpected ways during the transition to a neoliberal regime, as Chapter 5 discussed. But this legacy, however important in shaping continued conditions for informatics development, was carried out in a context where neoliberal economic policy dictated the official rules for development. Indeed, by 2001, the informatics policy focused primarily on attracting global capital to invest in the Brazilian market, a gesture designed to offset the costs of a mounting trade deficit rooted in the dependence on imported components.

The limitations of such nationalist development strategies raise questions about what Escobar (1995, 215) calls "alternatives to development." What possibilities appear if we reject the development paradigm? Escobar notes that local communities create their own models for economic, political, and cultural activity even in the context of dominant models. He recommends examining how grassroots movements and local knowledge work to transform conditions of development. Taking this kind of local or grassroots perspective means "investigating how external forces—capital and modernity, generally speaking—are processed, expressed, and refashioned by local communities" (98).

The grassroots perspective shifts the focus from struggles by national governments or local capital to strategies for resistance by social movements or community groups. The Brazilian informatics strategy was formulated within the state and implemented by government officials and local business executives. It sought to transform the dominance of global capital by developing local capital in a key industrial sector. During its heyday in the 1980s, the informatics policy's success implied success for Brazilian capital rather than for the kinds of grassroots groups that Escobar describes. The postdevelopment perspective emphasizes the interests of local communities rather than local capital, and thus calls for different kinds of strategies for change.

Gibson-Graham (1996) and Escobar (1995) advocate strategies that challenge globalization on both the material and discursive levels. Gibson-Graham emphasizes the importance of questioning the supposed inevitability of globalization, based on objective economic laws. By rejecting "the naturalization of power and violence that is conferred upon the [multinational corporation] by the globalization script" (146), it becomes possible to envision alternatives to existing forms of globalization and development. Gibson-Graham argues that such a process "queers" globalization by creating new interpretations of what globalization means and by exposing contradictions and vulnerabilities in the dominant globalization discourse. Indeed, "[by] querying globalization and queering the body of capitalism we may open up the space for many different scripts and invite many different actors to participate in the realization of different outcomes" (145).

Escobar (1995) and Gibson-Graham (1996) highlight the need for resistance to existing neoliberal models of globalization and development, a process that would involve a broader range of local groups in shaping discursive, economic, and political alternatives to development. These suggestions are well taken; however, they raise questions about which groups these would be and what kinds of strategies they might engage in during this process of transformation. Part of the reason for this vagueness about local struggles lies in the myriad possibilities for such struggles in different national contexts. Particular struggles, however, provide insights into possible futures for resistance to globalization, neoliberalism, and development.

For example, Walton and Seddon (1994) analyze food riots that protest neoliberal state policies to open markets and comply with austerity measures dictated by the International Monetary Fund. These policies were designed to "structurally adjust" markets in the former Third World. In many countries, they led to government cutbacks in key social supports such as food, health care, education, transportation, housing, and other services critical for poor and working-class populations, particularly in large urban areas. Walton and Seddon document 146 cases of such austerity protests between 1976 and 1992, in Latin America, Eastern Europe, and Africa. These protests are examples of the kinds of grassroots local struggles advocated by Escobar (1995) and Gibson-Graham (1996). They involve social movements organized across a range of urban centers, to pressure the government to address the social inequalities that have intensified in the wake of neoliberal economic reforms.

These inequalities were also targeted by what Moody (1997) calls "social movement unionism." Inspired by labor movements in South Africa, Brazil, and other former Third World countries, Moody views this kind of unionism as "asserting the centrality of union democracy as a source of power and broader social vision, and outreach as a means of enhancing that power" (4). Social-movement unionism seeks to mobilize large numbers of workers through a deep commitment to democracy and participation, and through militant collective bargaining. It rejects the tendency of unions in the United States and elsewhere to give in to corporate demands in a bid to "save jobs" and keep firms from moving production to other countries. By contrast, social-movement unionism is based on the belief that "retreat anywhere only leads to more retreats—an injury to one is an injury to all. It seeks to craft bargaining demands that create more jobs and aid the whole class" (4). Social-movement unionists view workers' power as rooted in their jobs; they are militant about not giving up jobs in the face of corporate pressures to do so. In addition to organizing at the workplace, these unionists target the larger political arena. They build political and social power by forging alliances with other sectors of the working class, such as other unions, neighborhood or community groups, and other social movements. They place less emphasis on alliances with existing political parties and seek independence from such parties as they focus on grassroots groups. Social-movement unionism "fights for all the oppressed and enhances its own power by doing so" (5). Moody documented the activities of such unions around the globe in the 1990s, as they organized against neoliberal policies that threatened to dismantle social protections for working people. General or mass political strikes were conducted in many countries, including Nigeria (1994), Indonesia (1994), Paraguay (1994), Taiwan (1994), Bolivia (1995), France (1995), Canada (1995), South Africa (1996), Brazil (1996), Greece (1996, 1997), Spain (1994, 1996), Argentina (twice in 1996), Venezuela (1996), Italy (1996), Haiti (1997), Colombia (1997), Ecuador (1997), South Korea (1997), and Belgium (1997).

Social-movement unionism is thus a key force of resistance against neoliberal globalization, which pressures governments to open markets to global capital, "structurally adjust" former Third World economies, and allow multinationals to expand their global operations without regard for the effects on local workers and communities. These trends are threatening the living standards of working people around the world and creating conditions for mobilization and protest in a range of different countries. To date, national governments or groups of governments have failed to develop economic policies that have succeeded in challenging the rise of neoliberal globalization. Moody (1997) does not expect them to do so. Instead, he argues, "If it is to come, relief will come at the hands of the working class pulling itself together both 'at home' and abroad. The first line of resistance in the South is taking shape in new or changing labor movements. The challenge for workers in the North is to reach out to these workers and their organizations—unions, parties, social-movement organizations—and forge alliances" (226). For such alliances to succeed, they must develop innovative forms of organizing that transcend the limits of past efforts at labor internationalism, expanding alliances to include a broader range of social movements and sectors of the working class.

Examples of such innovative organizing abounded during protests at the World Trade Organization (WTO) meeting in Seattle in November 1999. As trade ministers from 135 countries met to negotiate conditions for "free and fair" international trade, members of at least 750 organizations flocked to Seattle to challenge the WTO's commitment to neoliberalism and the expansion of global capital. This grassroots mobilization was much greater than at previous negotiations over international trade. Indeed, only 12 such organizations were present during GATT negotiations in Uruguay in 1986. In 1999 in Seattle, protesters against neoliberalism exemplified Moody's (1997) social-movement unionism, representing alliances of labor, environmental, consumer protection, and other community groups. These novel alliances pursued creative, nontraditional organizing strategies such as street theater with giant puppet shows. Huge caricatures of world leaders and antitrade heroes acted out the drama of resistance to neoliberal globalization in the streets. In one performance, the WTO was depicted as a giant octopus with tentacles strangling clean air, old-growth forests, and workers around the world. Guerrilla theater also extended into actual confrontations with riot police, as protesters dressed as sea turtles faced armed officers wearing gas masks. The significance of these imaginative forms of protest was highlighted by Noah Kenneally, a twenty-four-year-old, full-time volunteer for the Direct Action Network, a leading anti-WTO group. Kenneally remarked, "People are putting their bodies on the line and taking risks, but we can also do it in a festive and celebratory way" (Iritani 1999, A28).

Festive, celebratory protest, where people forge new alliances through social-movement unionism, where they take risks and "put their bodies on the line," may be the key to resisting neoliberal globalization. The seeds for such alliances are breaking ground in many corners of the world, and may continue to spread in contradictory and unexpected ways. Future studies would do well to document these alliances, their organizing strategies, their successes and setbacks. The anti-globalization movement sparked by the protesters in Seattle, social-movement unionists around the world, and other local community groups offer hope for a new form of creative internationalism. Such a movement would be informed by an understanding of the economic, political, and discursive complexities of neoliberal globalization. This understanding would help activists find innovative ways to combine international solidarity with deeply democratic local struggles. This process could lead to a transformation of neoliberal conditions of globalization and development, and to the creation of alternatives rooted in the myriad visions of local communities.

Abbreviations

ABES	Associação Brasileira de Empresas de Software (Brazilian Association of Software Firms)
ABICOMP	Associação Brasileira da Industria de Computadores e Periféricos (Brazilian Computer and Peripherals Industry Association)
ABINEE	Associação Brasileira da Indústria Elétrica e Eletrônica (Brazilian Association of Electrical and Electronics Industries)
ADAPSO	Computer Software and Services Industry Association (Now ITAA [Information Technology Association of America])
AEA	American Electronics Association
AEB	Associação de Comércio Exterior do Brasil (Brazilian Association of Foreign Trade)
ASSESPRO	Associação de Empresas Brasileiras de Software e Servicios de Informática (Association of Brazilian Informatics Software and Services Firms)
CBEMA	Computer and Business Equipment Manufacturers Association
CCIA	Computer and Communications Industry Association
CONIN	Conselho Nacional de Informática (National Informatics Council)
DEPIN	Departamento de Política de Informática e Automação (Department of Informatics and Automation Policy)
FIESP	Federação das Industrias do Estado de São Paulo (Federation of Industries of the State of São Paulo)
GATT	General Agreement on Tariffs and Trade
IBI	Intergovernmental Bureau for Informatics
IPI	Impôsto sobre Produtos Industrializados (Tax on Industrialized Products)
MBI	Movimento Brasil Informática (Brazilian Informatics Movement)
MCT	Ministério da Ciência e Tecnologia (Ministry of Science and Technology)
MITI	Japanese Ministry of International Trade and Industry

Abbreviations

SEI	Secretaría Especial de Informática (Special Secretariat of Informatics)
SPIN I	Intergovernmental Conference on Strategies and Policies for Informatics
SUCESU	Sociedade dos Usuários de Computadores e Equipamentos Subsidiários (Society of Computer and Subsidiary Equipment Users)
SUFRAMA	Superintendência da Zona Franca de Manaus (Superintendency of the Free-Trade Zone of Manaus)
UFRJ	Universidade Federal do Rio de Janeiro (Federal University of Rio de Janeiro)
UNCTAD	United Nations Conference on Trade and Development
UNESCO	United Nations Educational, Scientific and Cultural Organization
USTR	United States Trade Representative
WTO	World Trade Organization

Notes

Chapter 1: Globalization, Neoliberalism, and the Brazilian Informatics Case

1. Calls for a new information order included proposals to regulate transborder data flows and counteract information dependency. The first formal discussions about the need for transborder data-flow policies were held at the first Intergovernmental Conference on Strategies and Policies for Informatics (SPIN I) in 1978. In 1979 the Intergovernmental Bureau for Informatics held conferences for delegates from Latin America and Africa. These delegates passed resolutions to use transborder data-flow policies to promote the development of their national computer industries and processing facilities. Some delegates asserted that data pertaining to their countries should be protected from use by other countries, particularly in the case of remote sensing of geographical data by satellites (Sauvant 1984b; Intergovernmental Bureau for Informatics 1982).

2. For example, Adler (1987) emphasizes the role of nationalist ideology as a motivation for the military, scientists, and technicians to support informatics development in Brazil. Langer (1989) notes how Brazilian informatics development was supported by Brazil's prior experience with scientific and technological development in nuclear and solid-state physics during the 1950s and 1960s, while Evans (1995) analyzes how the Brazilian, Indian, and South Korean states intervened in the information-technology industry. Fadul and Straubhaar (1991) emphasize the historical development of communications structures in Brazil, from the construction of a modern telecommunications system in the 1960s to the development of cultural industries in the 1970s.

Chapter 2: Information Trade Politics: From Telecommunications to Trade Policy

1. Other task forces and working groups included the Interdepartmental Radio Advisory Committee, chaired by the National Telecommunications Information Administration in the Department of Commerce; the interagency Preparatory Committee for the International Telecommunications Union Plenipotentiary Conference, chaired by the State Department; the interagency Working Group on the Legal Subcommittee of the United Nations Committee on Outer Space, chaired by the State Department; and the coordinating committee for

U.S. government instructions for ComSat, including the National Telecommunications Information Administration and the Federal Communications Commission, chaired by the State Department (U.S. House Committee on Government Operations 1982).

2. The text of the resolutions passed at the Third Conference of Latin American Informatics Authorities and the Conference on African Informatics Integration was reproduced in this United Nations report (United Nations 1982). These quotes are taken from the resolution passed at the Latin American conference.

3. The deregulation of the U.S. telecommunications industry and the break-up of AT&T's historical monopoly also involved the application of this different set of free-market principles to U.S. telecommunications policy. These principles reflected corporate strategies to enter new markets for advanced telecommunications services (see Batten and Schoonmaker 1987; Schiller 1982). Drawn from neoclassical economics, they viewed free-market competition as the most efficient means of providing telecommunications services. Corporate strategies to restructure U.S. telecommunications policy according to neoliberal economic principles required the development of new rules and decision-making procedures. Discussions arose over how to restructure U.S. telecommunications from a monopoly to a competitive industry. Different rules were needed to establish conditions for entry into unregulated markets, and to remove controls over rates and terms of entry into the U.S. market (United Nations Centre on Transnational Corporations 1990; U.S. House Committee on Government Operations 1981).

Chapter 3: Who's Afraid of Brazilian Informatics?

This chapter title is the English translation of the title of a monograph by Renato Archer (1987), former Brazilian Minister of Science and Technology. Archer's work is entitled *Quem Tem Medo da Informática Brasileira*. It is a collection of essays by, and interviews with, Archer concerning informatics policy and the challenges involved with implementing it in the mid-1980s.

The epigraph to this chapter is from "Administration Statement on International Trade Policy," issued September 23, 1985, by the Office of the U.S. Trade Representative. See U.S. House Committee on Ways and Means 1986a, 23.

1. These conclusions were largely based upon an analysis of responses by U.S. companies and trade associations to major tariff and nontariff barriers imposed by foreign governments to the sale of their products. This inquiry was not based upon a scientific sample designed to represent all U.S. exporters; instead, narrative responses were received from over half of a group of 500 trading firms contacted by the Subcommittee on Oversight and Investigations of the House Committee on Energy and Commerce. These responses indicate some general types of trade barriers encountered by these firms.

Respondents identified 751 foreign trade barriers, 30 percent of which involved tariff complaints and 70 percent nontariff complaints. Former Third World countries imposed 56 percent of all of these barriers, compared to 44 percent by their First World counterparts. This supported the general perception of former Third World countries as more likely to implement protective economic policies. They were particularly likely to impose higher tariff rates as a means both to protect local industry and to raise revenues. First World countries reduced their tariff rates over the course of seven rounds of GATT trade negotiations, making tariff barriers to trade of lesser general concern to U.S. exporters.

By contrast, nontariff barriers were viewed as the major obstacle to the entrance of U.S. goods into foreign markets. Such barriers included any practices by governments or private firms that offered advantages to domestic producers over foreign ones, and thus altered the flow of trade. Over half of the nontariff barrier complaints in the study concerned five types of such barriers, including import licensing, product standards, embargoes, government subsidies, and offset barter arrangements. In general, nontariff barriers were also encountered more frequently in former Third World countries; complaints pertaining to these countries accounted for 55 percent of all nontariff complaints, compared to 45 percent for First World countries.

Both tariff and nontariff complaints by U.S. exporters focused upon a particular group of U.S. trading partners. The European Community, Japan, and Canada accounted for 72 percent of all the tariff complaints against First World countries; with the addition of France, this group accounted for half of the nontariff complaints against such countries. Korea, Taiwan, Brazil, Mexico, and Venezuela were the focus of 53 percent of all tariff complaints against former Third World countries, and 45 percent of all nontariff complaints against them (U.S. House Committee on Energy and Commerce 1986).

2. For example, the Reciprocal Trade and Investment Act of 1983 was designed to amend the Trade Act of 1974 by establishing measures to counter foreign trade barriers in targeted sectors. It was formulated to provide presidential authority to negotiate the expansion of trade and foreign direct investment, particularly in services and high-technology products. Its goal was to promote open access to foreign markets for U.S. exports by improving the President's ability to identify and eliminate foreign barriers to trade in those areas (U.S. House Committee on Ways and Means 1984).

The 1983 bill was based upon a sectoral approach to trade reciprocity, which made it difficult to implement given the existence of other U.S. trade agreements. First, its provisions were intended to be applied irrespective of any such agreements, which posed the danger of violating existing U.S. treaty obligations. Sectoral reciprocity would be triggered automatically if it were found that U.S. products had been excluded from a foreign market, a provision that allowed little flexibility to withhold sanctions to avoid foreign policy problems. Second, these sanctions risked violating GATT by bypassing existing complaint procedures and establishing trade barriers that countermanded GATT rules. Finally, reciprocity legislation offered legal grounds for U.S. trading partners to retaliate in other sectors; it thus raised the prospect of increasing U.S. involvement in trade disputes. For these and other reasons, the Reagan administration strongly opposed such a sectoral approach toward reciprocity (U.S. Senate Committee on Commerce, Science, and Transportation 1983).

3. Section 103 of the Revenue Act of 1971 also provides for presidential authority to suspend eligibility of foreign-made products for an investment tax credit, if the President finds

that U.S. trade has been limited unjustifiably by a foreign government that "tolerates international cartels" (U.S. Senate Committee on Commerce, Science, and Transportation 1983, 163).

4. See U.S. House Committee on Ways and Means 1989, 20–50, for a table of all Section 301 cases. It describes the status of alleged unfair foreign-trade practices affecting U.S. industries.

5. Evans (1989a) analyzed this conflict between the Brazilian and U.S. governments as indicative of the status of the United States as a declining hegemonic power. In this position, the U.S. government cannot afford to defend free-market principles in every case of international commerce. However, it is "easily threatened by industrial prowess and ideologically disposed to attack policies aimed explicitly at promoting it" (236). In the investigation of Brazilian informatics, the Reagan administration pressured for open-market policies in an area where the United States had a history of comparative advantage. Maintaining high-technology exports to former Third World countries was one potential avenue to counteract the massive U.S. trade deficit (236).

6. Statement of Ralph Johnson, Deputy Assistant Secretary for Trade and Commercial Affairs, Bureau of Economic and Business Affairs, U.S. Department of State (U.S. House Committee on Energy and Commerce 1988, 22–23).

7. IBM and Burroughs (now Unisys) have manufactured computers in Brazil since 1924 (Evans 1986, 792).

8. Manufacturers of personal computers like Apple were completely excluded from the Brazilian market because of the market reserve. These firms were more vocal in their support of the 301 investigation (Evans 1989a).

9. Similar reasons sparked the initiation or acceleration of three other 301 cases in September 1985. An investigation of Korean insurance laws offered the chance to pursue openness in services. Agricultural exports to First World countries were promoted through examinations of Japanese restrictions on tobacco imports and European Community regulations on canned fruits (Evans 1989a).

10. The informatics law defined the informatics sector very broadly, as including computers, computer parts, and all other devices that incorporated a digital instrument. It thus potentially applied to communications switching equipment, controls for automated processes, optical and electronic components, and software (U.S. Trade Representative 1986; U.S. House Committee on Energy and Commerce 1988).

Chapter 4: The Double Desire: Mediation and Resistance through Software Policy

1. Although software piracy is hard to measure, the U.S. Software Publishers Association has estimated that between three and seven illegal copies are made and distributed for each copy of a software program sold through legitimate channels in the United States (Lewis 1989). Piracy of Datalogica software would thus be considerably below estimated U.S. levels, while piracy of Brasoft could be considered high but not above U.S. levels.

2. The Movimento Brasil Informática (Brazilian Informatics Movement) (MBI) is a coalition of domestic professional associations and firms involved in the informatics industry. It was formed in 1983 to influence the formation of Brazil's informatics policy (Calicchio 1990, interview).

3. Scopus was also cited for piracy of a few lines of code from MS-DOS that appeared in version 3.0 of its Sisne operating system. It promptly admitted that one of its engineers had copied the lines, and developed original lines to replace them.

It is important to note that Scopus's piracy was not due to lack of technical knowledge; the lines were relatively simple and had been copied for convenience by the engineer involved. Concerned to eliminate any doubt about the legitimacy of Sisne's authorship after successive attacks by Microsoft, Scopus made a special offer to owners of Scopus 16-bit computers and their licensees. These owners would receive a free copy of Sisne 3.0 that did not contain the lines that had been copied from MS-DOS (1990 interview with Josef Manasterski, vice-president of Scopus; 1990 interview with Ivan da Costa Marques, former president of Cobra; *Data News* 1987b).

4. Even some of Microsoft's own firms concurred with this judgment. Its French subsidiary stated that it did not really need the new version (Henrique 1990, interview).

5. Pseudonyms have been used to protect the confidentiality of interviews with IBM and Unisys executives, as well as some other business executives and government officials.

References

Interviews

Araujo, João (pseud., Unisys executive). 1992. Interview by author. Rio de Janeiro.
Archer, Renato (former Minister of Science and Technology). 1990. Interview by author. Rio de Janeiro.
Calicchio, Fernando (Secretary-general of MBI [1990] and representative of ABICOMP [1992]). July and August 1990, 1992. Interviews by author. Rio de Janeiro.
Campos, José (pseud., Unisys executive). 1992. Interview by author. Rio de Janeiro.
Costa Marques, Ivan da (former president of Cobra). 1990. Interview by author. Rio de Janeiro.
Fregni, Edson (former president of Scopus). 1990 and 1992. Interviews by author. São Paulo.
Gomes, Ricardo (pseud., IBM executive). 1992. Interview by author. Rio de Janeiro.
Guaranys, José Fernando Halfeld dos (main negotiator for ABICOMP). 1990 and 1992. Interviews by author. Rio de Janeiro.
Henrique, Carlos Antonio (pseud., former informatics advisor to President José Sarney). 1990 and 1992. Interviews by author. São Paulo.
Manasterski, Josef (former vice-president of Scopus). 1990 and 1992. Interviews by author. São Paulo.
Moraes, Fernando de (pseud., IBM executive). 1992. Interview by author. Brasília.
Mourão, Rubens (pseud., Chief of the Divisão de Programmas de Computador e Serviços Técnicos [Computer Programs and Technical Services Division], DEPIN). 1992. Interview by author. Brasília.
Nunes, Artur Pereira (representative of ABICOMP). 1990 and 1992. Interviews by author. Rio de Janeiro.
Porto, José Rubens Doria (former Secretary of Informatics). 1992. Interview by author. São Paulo.
Ripper, Mário Dias (former president of Brazilian computer company). 1990. Interview by author. Rio de Janeiro.
Rocha, José Ezil Veiga da (former Secretary of Informatics). June and July 1992. Interviews by author. Brasília.
Sousa, Paulo de (pseud., Unisys executive). 1992. Interview by author. Rio de Janeiro.
Velloso, Sergio (pseud., Itautec executive). 1992. Interview by author. São Paulo.

References

Published Resources

Adler, Emanuel. 1987. *The Power of Ideology: The Quest for Technological Autonomy in Argentina and Brazil.* Berkeley: University of California Press.

———. 1988. "State Institutions, Ideology, and Autonomous Technological Development: Computers and Nuclear Energy in Argentina and Brazil." *Latin American Research Review* 23, no. 2: 59–90.

Aglietta, Michel. 1987. *A Theory of Capitalist Regulation: The U.S. Experience.* London: Verso.

Appelbaum, Richard, and Gary Gereffi. 1994. "Power and Profits in the Apparel Commodity Chain." In *Global Production: The Apparel Industry in the Pacific Rim*, ed. Edna Bonacich, Lucie Cheng, Norma Chinchilla, Nora Hamilton, and Paul Ong, 42–62. Philadelphia: Temple University Press.

Appiah, Kwame Anthony. 1995. "The Postcolonial and the Postmodern." In *The Post-colonial Studies Reader*, ed. Bill Ashcroft, Gareth Griffiths, and Helen Tiffin, 119–25. New York: Routledge.

Aquino, Miriam de. 1987. "Momento de decisão." *Dados e Ideias*, September, pp. 31–33.

Archer, Renato. 1987. *Quem tem medo da informática brasileira.* Brasília: Ministério da Ciência e Tecnologia.

Aronson, Jonathan D., and Peter F. Cowhey. 1984. *Trade in Services: A Case for Open Markets.* Washington, D.C.: American Enterprise Institute.

Arrighi, Giovanni. 1999. "Globalization, State Sovereignty, and the Endless Accumulation of Capital." In *States and Sovereignty in the Global Economy*, ed. David A. Smith, Dorothy J. Solinger, and Steven C. Topik, 53–73. London: Routledge.

Ashcroft, Bill, Gareth Griffiths, and Helen Tiffin. 1995a. "Postmodernism and Post-colonialism: Introduction." In *The Post-colonial Studies Reader*, ed. Bill Ashcroft, Gareth Griffiths, and Helen Tiffin, 117–18. New York: Routledge.

———. 1995b. "Issues and Debates: Introduction." In *The Post-colonial Studies Reader*, ed. Bill Ashcroft, Gareth Griffiths, and Helen Tiffin, 7–11. New York: Routledge.

Associação Brasileira da Indústria Elétrica e Eletrônica (ABINEE). 2001. "Balança comercial de produtos do setor Jan–Nov/00." Available from www.abinee.org.br/abinee/decon/decon12.htm. Accessed 26 January 2001.

Azevedo, Carlos, and Guerino Zago, Jr. 1989. *Do tear ao computador: As lutas pela industrialização no Brasil.* São Paulo: Editora Política.

Baran, Paul. 1973. "On the Political Economy of Backwardness." In *The Political Economy of Development and Underdevelopment*, ed. Charles K. Wilbur, 82–93. New York: Random House.

Batten, Dick, and Sara Schoonmaker. 1987. "Deregulation, Technological Change, and Labor Relations in Telecommunications." In *Workers, Managers, and Technological Change: Emerging Patterns of Labor Relations*, ed. Daniel Cornfield, 311–27. New York: Plenum Press.

Baudrillard, Jean. 1975. *The Mirror of Production.* St. Louis: Telos Press.

———. 1983. *Simulations.* New York: Semiotext(e).

Becker, David G. 1983. *The New Bourgeoisie and the Limits of Dependency: Mining, Class, and Power in "Revolutionary" Peru.* Princeton: Princeton University Press.

References

Bell, Daniel. 1976. *The Coming of Post-Industrial Society.* New York: Basic Books.

Benakouche, Rabah. 1985. *A questão da informática no Brasil.* São Paulo: Editora Brasiliense, S.A.

Beniger, James R. 1986. *The Control Revolution: Technological and Economic Origins of the Information Society.* Cambridge: Harvard University Press.

Bennett, Colin J. 1992. *Regulating Privacy: Data Protection and Public Policy in Europe and the United States.* Ithaca: Cornell University Press.

Bhagwati, Jagdish N. 1989. "The Role of Services in Development." In *Services and Development: The Role of Foreign Direct Investment and Trade,* ed. United Nations Centre on Transnational Corporations, 5–8. New York: United Nations.

Bhalla, Surjit. 1990. "India." In *The Uruguay Round: Services in the World Economy,* ed. Karl P. Sauvant and P. A. Messerlin, 188–96. Washington, D.C.: World Bank.

Bierling, Jacques, and Georgina Murray. 1995. "The 'Emerging Powers': China, Singapore, Hong Kong and Taiwan." *Current Sociology* 43: 65–96.

Block, Fred. 1996. *The Vampire State and Other Myths and Fallacies about the U.S. Economy.* New York: New Press.

Bornschier, Volker, and Christopher Chase-Dunn. 1985. *Transnational Corporations and Underdevelopment.* New York: Praeger.

Boswell, Terry, and William J. Dixon. 1990. "Dependency and Rebellion: A Cross-National Analysis." *American Sociological Review* 55: 540–59.

Braga, Carlos Alberto Primo. 1990. "Brazil." In *The Uruguay Round: Services in the World Economy,* ed. Karl P. Sauvant and P. A. Messerlin, 197–209. Washington, D.C.: World Bank.

Braman, Sandra. 1990. "Trade and Information Policy." *Media, Culture and Society* 12: 361–85.

Buell, Frederick. 1994. *National Culture and the New Global System.* Baltimore: Johns Hopkins University Press.

Burns, E. Bradford. 1980. *A History of Brazil.* New York: Columbia University Press.

Business Roundtable. 1985. *International Information Flow: A Plan for Action.* New York: Business Roundtable.

Campos, Alda. 1992. "As estratégias da IBM diante do downsizing." *Data News,* 9 June, p. 6.

Canal Web. 2001a. "Lei de TI vai equilibrar produção de componentes e balança comercial, diz Funari." *Canal Web,* 11 January.

———. 2001b. "Alcatel comemora Lei de TI e diz que Zona Franca não será prejudicada." *Canal Web,* 11 January.

Cardoso, Fernando H., and Enzo Faletto. 1979. *Dependency and Development in Latin America.* Trans. M. M. Urquidi. Berkeley: University of California Press.

Castells, Manuel. 1996. *The Rise of the Network Society.* Oxford: Blackwell.

Castells, Manuel, and Roberto Laserna. 1989. "The New Dependency: Technological Change and Socioeconomic Restructuring in Latin America." *Sociological Forum* 4, no. 4: 535–60.

Chaves, Antonio. 1988. *Software brasileiro sem mistério.* São Paulo: Julex Livros.

Cleveland, Harland. 1985. *The Knowledge Executive.* New York: Dutton.

Cline, William. 1987. *Informatics and Development: Trade and Industrial Policy in Argentina, Brazil, and Mexico.* Washington, D.C.: Economics International.

Collier, George A., with Elizabeth Lowery Quaratiello. 1994. *Basta! Land and the Zapatista Rebellion in Chiapas*. Monroe, Ore.: Institute for Food and Development Policy.

Collins, Patricia Hill. 1990. *Black Feminist Thought: Knowledge, Consciousness, and the Politics of Empowerment*. New York: Routledge.

Coombe, George W. 1985a. "Legal Aspects of Transborder Data Flows: The View from the Office of General Counsel." Paper presented at the meetings of the American Society of International Law, New York, April.

———. 1985b. "Transborder Data Flow Legal Issues: The Case for Economic Analysis." Paper presented at the meetings of the American Society of International Law, New York, April.

Correa, Carlos Maria. 1990. "Software Industry: An Opportunity for Latin America?" *World Development* 18, no. 11: 1587–98.

Cowhey, Peter F., and Jonathan D. Aronson. 1989. "Global Diplomacy and National Policy Options for Telecommunications." In *Changing Networks: Mexico's Telecommunications Options*, ed. Peter F. Cowhey, Jonathan D. Aronson, and Gabriel Szekely, 51–78. San Diego: Center for U.S.-Mexican Studies.

Dantas, Marcos. 1989. *O crime de Prometeu: Como o Brasil obteve a tecnologia da informática*. Rio de Janeiro: ABICOMP.

Dantas, Vera. 1987a. "Mais ação, menos discurso." *Data News*, 25 May, p. 2.

———. 1987b. "Um novo capítulo." *Data News*, 29 June, p. 2.

———. 1987c. "Uma situação insustentável." *Data News*, 10 August, p. 2.

———. 1987d. "Para Gregos e Troianos." *Data News*, 26 October, p. 2.

———. 1987e. "Fim do mundo." *Data News*, 23 November, p. 2.

———. 1987f. "Papai Noel." *Data News*, 28 December, p. 2.

———. 1988. *Guerrilha tecnológica: A verdadeira história da política nacional de informática*. Rio de Janeiro: Livros Técnicos e Científicos Editora.

———. 1992a. "Novas empresas enfatizam a comercialização por revendas." *Data News*, 28 January, pp. 6–7.

———. 1992b. "Liberou geral." *Data News*, 24 March, p. 4.

———. 1992c. "Fazer ou não fazer." *Data News*, 7 April, p. 4.

———. 1992d. "Importação." *Data News*, 14 April, p. 4.

———. 1992e. "Radiografia." *Data News*, 28 April, p. 4.

———. 1992f. "Tarefa ardua." *Data News*, 28 April, p. 3.

———. 1992g. "Fim de um pesadelo." *Data News*, 28 April, p. 4.

———. 1992h. "Acordo." *Data News*, 5 May, p. 4.

———. 1992i. "Mão na massa." *Data News* 5 May, p. 4.

———. 1992j. "Aquém da expectativa." *Data News*, 12 May, p. 4.

———. 1992k. "Barulho." *Data News*, 12 May, p. 4.

———. 1992l. "Indigestão." *Data News*, 9 June, p. 4.

Data News. 1987a. "MS-DOS: Novo capitulo." *Data News*, 31 August, p. 4.

———. 1987b. "Vale-sisne na feira." *Data News*, 31 August, p. 4.

———. 1987c. "Na platéia." *Data News*, 28 September, p. 2.

———. 1987d. "Retaliação, perigo real." *Data News*, 9 November, p. 1.

———. 1992a. "Uma evolução natural no mercado de commodities." *Data News*, 29 January, p. 7.
———. 1992b. "Mudança para baixar custo dos produtos." *Data News*, 16 June, p. 3.
Davis, Jim, Thomas A. Hirschl, and Michael Stack, eds. 1997. *Cutting Edge: Technology, Information, Capitalism and Social Revolution*. London: Verso.
Dicken, Peter. 1992. *Global Shift*. New York: Guilford Press.
Dixon, William J., and Terry Boswell. 1996. "Dependency, Disarticulation, and Denominator Effects: Another Look at Foreign Capital Penetration." *American Journal of Sociology* 102, no. 2: 543–62.
Eger, John M. 1978. "Emerging Restrictions on Transnational Data Flows: Privacy Protection, or Non-Tariff Trade Barriers?" *Law and Policy in International Business* 10: 1055–1103.
Epstein, Gerald, Julie Graham, and Jessica Nembhard, eds. 1993. *Creating a New World Economy: Forces of Change and Plans for Action*. Philadelphia: Temple University Press.
Escobar, Arturo. 1995. *Encountering Development: The Making and Unmaking of the Third World*. Princeton: Princeton University Press.
Evans, Peter B. 1979. *Dependent Development: The Alliance of Multinational, State, and Local Capital in Brazil*. Princeton: Princeton University Press.
———. 1986. "State, Capital, and the Transformation of Dependence: The Brazilian Computer Case." *World Development* 14: 791–808.
———. 1989a. "Declining Hegemony and Assertive Industrialization: U.S.-Brazil Conflicts in the Computer Industry." *International Organization* 43, no. 1: 207–38.
———. 1989b. "Predatory, Developmental and Other Apparatuses: A Comparative Political Economy Perspective on the Third World State." *Sociological Forum* 4, no. 4: 561–87.
———. 1992. "Greenhouses and Strategic Nationalism: A Comparative Analysis of Brazil's Informatics Policy." In *High Technology and Third World Industrialization: Brazilian Computer Policy in Comparative Perspective*, ed. Peter B. Evans, Claudio R. Frischtak, and Paulo Bastos Tigre, 1–37. Research Series no. 85. Berkeley: University of California, International and Area Studies.
———. 1995. *Embedded Autonomy: States and Industrial Transformation*. Princeton: Princeton University Press.
Evans, Peter B., Claudio R. Frischtak, and Paulo Bastos Tigre, eds. 1992. *High Technology and Third World Industrialization: Brazilian Computer Policy in Comparative Perspective*. Research Series no. 85. Berkeley: University of California, International and Area Studies.
Evans, Peter B., and Michael Timberlake. 1980. "Dependence, Inequality and the Growth of the Tertiary: A Comparative Analysis of Less Developed Countries." *American Sociological Review* 45: 531–52.
Fadul, Anamaria, and Joseph Straubhaar. 1991. "Communications, Culture, and Informatics in Brazil: The Current Challenges." In *Transnational Communications: Wiring the Third World*, ed. Gerald Sussman and John A. Lent, 214–33. Newbury Park, Calif.: Sage.
Fanon, Frantz. 1968. *The Wretched of the Earth*. New York: Grove Press.
Farias, Andréa. 2000. "Lei de TI enfrenta novas pressoes." *Computerworld*, 10 January.
Farnsworth, Clyde H. 1987. "Reagan Imposes Punitive Tariffs against Brazil." *New York Times*, 14 November, p. A38.

Fejes, Fred. 1983. "The U.S. in Third World Communications: Latin America, 1900–1945." *Journalism Monographs* 86: 1–28.
Feketekuty, Geza. 1988. *International Trade in Services: An Overview and Blueprint for Negotiations*. Cambridge: Ballinger.
———. 1992. *The New Trade Agenda*. Washington, D.C.: Group of Thirty.
Feketekuty, Geza, and Jonathan D. Aronson. 1984. "Restrictions on Trade in Communication and Information Services." *The Information Society* 2: 217–47.
Ferreira, Aldo Soares. 1992. "O contrabando e a reserva de mercado na informática." *O Estado de São Paulo*, 3 February, p. 4.
Firebaugh, Glenn. 1992. "Growth Effects of Foreign and Domestic Investment." *American Journal of Sociology* 98, no. 1: 105–30.
Flaherty, David H. 1989. *Protecting Privacy in Surveillance Societies: The Federal Republic of Germany, Sweden, France, Canada, and the United States*. Chapel Hill: University of North Carolina Press.
Foucault, Michel. 1970. *The Order of Things: An Archeology of the Human Sciences*. New York: Vintage Books.
———. 1978. *The History of Sexuality. Volume I: An Introduction*. Trans. Robert Hurley. New York: Vintage Books.
———. 1980. *Power/Knowledge: Selected Interviews and Other Writings, 1972–1977*. Trans. Colin Gordon, Leo Marshall, John Mepham, and Kate Super. New York: Pantheon Books.
Fowler, Mark S. 1985. "Free Markets for Telecommunications: U.S. View." *Transnational Data Report* 8 (June): 220–24.
Frank, André Gunder. 1967. *Capitalism and Underdevelopment in Latin America*. New York: Monthly Review Press.
Fregni, Edson. 1987. "Building Endogenous Data Capacities in Brazil." In *Information Economy and Development*, ed. Dorothy Riddle. Bonn: Friedrich Ebert Stiftung.
Fritsch, Winston. 1992. "Informatics Policy in the New Industrial Strategy: A Reform Proposal." In *High Technology and Third World Industrialization: Brazilian Computer Policy in Comparative Perspective*, ed. Peter B. Evans, Claudio R. Frischtak, and Paulo Bastos Tigre, 144–64. Research Series no. 85. Berkeley: University of California, International and Area Studies.
Fujii, Hiroshi. 1987a. "Acordo cooperativo distância licenciamento do DOS." *Data News*, 28 September, p. 10.
———. 1987b. "Retaliações: O que pensam as entidades." *Data News*, 23 November, p. 10.
———. 1987c. "Retaliaçoes, só em 1988." *Data News*, 14 December, p. 10.
———. 1987d. "Vale a pena vetar o licenciamento do DOS?" *Data News*, 14 December, pp. 10–11.
Gazeta Mercantil. 2001. "Lei de informática atrai investimentos ao pais." *Gazeta Mercantil*, 12 January.
Gereffi, Gary. 1989. "Rethinking Development Theory: Insights from East Asia and Latin America." *Sociological Forum* 4, no. 4: 505–33.
———. 1990. "Paths of Industrialization: An Overview." In *Manufacturing Miracles: Paths of*

Industrialization in Latin America and East Asia, ed. Gary Gereffi and Donald L. Wyman, 3–31. Princeton: Princeton University Press.

Gereffi, Gary, and Miguel Korzeniewicz, eds. 1994. *Commodity Chains and Global Capitalism.* Westport, Conn.: Praeger.

Gibson-Graham, J. K. 1996. *The End of Capitalism (As We Knew It): A Feminist Critique of Political Economy.* Malden, Mass.: Blackwell.

Giurlani, Silvia. 1992. "Medidas do governo não entusiasmam empresários." *Data News,* 5 May, p. 3.

Gordon, Avery F. 1997. *Ghostly Matters: Haunting and the Sociological Imagination.* Minneapolis: University of Minnesota Press.

Greenberg, Allen. 1985. "Impasse? The U.S. Stake in Third World Telecommunications Development." *Journal of Communication* (Spring): 42–49.

Grieco, Joseph. 1984. *Between Dependency and Autonomy: India's Experience with the International Computer Industry.* Berkeley: University of California Press.

Guaranys, José Fernando Halfeld dos. 1992. "Textos em negociação no GATT: Conheca a posição da Abicomp." *O Estado de São Paulo,* 20 January, p. 4.

Guback, Thomas, ed. 1994. *Counterclockwise: Perspectives on Communication/Dallas Smythe.* Boulder, Colo.: Westview Press.

Haggard, Stephan, and Robert Kaufman. 1992. Institutions and Economic Adjustment. In *The Politics of Economic Adjustment,* ed. Stephan Haggard and Robert Kaufman, 3–37. Princeton: Princeton University Press.

Harvey, David. 1989. *The Condition of Postmodernity.* Oxford: Basil Blackwell.

———. 1995. "Globalization in Question." *Rethinking Marxism* 8, no. 4: 1–17.

Helleiner, Eric. 1999. "Sovereignty, Territoriality, and the Globalization of Finance." In *States and Sovereignty in the Global Economy,* ed. David A. Smith, Dorothy J. Solinger, and Steven C. Topik, 138–57. London: Routledge.

Henderson, Jeffrey. 1993. "Against the Economic Orthodoxy: On the Making of the East Asian Miracle." *Economy and Society* 22, no. 2: 200–217.

Herédia, Mari-Angela. 1987a. "Roberto Campos abre baterías contra projeto de software." *Data News,* 10 August, p. 6.

———. 1987b. "Projeto de software: Muitas críticas e nenhum consenso." *Data News,* 17 August, p. 7.

———. 1987c. "A última cartada do governo em um jogo decisivo." *Data News,* 31 August, p. 6.

———. 1987d. "Com base na similaridade, SEI veta o MS-DOS da Microsoft." *Data News,* 5 October, pp. 6–7.

———. 1987e. "Veto a DOS traz de volta as ameaças norte-americanas." *Data News,* 12 October, p. 6.

———. 1987f. "Projeto de software, o expectativa continua." *Data News,* 2 November, p. 7.

———. 1987g. "Retaliações: Agora ficou mais difícil para o pais." *Data News,* 9 November, p. 6.

———. 1987h. "Novos desencontros no jogo das retaliações." *Data News,* 16 November, p. 6.

———. 1987i. "Os ajustes finais na lei de software." *Data News,* 16 November, p. 3.

———. 1987j. "Projeto de proteção juridica: Agora nas mãos dos deputados." *Data News*, 23 November, p. 18.

———. 1987k. "Retaliaçoes: Semana agitada, sem definição." *Data News*, 23 November, p. 6.

———. 1987l. "Na constituinte, A opção verde-amarela." *Data News*, 23 November, p. 7.

———. 1987m. "Presidente sanciona lei de software com vetos." *Data News*, 28 December, p. 6.

Hettne, Bjorn. 1995. *International Political Economy: Understanding Global Disorder*. London: Zed.

Hirschman, Albert O. 1987. "The Political Economy of Latin American Development: Seven Exercises in Retrospection." *Latin American Research Review* 22, no. 3: 7–36.

Hirst, Paul, and Grahame Thompson. 1992. "The Problem of 'Globalization': International Economic Relations, National Economic Management and the Formation of Trading Blocs." *Economy and Society* 21, no. 4: 357–96.

———. 1999. *Globalization in Question*. Malden, Mass.: Blackwell.

Hoogvelt, Ankie. 1997. *Globalization and the Postcolonial World: The New Political Economy of Development*. Baltimore: Johns Hopkins University Press.

Inter-American Development Bank (IADB). 1988. *Economic and Social Progress in Latin America*. Washington, D.C.: Inter-American Development Bank.

Intergovernmental Bureau for Informatics (IBI). 1982. "Latin American Regional Meeting on Transborder Data Flows." Rome: Intergovernmental Bureau for Informatics.

Iritani, Evelyn. 1999. "Storm Is Brewing in Seattle over Trade." *Los Angeles Times*, 14 November, pp. A1, A28.

IT Web. 2001. "FHC sanciona Lei de Informática, vetando artigo que prejudicaria São Paulo." *IT Web*, 11 January.

Jaikumar, Ramchandran. 1986. "Post-industrial Manufacturing." *Harvard Business Review* 64 (November/December): 69–76.

Jaramillo, Felipe. 1989. "Multilateral Negotiations on Trade in Services: Perspectives for the Future." In *Services and Development: The Role of Foreign Direct Investment and Trade*, ed. United Nations Centre on Transnational Corporations, 163–66. New York: United Nations.

Jessop, Bob. 1988. "Regulation Theory, Post-Fordism and the State: More Than a Reply to Werner Bonefield." *Capital and Class*, no. 34: 147–68.

———. 1990a. *State Theory: Putting Capitalist States in Their Place*. University Park: Pennsylvania State University Press.

———. 1990b. "Regulation Theories in Retrospect and Prospect." *Economy and Society* 19, no. 2: 153–216.

Jimenez, Carla. 2001. "Empresas defendem veto na Lei de Informática." *O Estado de São Paulo*, 11 January.

Jimenez, Carla, and Helena Akikusa. 2001. "Empresas garantem investimentos no pais." *O Estado de São Paulo*, 12 January.

Jornal de Comércio. 2001a. "Criação da Alca reformula estratégias de eletroeletronicos e bens de capital." *Jornal de Comércio*, 14 January.

———. 2001b. "Lei de Informática." *Jornal de Comércio*, 14 January.

Kahler, Miles. 1990. "Orthodoxy and Its Alternatives: Explaining Approaches to Stabilization and Adjustment." In *Economic Crisis and Policy Choice: The Politics of Adjustment in the Third World*, ed. Joan M. Nelson, 33–61. Princeton: Princeton University Press.

Kakabadse, Mario A. 1987. *International Trade in Services: Prospects for Liberalisation in the 1990s*. London: Croom Helm.

Kane, Michael J. 1985. "The Impact of Transborder Data Flow Regulation on Large U.S. Corporations." *Transnational Data Report* 8 (September): 315–16.

Katzenbach, Nicholas de. 1985. "Framing Telecommunication Policy: An IBM View." *Transnational Data Report* 8 (April): 167–68.

Kelly, Margaret, Naheed Kirmani, Miranda Xafa, Clemens Boonekamp, and Peter Winglee. 1988. *Issues and Developments in International Trade Policy*. Washington, D.C.: International Monetary Fund.

Krasner, Stephen D. 1985. *Structural Conflict: The Third World against Global Liberalism*. Berkeley: University of California Press.

———. 1999. "Globalization and Sovereignty." In *States and Sovereignty in the Global Economy*, ed. David A. Smith, Dorothy J. Solinger, and Steven C. Topik, 34–52. London: Routledge.

Langer, Erick D. 1989. "Generations of Scientists and Engineers: Origins of the Computer Industry in Brazil." *Latin American Research Review* 24, no. 2: 95–111.

Latin America Regional Reports Brazil. 1987. "U.S. Threatens Trade Sanctions." *Latin America Regional Reports Brazil*, 26 November, pp. 4–5.

———. 1988. "Government Seeks to Avert U.S. Sanctions." *Latin America Regional Reports Brazil*, 7 January, p. 6.

Lemos, Salette. 1987. "Soberania ou interesse, O que fala mais alto?" *Data News*, 23 November, p. 6.

Lewis, Paul H. 1997. "Political Scholarship." *Journal of Interamerican Studies and World Affairs* 38 (Winter): 193–200.

Lewis, Peter. 1989. "Cracking Down on Software Pirates." *New York Times*, 9 July.

Lipietz, Alain. 1986. "New Tendencies in the International Division of Labor: Regimes of Accumulation and Modes of Regulation." In *Production, Work, Territory: The Geographical Anatomy of Industrial Capitalism*, ed. Allen J. Scott and Michael Storper, 16–40. Boston: Allen and Unwin.

Lobo, Ana Paula. 2000a. "Sai acordo da lei de informática no Senado." *Computerworld*, 12 January.

———. 2000b. "MCT quer incentivar P&D nas pequenas e médias empresas através da lei de TI." *Computerworld*, 18 January.

Lyon, David. 1988. *The Information Society: Issues and Illusions*. New York: Polity Press.

Lyotard, Jean-François. 1984. *The Postmodern Condition: A Report on Knowledge*. Minneapolis: University of Minnesota Press.

Machlup, Fritz. 1962. *The Production and Distribution of Knowledge in the United States*. Princeton: Princeton University Press.

Maciel, Ricardo Oliveira. 1981. "Impact of the Information Industry and Transborder Data Flows on the Brazilian Economy." Paper presented at the first meeting of the Interna-

tional Working Groups for the Analysis of Economic and Commercial Impacts of Transborder Data Flows, Paris, April.
Mahlmeister, Ana Luiza. 1987. "Sistemas operacionais dividem os fabricantes." *Dados e Ideias* (May): 42–44.
Mahoney, Eileen. 1988. "The Intergovernmental Bureau for Informatics: An International Organization within the Changing World Political Economy." In *The Political Economy of Information*, ed. Vincent Mosco and Janet Wasco, 297–315. Madison: University of Wisconsin Press.
Manzoni, Ralphe. 1999a. "Lei de informática vira colcha de retalhos." *Computerworld*, 22 November.
———. 1999b. "Indústria critica nova fórmula de P&D." *Computerworld*, 11 November.
———. 2000. "Disputas regionais emperram lei de TI." *Computerworld*, 27 July.
Marconini, Mario. 1990. "The Uruguay Round Negotiations on Services: An Overview." In *The Uruguay Round: Services in the World Economy*, ed. Karl P. Sauvant and Patrick A. Messerlin, 19–26. Washington, D.C.: World Bank.
Maturo, Jussara. 1987a. "Aprovada a lei, cuidados dos usuários." *Data News*, 6 July, pp. 6–7.
———. 1987b. "Assespro: Taxação sobre os estrangeiros." *Data News*, 10 August, p. 19.
———. 1987c. "Equivalência ou taxação: As opções para o projeto de lei." *Data News*, 31 August, p. 16.
McMichael, Philip. 2000a. *Development and Social Change: A Global Perspective*. Thousand Oaks, Calif.: Pine Forge Press.
———. 2000b. "Globalisation: Trend or Project?" In *Global Political Economy: Contemporary Theories*, ed. Rolan Palan, 100–113. London: Routledge.
Melody, William H. 1991. "The Information Society: The Transnational Economic Context and Its Implications." In *Transnational Communications: Wiring the Third World*, ed. Gerald Sussman and John A. Lent, 27–41. Newbury Park, Calif.: Sage.
Memmi, Albert. 1965. *The Colonizer and the Colonized*. New York: Orion.
Ministério da Ciência e Tecnologia. 1999. *Panorama do setor de informática*. Available from http://www.mct.gov.br/temas/info/Dsi/panorama.htm. Accessed 9 January 2001.
Mitchell, W. J. T. 1995. "Postcolonial Culture, Postimperial Criticism." In *The Post-colonial Studies Reader*, ed. Bill Ashcroft, Gareth Griffiths, and Helen Tiffin, 475–79. New York: Routledge.
"Mixed Reaction to New Software Law." 1988. *Latin America Regional Reports Brazil*, 17 March, p. 4.
Moody, Kim. 1997. *Workers in a Lean World: Unions in the International Economy*. London: Verso.
Murphy, Brian M. 1986. *The International Politics of New Information Technology*. New York: St. Martin's Press.
"Nationalists Decry Software Decision." 1986. *Latin America Weekly Report*, 11 September, pp. 4–5.
Neto, Raul Fagundes. 1992. "PS/2 vive momento decisivo no Brasil." *Data News*, 23 June, p. 6.
Nicolaides, Phedon. 1989. *Liberalizing Service Trade: Strategies for Success*. London: Royal Institute of International Affairs.

Nunes, Artur Pereira. 1992. "As mudanças no setor de informática: 1984 a 1991." *O Estado de São Paulo*, 16 March.
O'Brien, Rita Cruise, ed. 1983. *Information, Economics, and Power*. London: Hodder and Stoughton.
O'Connor, Walter F. 1986. "Information—The Next Trade Problem?" *Data Communication* (April): 185–89.
O'Connor, Walter F., and S. Thomas Moser. 1987. "Trade Barriers to Information." *CFO* 3, no. 7: 2–3.
O Estado de São Paulo. 2001a. "FHC veta restrição na Lei da Informatica." *O Estado de São Paulo*, 11 January.
——. 2001b. "Empresas garantem investimentos no pais." *O Estado de São Paulo*, 12 January.
Organization for Economic Cooperation and Development (OECD). 1979. "Transborder Data Flows and the Protection of Privacy." Paris: Organization for Economic Cooperation and Development.
Packenham, Robert A. 1992. *The Dependency Movement: Scholarship and Politics in Development Studies*. Cambridge: Harvard University Press.
Panorama Brasil. 2001. "Abinee está em Brasilia e apóia veto ao artigo 10 da lei de informática." *Panorama Brasil*, 11 January.
Peñaranda, César N. 1989. "The Services Sector in the Andean Pact Countries: Diagnostic and General Outline for Actions of Co-operation and Integration." In *Services and Development: The Role of Foreign Direct Investment and Trade*, ed. United Nations Centre on Transnational Corporations, 122–31. New York: United Nations.
Pereira de Lucena, Carlos. 1990. "O software na política nacional de informática." Unpublished paper, Universidade Estadual de Campinas.
Piera, Fernando. 1986. "Informatics: Development over Dependence." *Transnational Data and Communications Report* 9 (April): 17–18.
Piore, Michael J., and Charles F. Sabel. 1984. *The Second Industrial Divide: Possibilities for Prosperity*. New York: Basic Books.
Pipe, G. Russell. 1983. "Latin America and TDF: Regional TDF Agreement Wanted." *Transnational Data Report* 6 (June): 193–95.
——. 1985. "South-South Cooperation: The Solution?" *Transnational Data Report* 8 (July): 227–28.
Portes, Alejandro. 1996. "Embedded Autonomy: States and Industrial Transformation" (book review). *Contemporary Sociology* 25: 175–76.
——. 1997. "Neoliberalism and the Sociology of Development: Emerging Trends and Unanticipated Facts." *Population and Development Review* 23, no. 2: 229–59.
Presidência da República. 2001. "Sancionada Lei de Informática—11.01.01." Brasília: Presidência da República.
Queiroz, Luiz. 2000a. "Ericsson: Investimentos superam percentual da lei de TI." *Computerworld*, 29 June.
——. 2000b. "Governo reedita pela 11a vez MP da lei de TI." *Computerworld*, 31 July.
——. 2000c. "Relator da lei de informática contraria governo." *Computerworld*, 1 August.

———. 2000d. "Lei de TI: Saussuna quer nova reunião com o governo." *Computerworld*, 2 August.

———. 2000e. "Nova legislação busca equilíbrio." *Computerworld*, 3 August.

———. 2001. "Abinee lamenta posicionamento da indústra de Manaus." *Computerworld*, 11 January.

Rada, Juan F. 1981. "The Microelectronics Revolution: Implications for the Third World." *Development Dialogue* 2: 41–67.

Rahnema, Majid, and Victoria Bawtree. 1997. *The Post-Development Reader*. London: Zed Books.

Regan, Priscilla M. 1992. "The Globalization of Privacy: Implications of Recent Changes in Europe." Paper presented at the 87th annual meeting of the American Sociological Association, Pittsburgh, August.

Richardson, John B. 1989. "The Characteristics of a Successful Agreement on Trade in Services." In *Services and Development: The Role of Foreign Direct Investment and Trade*, ed. United Nations Centre on Transnational Corporations, 175–81. New York: United Nations.

Richardson, John B., and Jonathan Scheele. 1989. "Appropriate Regulation and Other Concepts." In *Services and Development: The Role of Foreign Direct Investment and Trade*, ed. United Nations Centre on Transnational Corporations, 151–55. New York: United Nations.

Riding, Alan. 1986. "U.S., Brazil Computer Dispute Brews." *New York Times*, 5 May.

———. 1987. "Brazil Exporters Move to Stop U.S. Sanctions." *New York Times*, 23 November.

———. 1988. "Brazil Accepts One U.S. Software Product." *New York Times*, 25 January.

Ripper, Mario Dias. 1993. "Corporate Strategies Post-Market Reserve." Paper presented at "The Future of Information Technology in Brazil" conference, University of California, Berkeley, January.

Rocha, Carlos. 1992. "Governo precisa reestruturar seu poder de compra." *O Estado de São Paulo*, 30 March, p. 4.

Rostow, W. W. 1960. *The Stages of Economic Growth: A Noncommunist Manifesto*. London: Cambridge University Press.

Rustin, Michael. 1989. "The Politics of Post-Fordism: or, The Trouble with 'New Times.'" *New Left Review*, no. 175: 54–77.

"Sarney poderá rever sua decisão de vetar emendas do Conin." 1986. *O Estado de São Paulo*, 28 September.

Sassen, Saskia. 1988. *The Mobility of Labor and Capital: A Study in International Investment and Labor Flow*. Cambridge: Cambridge University Press.

———. 1991. *The Global City: New York, London, Tokyo*. Princeton, N.J.: Princeton University Press.

———. 1999. "Embedding the Global in the National: Implications for the Role of the State." In *States and Sovereignty in the Global Economy*, ed. David A. Smith, Dorothy J. Solinger, and Steven C. Topik, 158–71. London: Routledge.

Sauvant, Karl P. 1984a. *Trade and Foreign Direct Investment in Data Services*. Boulder, Colo.: Westview Press.

———. 1984b. "Transborder Data Flows: Importance, Impact, Policies." *Information Services and Use* 4: 3–30.
———. 1986. *International Transactions in Services: The Politics of Transborder Data Flows.* Boulder, Colo.: Westview Press.
Sayer, Andrew. 1989. "Postfordism in Question." *International Journal of Urban and Regional Research* 13, no. 4: 666–95.
Schiller, Dan. 1982. *Telematics and Government.* Norwood, Conn.: Ablex.
Schoonmaker, Sara. 1993. "Trading On-Line: Information Flows in Advanced Capitalism." *The Information Society* 9: 39–49.
———. 1994. "Capitalism and the Code: A Critique of Baudrillard's Third-Order Simulacrum." In *Baudrillard: A Critical Reader,* ed. Douglas Kellner, 168–88. Cambridge: Basil Blackwell.
———. 1995a. "Regulation Theory and the Politics of Global Restructuring." *Current Perspectives in Social Theory* 15: 213–44.
———. 1995b. "High-Tech Development Politics: New Strategies and Persistent Structures in Brazilian Informatics." *Sociological Quarterly* 36, no. 2: 369–95.
———. 1996. "Annihilating Space with Time: Digital Trade, Services, and Capitalist Development." Paper presented at the 89th annual meeting of the American Sociological Association, New York, August.
———. 1997. "Postcolonial/Postimperial: Tracing Power, History, Capitalism." Paper presented at the 68th annual meeting of the Pacific Sociological Association, San Diego, April.
Secretaria de Ciência e Tecnologia (DEPIN). 1992. *Panorama do setor de informática.* Brasília: Secretaria de Ciência e Tecnologia.
Serro, Rosane. 1987a. "O peso da Assesspro no projeto de software." *Data News,* 17 August, p. 3.
———. 1987b. "Assespro e Sucesu entregam sugestões ao Senado." *Data News,* 31 August, pp. 16–17.
Shukla, Shrirang P. 1989a. "The Regulatory and Policy Framework for Services: Comments." In *Services and Development: The Role of Foreign Direct Investment and Trade,* ed. United Nations Centre on Transnational Corporations, 156–58. New York: United Nations.
———. 1989b. "International Discussions on Trade in Services: The Perspective of Developing Countries." In *Services and Development: The Role of Foreign Direct Investment and Trade,* ed. United Nations Centre on Transnational Corporations, 170–74. New York: United Nations.
Shultz, George P. 1986. "Consequences of the Age of Information." *Transnational Data and Communications Report* 9 (May): 16–19.
Sklair, Leslie. 1994. "Capitalism and Development in Global Perspective." In *Capitalism and Development,* ed. Leslie Sklair, 165–85. New York: Routledge.
Slemon, Stephen. 1995. "The Scramble for Post-colonialism." In *The Post-colonial Studies Reader,* ed. Bill Ashcroft, Gareth Griffiths, and Helen Tiffin, 45–52. New York: Routledge.
Smith, Anthony. 1980. *The Geopolitics of Information: How Western Culture Dominates the World.* New York: Oxford University Press.

Smith, David A., and Douglas R. White. 1992. "Structure and Dynamics of the Global Economy: Network Analysis of International Trade, 1965–1980." *Social Forces* 70, no. 4: 857–93.

Stallings, Barbara. 1990. "The Role of Foreign Capital in Economic Development." In *Manufacturing Miracles: Paths of Industrialization in Latin America and East Asia*, ed. Gary Gereffi and Donald L. Wyman, 55–89. Princeton: Princeton University Press.

———. 1992. "International Influence on Economic Policy: Debt, Stabilization, and Structural Reform." In *The Politics of Economic Adjustment*, ed. Stephan Haggard and Robert R. Kaufman, 41–88. Princeton: Princeton University Press.

Sussman, Gerald, and John A. Lent. 1991. "Introduction: Critical Perspectives on Communication and Third World Development." In *Transnational Communications: Wiring the Third World*, ed. Gerald Sussman and John A. Lent. 27–41. Newbury Park, Calif: Sage.

Tapscott, Don. 1996. *The Digital Economy: Promise and Peril in the Age of Networked Intelligence*. New York: McGraw-Hill.

Tigre, Paulo Bastos. 1983. *Technology and Competition in the Brazilian Computer Industry*. New York: St. Martin's Press.

———. 1992. "Current Dilemmas and Future Options for Informatics Policy." In *High Technology and Third World Industrialization: Brazilian Computer Policy in Comparative Perspective*, ed. Peter B. Evans, Claudio R. Frischtak, and Paulo Bastos Tigre, 117–43. Research Series no. 85. Berkeley: University of California, International and Area Studies.

———. 1993. "Brazil's IT Sector—The Profile in 1992." Paper presented at "The Future of Information Technology in Brazil" conference, University of California, Berkeley, January.

Transnational Data Report. 1985. "Nations Restricting TDF Run Risks." *Transnational Data Report* 8 (April): 170.

Transnational Data Reporting Service. 1980. "Strategic Responses to Regulation of Transnational Data Flows." Washington, D.C.: Transnational Data Reporting Service.

Tucker, Robert C. 1978. *The Marx-Engels Reader*. New York: W. W. Norton.

United Nations Centre on Transnational Corporations (UNCTC). 1982. *Transnational Corporations and Transborder Data Flows: A Technical Paper*. New York: United Nations.

———. 1983. *Transborder Data Flows and Brazil*. New York: United Nations.

———. 1988. *Transnational Corporations in World Development: Trends and Prospects*. New York: United Nations.

———. 1990. *Transnational Corporations, Services and the Uruguay Round*. New York: United Nations.

U.S. House Committee on Energy and Commerce. 1981. Hearings on Telecommunications and Information Products and Services in International Trade before the Subcommittee on Telecommunications, Consumer Protection, and Finance of the Committee on Energy and Commerce. 97th Cong., 1st sess., 29 April and 22 July 1981. Washington, D.C.: U.S. Government Printing Office.

———. 1986. *Report on Unfair Foreign Trade Practices: Barriers to U.S. Exports by the Subcommittee on Oversight and Investigations of the Committee on Energy and Commerce Together with Reports Prepared by the Congressional Research Service*. 99th Cong., 2d sess. Washington, D.C.: U.S. Government Printing Office.

———. 1988. Hearing on Informatics Trade Problems with Brazil before the Subcommittee on Commerce, Consumer Protection, and Competitiveness of the Committee on Energy and Commerce. 100th Cong., 1st sess., 15 July 1987. Washington, D.C.: U.S. Government Printing Office.

U.S. House Committee on Foreign Affairs. 1982. Hearings and Markup on the International Communication and Reorganization Act before the Committee on Foreign Affairs and Its Subcommittees on International Operations and on H.R. 1957. 97th Cong., 1st sess., 8, 13, and 14 July 1981. Washington, D.C.: U.S. Government Printing Office.

U.S. House Committee on Government Operations. 1981. Hearings on the International Communications Reorganization Act of 1981 before a Subcommittee of the Committee on Government Operations. 97th Cong., 1st sess., 31 March and 2 April 1981. Washington, D.C.: U.S. Government Printing Office.

———. 1982. Hearings on International Telecommunications and Information Policy before the Subcommittee of the Committee on Government Operations. 97th Cong., 1st and 2d sess., 2 December 1981 and 29 April 1982. Washington, D.C.: U.S. Government Printing Office.

———. 1991. Hearings on Data Protection, Computers, and Changing Information Practices before the Government Information, Justice, and Agriculture Subcommittee of the Committee on Government Operations. 101st Cong., 2d sess., 16 May 1990. Washington, D.C.: U.S. Government Printing Office.

———. 1992. Hearings on Domestic and International Data Protection Issues before the Government Information, Justice, and Agriculture Subcommittee of the Committee on Government Operations. 102d Cong., 1st sess., 10 April and 17 October 1991. Washington, D.C.: U.S. Government Printing Office.

U.S. House Committee on Ways and Means. 1984. Hearing on Trade Reciprocity Legislation before the Subcommittee on International Economic Policy and Trade of the Committee on Ways and Means. 98th Cong., 1st sess., 2 and 9 November 1983 and 2 March 1984. Washington, D.C.: U.S. Government Printing Office.

———. 1986a. Hearing on Trade Policy Agenda and Outlook for 1986 before the Subcommittee on Trade of the Committee on Ways and Means. 99th Cong., 2d sess., 20 February 1986. Washington, D.C.: U.S. Government Printing Office.

———. 1986b. Hearing on Telecommunications Trade Act of 1985 before the Subcommittee on Trade of the Committee on Ways and Means. 99th Cong., 2d sess., 11 and 13 March 1986. Washington, D.C.: U.S. Government Printing Office.

———. 1989. Hearings on National Trade Policy Agenda before the Subcommittee on Trade of the Committee on Ways and Means. 100th Cong., 2d sess., 29 February and 26 April 1989. Washington, D.C.: U.S. Government Printing Office.

U.S. Senate Committee on Commerce, Science, and Transportation. 1983. *Long Range Goals in International Telecommunications and Information: An Outline for United States Policy.* 98th Cong., 1st sess. Washington, D.C.: U.S. Government Printing Office.

U.S. Trade Representative. 1986. *National Trade Estimate: 1986 Report on Foreign Trade Barriers.* Washington, D.C.: U.S. Government Printing Office.

Valor. 2001a. "Texto final mantém possibilidade de SP oferecer incentivo." *Valor,* 12 January.

———. 2001b. "Fernando Henrique defende adoção de uma política industrial adequada." *Valor*, 12 January.

———. 2001c. "Atenção nos componentes." *Valor*, 12 January.

Vessuri, Hebe M. C. 1990. "O inventamos o erramos: The Power of Science in Latin America." *World Development* 18 (November): 1543–53.

"Veto presidencial restabelece texto original sobre 'software.'" 1986. *Jornal do Brasil*, 27 September, p. 4.

Villareal, René. 1990. "The Latin American Strategy of Import Substitution: Failure or Paradigm for the Region?" In *Manufacturing Miracles: Paths of Industrialization in Latin America and East Asia*, ed. Gary Gereffi and Donald L. Wyman, 292–320. Princeton: Princeton University Press.

Wallerstein, Immanuel. 1974. *The Modern World System*. New York: Academic Press.

———. 1999. "States? Sovereignty? The Dilemmas of Capitalists in an Age of Transition." In *States and Sovereignty in the Global Economy*, ed. David A. Smith, Dorothy J. Solinger, and Steven C. Topik, 20–33. London: Routledge.

Walton, John, and David Seddon. 1994. *Free Markets and Food Riots: The Politics of Global Adjustment*. Oxford: Blackwell.

Weber, Max. 1978. *Economy and Society: An Outline of Interpretive Sociology*. Vol. I. Edited by Guenther Roth and Claus Wittich. Berkeley: University of California Press.

Wigand, Rolf T., Carrie Shipley, and Dwayne Shipley. 1984. "Transborder Data Flow, Informatics, and National Policies." *Journal of Communication* 34 (Winter): 153–75.

Wimberly, Dale W. 1990. "Investment Dependence and Alternative Explanations of Third World Mortality: A Cross-National Study." *American Sociological Review* 55: 75–91.

Wood, Stephen. 1989. "The Transformation of Work?" In *The Transformation of Work? Skill, Flexibility, and the Labor Process*, ed. Stephen Wood, 1–43. London: Unwin Hyman.

Worsely, Peter. 1964. *The Three Worlds*. Chicago: University of Chicago Press.

Wright, Robin. 2000. "Clinton Urges Dialogue on Globalization." *Los Angeles Times*, 30 January, pp. A1, A10.

Zanabria, Luzmilla. 1989. "The Policy Framework for Services: Comments." In *Services and Development: The Role of Foreign Direct Investment and Trade*, ed. United Nations Centre on Transnational Corporations, 159–60. New York: United Nations.

Index

ABES (Brazilian Association of Software Firms), 102, 120
ABICOMP (Brazilian Computer and Peripherals Industry Association), 26–27; and transition to open market, 122, 124, 127, 139–41, 143, 145–47, 149–50
ABINEE (Brazilian Association of Electrical and Electronics Industries), 29, 165–66
ADAPSO (Computer Software and Services Industry Association), 99–100
AEA (American Electronics Association), 99–100
Africa and African countries, 14, 21, 47, 48, 64, 88, 185–86
alliances: between Brazilian and foreign firms, 131–37, 142, 146–48, 153; between capital and the state, 133, 144–46
Amazonas (state), 160, 165
Amazon region, 160–61, 163, 165, 170
Apple Computer Corporation, 85–86, 92, 144, 194n8
Archer, Renato, 27, 104, 113
Argentina, 63, 89, 186
Asia and Asian countries, 46–47, 64, 72, 88, 89, 186, 193n1
ASSESPRO (Association of Brazilian Informatics Software and Services Firms), 27, 102, 120
AT&T, 74, 192n3

banks, 12, 34, 53, 56, 62, 112; Brazilian, 108, 135

Belgium, 46, 186
Biddle, A. G. W., 86, 98
Brasoft, 92, 194n1
Brazil, 22, 27–28, 89, 105, 159–65, 170, 186; states and regions of, 29, 114, 152, 160–67, 170
Brazilian Congress, 25, 85, 138, 159–62, 165; House, 101–2, 104, 105; Senate, 97, 100–102, 104–5, 112, 165; and software policy, 90, 95–97, 110
Brazilian constitution, 100, 112
Brazilian government. *See* Brazilian Congress; Brazilian government officials; DEPIN; MCT; SEI
Brazilian government officials, 27–29, 91, 93, 110–11, 119, 121, 167; and transition to open market, 124–27, 138, 143, 151
Brazilian military, 27, 49, 90
Brazilian policies: investigations of, 17–19, 23, 80–81, 83–86, 89–91, 114; mediation of, 94, 96, 105; and Reagan administration, 82, 95, 104, 118, 194n5; suspension of, 96, 97–100
business executives, Brazilian, 26–29, 84, 125–26

Campos, Roberto, 101–2, 103, 104
Canada, 21, 46, 62, 73–74, 76, 186, 193n1
capital, 67, 123, 144, 170, 175. *See also* foreign investment
capital, global, 11–12, 124–25, 133, 147, 170; incentives for, 159, 164–65, 172
capitalism, 2, 5, 7, 9, 174

213

Cardoso, Fernando Henrique, 25, 158–59, 165, 167–70, 180; administration of, 20, 20, 159–60, 163–64, 170
CBEMA (Computer and Business Equipment Manufacturers Association), 85, 99–100
CCIA (Computer and Communications Industry Association), 86, 98
cellular phone industry, 161–63, 167
Collor, Fernando, 19–20, 24, 121, 159; administration of, 122–27, 131–33, 136, 138, 147, 151; and end of 1984 informatics law, 24, 26, 28, 116, 146
Colombia, 64, 186
communications technologies, 5–6, 33, 36–37. *See also* telecommunications
community groups, 184–88
competition, 45, 52, 117, 137; foreign, 15, 61, 73–75, 127, 138; global, 14, 77–78; protection from, 15, 95, 112
competitiveness of United States, 22, 72, 75, 78–80, 83, 86, 178
computer firms, 123, 128; and agreement on policy, 138–39, 147, 149–50; and distribution, 124–25, 131, 134–37, 145, 149–50; and production, 16–17, 124, 133–42, 145, 147–50, 161–62, 166–68; and the state, 133, 137–39, 144–46, 151–52; U.S., 81–85, 96, 98–100, 111, 129, 164, 166. *See also* Apple; Digital; Hewlett-Packard; IBM; NCR; Unisys
computer firms, Brazilian, 23, 92, 105–8, 111, 161, 194*n1*; and alliances with foreign firms, 131–37, 142, 146–48, 153; and 2001 informatics law, 166; and transition to open market, 126, 128–30, 136. *See also* Edisa; Itautec; Scopus; SID
computer industry associations, 102–3. *See also* ABES; ABICOMP; ABINEE; ADAPSO; ASSESPRO; CBEMA; CCIA; MBI
computers: and monitors, 161–63; and operating systems, 105–8, 115, 195*n3*;

prices and sales of, 129–33, 141, 145–46; quality of, 128–29, 131, 145–46
computer technology, 13, 33, 35–36, 76
computer users, 101–4, 111, 125, 134, 136–37, 139; and foreign products, 128–32
conferences, 46–49, 50, 152, 191*n1*
CONIN (National Informatics Council), 94–96, 115
contraband, 20, 24, 128, 137, 141–44, 149–50
copyright, 23, 83, 85, 91, 94–96, 99, 107
cultural values, 6–7, 11, 13, 17, 44, 51, 173; nationalist, 16, 43, 49, 158. *See also* free-market competition; free trade; neoliberalism; sovereignty, national

Datalogica (firm), 92, 194*n1*
deindustrialization, 139–40
denationalization, 12, 120–21, 164–65, 170, 174–76; and shift to open market, 124, 133, 140, 147, 156
DEPIN (Department of Informatics and Automation Policy), 28, 116, 124, 169
deregulation, 74, 75, 122, 192*n3*
development: national, 16–18, 49, 56–58, 68, 94, 100, 183–84; nationalist, 20, 112, 117
development, neoliberal: alternatives to, 25, 171, 184; of Brazilian informatics industry, 18, 28, 91–93, 132, 138, 151, 158–59; of Brazilian software industry, 92, 97, 101–2, 106–7; discourse of, 6, 7, 173; economic, 3, 12, 53, 65–66, 73, 112, 141; resistance to, 184–88; of technology, 16, 72, 108, 112, 158. *See also* neoliberalism; open market, transition to
development policy, 3, 25, 88, 179–81; transition from nationalist to neoliberal, 20, 24, 28–29, 116. *See also* open market, transition to
development project, 43, 45, 49–50, 61, 67
digital advertising, 35–36

Index

Digital (firm), 118–19, 136, 140, 150
digital trade and communication, 20–21, 34, 36–38, 43, 69–70; discourse of, 32–33, 37–38, 54–55
discourse: of Brazilian informatics industry, 18, 28, 91–93, 101–2, 119; of development, 6, 7, 173; of economic policy, 21, 43–44, 123; of free trade, 50, 54, 65, 126; of globalization, 3–9, 11, 17–18, 87–88, 172–73, 175–76, 179–80; nationalist, 16, 18, 158; of national sovereignty, 49–50, 55–56, 61, 65; neoliberal, 5–7, 13, 17–18, 22, 59, 133, 168; and power, 4, 32–33, 66; of services trade, 57, 58–60; of transborder data flows, 44, 49, 50–51
distribution of computer products, 124–25, 131, 134–37, 140–42, 145, 149–50
division of labor, international, 16, 18, 82
Dresser Corporation, 46–47

economic development, 3, 12, 53, 65–66, 73, 112, 141
economic policy. *See* informatics policies, Brazilian
economics, 8, 148, 152; neoclassical, 5–7, 51, 53, 54, 59, 61; neoliberal, 3, 11, 12, 192n3
economy, 12, 53, 68, 187; global, 2, 5–6, 8, 50, 56–57, 60, 87
Edisa (firm), 136, 141–42
efficiency, 41, 42, 73
Escobar, Arturo, 6–8, 25, 39, 51, 54, 126, 173, 183–86
European Community, 42, 62–64, 76, 80, 193n1, 194n9
Europe and European countries, 1, 9, 21, 60–63, 76, 128–29, 185–86. *See also* France; Germany; Spain; United Kingdom; West Germany
Evans, Peter B., 18–20, 83, 194n5; and shift to open market, 132, 134, 137, 142, 144–46, 151
exports, 119–20, 158; Brazilian, 108, 111, 113–15, 132, 167–68; U.S., 73–74, 81, 83–84, 100

First World, 8–9, 16, 30, 172, 186, 192–93n1; and clash with Third World, 18, 33; and services trade, 56, 57–59, 66–68; and transborder data flows, 41, 44–45, 50–51, 53. *See also* Europe; U.S. government
foreign competition, 61, 74, 75, 77, 117, 138; protection from, 95, 112
foreign firms. *See* multinational corporations
foreign investment, 9, 11–12, 36, 52–53, 60, 87, 96, 167; dependence on, 120, 155, 169, 180; facilitation of, 3–4, 25, 67, 73, 123, 163–65, 168; restrictions on, 3–4, 15, 73–74, 76, 82–84, 101; and U.S., 87, 96
Foucault, Michel: discursive theory of, 4, 31–33, 57, 58, 171–72; *History of Sexuality*, 4, 32
France, 46–47, 62, 73–74, 186, 193n1, 195n4
free-market competition, 45, 50, 52, 67
free trade, 11, 18, 53, 60, 88, 123, 173; discourse of, 50, 54, 65, 126; and GATT, 22, 54, 78; U.S. promotion of, 2, 52, 73, 76–77
free-trade zone, 139, 141, 143, 160–63, 165
Fregni, Edson, 107, 115–16, 117, 128
functional equivalency, 97, 101–3, 104–5, 115–16

GATT (General Agreement on Tariffs and Trade), 17, 22, 76, 78, 103, 187, 193n2; discourse of, 54, 57; First World delegates to, 53, 55, 58, 59, 62, 66, 68; former Third World delegates to, 56, 58, 60–61, 63–64, 66–68; and services trade, 57–66, 70–71, 176
Germany, 40–41, 42. *See also* West Germany

Index

Gibson-Graham, J. K., 3–4, 178, 185–86
global economic management, 50, 53, 68. *See also* economy, global
globalization, neoliberal, 3, 75, 172–73; discourse of, 3–9, 11, 13, 17–18, 59, 87–88, 133, 172; economic aspects of, 8–13, 50, 124, 148–49, 173, 175, 179; political aspects of, 8–13, 18, 148, 175–79; process of, 2, 133, 164, 171, 179; resistance to, 13, 171, 185–88; theories of, 6, 10, 117 (*See also* McMichael, Philip; Sassen, Saskia)
globalization project, 22, 43, 50, 53, 61, 66; resistance to, 59, 68; and services trade policy, 57–58, 67
grassroots groups, 2, 184–88
Guaranys, José, 127–28, 145, 146, 152, 156

Hewlett-Packard (firm), 136, 141, 166

IBM (firm), 16, 27, 57, 84, 103, 118, 194*n*7; and transition to open market, 122, 125–26, 129–30, 135, 140, 147
imports, 15, 73, 74, 84, 115, 138, 141; Brazilian, 108, 140, 142, 167; dependence on, 132, 145, 162, 167–69, 180; restrictions on, 78, 82, 85, 96–97, 102, 105, 110–11; tariffs on, 139–42, 144, 149–52, 192–93*n*1; taxes on, 51, 55, 103–4, 115, 143–44, 150, 159–63
India, 22, 54, 62, 64–65, 132, 158
industrialization, 15, 26, 28, 131, 141–42, 145
informatics, definition of, 14, 163–64, 194*n*10
informatics firms, 138, 165, 167–68. *See also* computer firms
informatics industry, Brazilian: development of, 18, 28, 91–93, 101–2, 119, 168–69; preservation of, 127–28, 138, 145; regional tensions over, 159–65, 170. *See also* computer firms, Brazilian; computer industry, Brazilian; development, neoliberal; open market, transition to

informatics law of 1984, 15–16, 94, 110, 116, 159; end of, 19, 24, 26, 28, 116, 122, 124; implementation of, 18–19, 23, 28, 91, 96, 98, 105. *See also* Brazilian policy, investigations of
informatics law of 1991, 24, 138, 159–61
informatics law of 2001, 158–59, 162–68
informatics policies, Brazilian, 14–20, 76, 78, 80–84, 88–89, 95, 108; and concessions to U.S., 96–97, 115, 119, 122; constraints on, 119–21; development of, 28, 117; implementation of, 109, 124, 138–39, 152, 177–78; legacies of, 128, 157–58, 184; support for, 113, 122, 127–28. *See also* Brazilian policy, investigations of; software policy, Brazilian
information dependency, 13–14, 21, 31, 45–48, 50, 120
information technology, 5–6, 37
information trade politics, 17, 20, 21–22, 31, 38–39, 42–44, 53–56
intellectual property, 80, 87, 91–92, 96, 99–100, 107
international agreements, 11–12, 31–32, 61, 66, 79, 104, 179. *See also* GATT
internationalism, 187–88
internationalization, 20, 132, 137, 142
International Monetary Fund, 4, 11, 29, 53, 57, 183, 185
investment, 52–53, 138, 145, 159–66. *See also* foreign investment
Itaú (bank), 108, 135
Itautec (firm), 106, 108, 129, 131, 135, 136

Japan, 9, 62, 79, 80, 113, 124–25, 193*n*1; competition with, 127; policies of, 42, 72, 73–74, 75–76, 86, 194*n*9
joint ventures, 161; during shift to open market, 123, 126, 129–30, 132, 134, 141, 147

Korea, 80, 86, 89, 132, 193*n*1, 194*n*9. *See also* South Korea
Krasner, Stephen D., 12, 170, 176–77

labor movements, 186–88
Latin America and Latin American countries, 13, 63, 88–89, 166, 185–86, 191*n1*, 193*n1*; and GATT, 54, 64, 187; and transborder data flows, 14, 21, 47–48, 50
Lent, Norman F., 85, 98
liberalization of trade, 59–60, 63, 65–67, 76, 87; during shift to open market, 138, 150, 152
licensing accords, 129, 132

Manasterski, Josef, 107, 117
Manaus (city), 139, 141, 143, 160–63, 165
market forces, 2–3, 88
marketing, 35–36, 100, 101, 106–7, 129–30, 133, 136
market laws, 5, 123
market reserve, 15–16, 82, 84, 94, 97, 136; end of, 116, 122, 125–26, 138, 146, 150–51; negotiation of, 96, 113; opposition to, 85, 86, 98, 104; support of, 94, 101, 116
markets, 147; access to, 40, 67–68, 73–74, 81, 99, 118; Brazilian, 81–83, 85–86, 91, 92, 94, 100, 136; foreign, 74, 86–87; open, 2, 8, 24, 52, 73, 121; software, 100, 101, 105–7; U.S., 73, 75, 77, 81–82
Maxwell, William A., 99–100
MBI (Brazilian Informatics Movement), 27, 94–95, 101, 103–4, 108, 120, 195*n2*
MC&A Personal Systems, 130
McMichael, Philip, 11–12, 22, 30, 118, 120, 140, 147
MCT (Ministry of Science and Technology), 29, 107, 109–10
methodology, 25–30
Mexico, 13, 89, 193*n1*
microelectronics, 33–34, 70–71
Microsoft Corporation, 23, 106–7, 109–11, 115, 135, 195*nn3-4*. *See also* MS-DOS
Microtec (firm), 106, 136

minicomputers, 15, 76, 82, 118–19, 135
monopolies, 41, 42, 73, 74, 192*n3*
Motorola (firm), 51–52, 166
MS-DOS, 105–11, 115–16, 119, 122, 195*n3*
Multek (firm), 167–68
multinational corporations, 3–4, 14, 21, 29, 53, 165, 187; and alliances with Brazilian firms, 131–37, 142, 146–48, 153; and conflict with former Third World governments, 32, 39, 48, 82–86, 96, 98–100; and conflict with governments, 41–43, 49, 57, 125–26; foreign subsidiaries of, 45, 46–47, 51, 125–26, 132, 166; and policy, 8, 11, 18, 40; and public telecommunications networks, 40–41; and sales, 128–31; and services trade, 56–58, 67; and transborder data flows, 33, 44–45, 51–52; and transition to open market, 125–26, 128–29; U.S., 74, 81–86, 98–99, 116, 147. *See also* banks; computer firms, U.S.; foreign investment

national development, 16–18, 49, 56–58, 68, 94, 100, 183–84; discourse of, 16, 18, 158
national identity, 49, 90
National Informatics Law. *See* informatics law of 1984
nationalist cultural values, 16, 43, 49, 158
nationalist development strategies, 20, 112, 117
national security, 48, 68, 78
NCR (firm), 129, 136, 147
neoliberalism, 56, 78; and Cardoso regime, 159–60, 163–64; and Collor regime, 20, 116, 123–24, 126–27, 131, 151; discourse of, 5–7, 17–18, 22, 59, 133, 168, 173; and economics, 3, 8, 11, 12, 192*n3*; resistance to, 13, 67–68, 185–88; transition from nationalism to, 20, 24, 28–29, 116
Nigeria, 63, 88, 186
Nunes, Artur Pereira, 124–25, 139–40

open market, transition to, 117, 122–57, 170, 175; and alliances, 132–37, 142, 144–48; and Collor regime, 122–25, 127, 132–33, 136, 138, 147; and contraband, 137, 141–44, 149–50; and distribution, 134–37, 140–42, 145, 149–50; opposition to, 127, 138, 139–40; and policy implementation, 124, 138–39, 141, 152–53; and problems for foreign firms, 128–31; and production, 134–42, 145, 147–50; support for, 125, 126, 137, 139–42, 194$n5$; and tariffs, 139–42, 144, 149–52
operating systems, 105–8, 115, 195$n3$. *See also* MS-DOS

personal computers, 15, 76, 82, 118, 130, 135
Peru, 63, 88–89
Philippines, 64, 89
piracy, 83, 85, 91, 95, 194$n1$; of MS-DOS, 107, 111, 195$n3$
policy, state, 11–12; and telecommunications, 21, 37–38, 40, 41–44; and transborder data flows, 14, 17, 21–22, 47, 48, 50–52, 191$n1$. *See also* informatics policies, Brazilian; software policy, Brazilian; trade barriers
policy implementation, Brazilian: development, 3, 25, 88, 179–81; informatics, 109, 177–78; of 1984 informatics law, 18–19, 23, 28, 91, 96, 98, 105; during shift to open market, 124, 138–39, 141, 152–53
policy making, theory of, 87–89, 93–95, 110–11
political economy, 4, 6, 8–9, 179, 181
politics and globalization, 8–13, 18, 148, 175–79
Porto, José Rubens Doria, 27, 127
postdevelopment perspective, 183–84
poststructuralism, 4, 6–9, 28, 54, 66, 173, 179

power and knowledge, 4, 32–33, 54, 56, 66, 88
power relations, 4, 7, 8, 32–33, 45, 54, 56–57. *See also* Brazilian policy, investigations of; neoliberalism
privacy, 46, 48, 49
producer services, 10, 36
production, 6–8, 54, 122, 158, 178; of Brazilian informatics goods, 16–17, 124, 133–42, 145, 147–50, 161–62, 166–68; globalization of, 9, 10
protectionism, 59, 74, 86, 100, 105, 118
protest, 1, 184–88
public telecommunications networks, 40–42

Reagan, Ronald, 78; administration of, 58, 63; and investigations of Brazilian policy, 17, 80–82, 85, 89–90, 95–100, 104, 118, 194$n5$; and sanctions, 111–13
recession, economic, 123, 137
regulations, 9, 32; dismantling of, 124, 128, 147, 179; national, 11, 31, 47–48, 55, 57, 72, 76. *See also* trade barriers
research and development, 77, 94, 97, 131, 133, 135, 138; investment in, 159, 161–63
restrictions, 40, 42, 75, 81, 138; on foreign investment, 3–4, 15, 73–74, 76, 82–84, 101; on imports, 78, 85, 96–97, 102, 105, 110–11, 115
Rocha, José Ezil Veiga da, 27, 92–93, 109, 111

sanctions, trade, 23–24, 98, 111–15, 119; suspension of, 116, 122; threat of, 17, 63, 96, 104–5
São Paulo (city), 130, 163, 170
São Paulo (state), 114, 160, 162–67
Sardenberg, Ronaldo, 167
Sarney, President, 94, 95, 96, 98, 115–16
Sassen, Saskia, 10–13, 117, 153, 173–74; and denationalization, 120, 124, 133, 140, 147, 156, 170

Index

Scartezini, Vanda, 162, 164
Scopus Company, 105–11, 115, 129, 195$n3$
Seattle, 1, 187–88
SEI (Special Secretariat of Informatics), 28, 85, 94, 97, 101–4, 116, 124; and MS-DOS, 107, 109–10
services trade, 37, 56, 67–68; discourse of, 57, 58–60; and GATT, 57–66, 70–71, 176
SID (firm), 129–30, 136
Sisne (operating system), 105–8, 115, 195$n3$
Smith, Michael B., 81–82, 98
social movements, 13, 184–88
software, 23, 83, 85, 87, 158; functional equivalency of, 97, 101–3, 104–5, 115–16; marketing of, 100, 101, 106–7
software industry, Brazilian, 92, 95, 97, 101, 102–3
software policy, Brazilian, 91–121, 106–7, 181–82; criticism of, 100–104; and functional equivalency, 97, 101–5, 115–16; implementation of, 120–21; investigation of, 94, 96–100, 105, 114, 118; and MS-DOS, 106–11, 115–16, 119; and property rights, 93; and sanctions, 111–16; and U.S. demands, 91–92, 95–96
South Korea, 72, 186. *See also* Korea
sovereignty, national, 12–13, 68, 90, 170; challenges to, 41, 91, 177; as cultural value, 16–17, 39, 45, 145; discourse of, 49–50, 55–56, 61, 65; and transborder data flows, 46, 47–48
Soviet Union, former, 46–47
Spain, 46, 186
Stallings, Barbara, 87–89, 93–95, 110–11, 120, 179, 181–82
state: and computer firms, 133, 137–39, 144–46, 151–52; and policy implementation, 24–25. *See also* informatics industry, Brazilian; informatics law of 1984; informatics policies, Brazilian

structural adjustment, 87–88, 185, 187
SUCESU (Society of Computer and Subsidiary Equipment Users), 27, 102–3, 120

Taiwan, 72, 186, 193$n1$
Tápias, Alcides, 159, 167
tariffs, 86, 139–42, 144, 149–52, 192–93$n1$
Tavares, Cristina, 97, 102
taxation, 51, 55, 103–4, 115, 138, 143–44, 150
tax breaks, 159–63
technological autonomy, 145–46
technology: development of, 16, 72, 80, 108, 112, 158; foreign, 15, 123–24. *See also* development, neoliberal; informatics industry, Brazilian; multinational corporations
telecommunications, 15, 21, 31, 40–43, 66, 74, 192$n3$; and integration with computer technology, 33–34, 36, 37–38, 43–44; and policy, 21, 37–38, 40, 41–44
Third World, former, 3, 9, 30; and development policy, 3, 25, 88; and imports, 73, 78, 84, 192–93$n1$; and information dependency, 13–14, 31, 47; and services trade, 56, 58, 60, 63–68; and struggles with First World, 8, 17, 33, 186; and transborder data flows, 44–45, 48, 53. *See also* Africa; Asia; India
trade, international, 7, 21–22, 56–57; liberalization of, 59–60, 63, 65–67, 76, 87, 138, 150. *See also* exports; free trade; imports; services trade
trade, "unfair," 72–73, 77–80, 100; investigations of, 79–80, 100, 194$n9$
Trade Act of 1974, 17, 18, 56, 80
trade barriers, 5, 31, 58, 77, 86, 192–93$nn1–2$; measures to counteract, 54, 76, 79; tariff, 86, 139–42, 144, 149–52; and transborder data flows, 39–42, 46, 76
trade deficit, 83, 85, 162, 167–69, 194$n5$
trade in services. *See* services trade

trade policy, 38, 57, 61–62, 193*n*2. *See also* liberalization of trade; regulations; restrictions, on imports; sanctions, trade

trade surplus, 62, 64, 74

trade war, 17, 118, 120–22, 172, 177, 179–80, 182. *See also* Brazilian policy, investigations of

transborder data flows, 33–34, 36, 45, 53–55, 56; barriers to, 39, 41, 46, 76; discourse of, 44, 49, 50–51; laws and regulations regarding, 46, 48, 50–52, 191*n1*; and policy, 14, 17, 21–22, 50–51

transnational corporations. *See* multinational corporations

unions and unionism, 66, 113, 186–88

Unisys (firm), 27, 84, 122, 126, 147, 194*n*7, 195*n*5

United Kingdom, 46, 62

United Nations, 29, 47, 49

U.S. Congress, 72–75, 78, 85; Senate, 51–53, 73–75, 79

U.S. government, 37–38, 40, 50; and GATT, 53, 55–59, 62–63, 65; and policy, 16, 19, 21, 31, 39, 124, 178; and services trade, 56–59, 67–68; and transborder data flows, 50–51, 53. *See also* Brazilian policy, investigations of; U.S. Congress

U.S. State Department, 39, 82

U.S. Trade Representative, Office of, 39–42, 57–58, 76, 80–81, 83, 95, 97. *See also* Smith, Michael B.

United States, 1, 46–47, 128, 129, 187–88; competitiveness of, 72, 75, 78–80, 83, 86, 178; and promotion of free trade, 2, 52, 73, 76–77

Uruguay, 54, 64, 187

values. *See* cultural values

Velloso, Sergio, 131, 135, 143, 147, 149–50, 152

Venezuela, 186, 193*n1*

Wallerstein, Immanuel, 9, 174

West Germany, 62, 73–74

working class, 186–88

World Bank, 7, 11–12, 29, 53, 57, 183

World Trade Organization, 1, 4, 11, 176, 187–88